DISSONANT VOICES
IN SOVIET LITERATURE

DISSONANT VOICES

IN SOVIET

LITERATURE

Edited by PATRICIA BLAKE

and MAX HAYWARD

GREENWOOD PRESS, PUBLISHERS
WESTPORT, CONNECTICUT

Library of Congress Cataloging in Publication Data

Blake, Patricia, ed.
   Dissonant voices in Soviet literature.

   Reprint of the ed. published by Pantheon Books,
New York.
     "References to original Russian sources": p.
    1. Russian literature--20th century--Transla-
tions into English. 2. English literature--Trans-
lations from Russian. I. Hayward, Max, joint ed.
II. Title.
[PG3213.B55 1975]   891.7'08   75-8861
ISBN 0-8371-8109-7

All footnotes are by the editors.

Contents

INTRODUCTION *by Max Hayward*

Soviet Literature 1917–1962

This miscellany of Soviet writing covers a period of forty-four years, beginning with an early prose fragment by Boris Pasternak written in 1918 and ending with Evtushenko's "Babi Yar" and a short story, not so far published in the Soviet Union, "This Is Moscow Speaking," written by a Russian author under the pseudonym Nikolai Arzak.

Most of the voices represented here are dissonant, not in any political sense, but in that they do not speak in that trite and monotonous accent which, owing to the long and bitter years of Stalin's dictatorship, is still regarded by many people in the West as the sole voice of Soviet literature. The editors have given pride of place to writers who were murdered, hounded into silence, or otherwise persecuted (e.g. Babel, Pilnyak, and Pasternak) and to some others (e.g. Ehrenburg and Paustovsky) who despite their overtly "conformist" past have attempted, in the years since Stalin, to restore the literary and human values all but destroyed by him. The physical limits imposed on an anthology of this sort and, in some cases, the difficulty of finding hitherto untranslated pieces of suitable length, made it impossible to include specimens of the work of many writers such as Yuri Olesha, Leonid Leonov, Konstantin Fedin, and Alexander Tvardovsky, so that the picture which emerges is inevitably very incomplete, but the editors hope they may have succeeded in their principal aim of showing that the Soviet period has been by no means as barren in literary achievement as is often supposed. Apart from years of utter sterility—notably the years 1947 to 1953— there has been a fairly steady output of work, some of which is not unworthy of the great tradition from which it ultimately springs.

Needless to say, much Soviet writing can only be appreciated against the background in which it was produced, and the purpose of this introduction is to sketch the changing climate in which Soviet writers have lived and worked.

The Russian intelligentsia, not least the writers, were divided in their attitude to the Bolshevik Revolution of October 1917. Many, like Ivan Bunin, Leonid Andreyev, Alexander Kuprin, Boris Zaitsev, Dmitri Merezhkovsky, and others, could not reconcile themselves to Lenin's usurpation of power and emigrated at the earliest possible opportunity. Others like Ilya Ehrenburg, Alexei Tolstoy, and Maxim Gorky were more ambivalent in their attitude. At first skeptical of the new regime, they made their peace with it—for different reasons—and loyally served it, once they had convinced themselves that it was there to stay. It is interesting to note that it was the very few *Marxist* writers, such as Evgeni Zamyatin and Maxim Gorky, who were at the time the most implacably hostile to Lenin's *coup d'état*. Like Rosa Luxemburg, Gorky prophesied that the Bolshevik seizure of power would inevitably lead to the dictatorship of one man, and he violently denounced Lenin for his arrogance and "seigneurial" contempt for the Russian people. Zamyatin, as we can see from his article on "Literature, Revolution, and Entropy," clearly foresaw all the dangers of the Bolshevik monopoly of power for the free development of literature and the arts. Unlike Gorky, who had a fatal weakness for successful strongmen—one is reminded of G. B. Shaw—Zamyatin remained irreconcilably hostile and managed to emigrate from the Soviet Union in 1931—not long after Gorky finally returned to Moscow to become Stalin's confidant and advisor in literary matters. In the latter capacity Gorky was responsible for the formulation of the doctrine of "socialist realism."

There was a third category of writers, notably Alexander Blok, Andrei Bely, and Sergei Esenin, who greeted the October Revolution with unbridled enthusiasm as the secular consummation of a mystic vision. Politically naïve, they saw in the *grand chambardement* of October the beginning of a millennial "revolution of the spirit" which would somehow, out of the chaos, the squalor, and the bloodshed, produce a spiritual transfiguration of mankind ("Transfiguration" is the title of one of Esenin's poems in 1917) and the realization of ancient dreams. By a strange irony, therefore, Soviet literature had its beginnings in the religious ecstasy of a small group of poets who were the very antithesis of the cold-blooded engineers of October. An even greater paradox is that Blok, the ethereal, otherworldly symbolist, and Bely, the even more otherworldly esotericist (he was the leading Russian disciple of Rudolf Steiner), greeted the Revolution with poems steeped in Christian imagery. In Blok's "Twelve" (1918), Jesus Christ "in a white crown" leads the triumphal march of the Red Guards, and in Bely's "Christ Is Risen" (1918), Russia's ordeal by revolution is compared to Calvary: the martyrdom of the Cross will be followed by Resurrection. Esenin, too, used religious symbols to convey his vision of the Revolution as the dawn of a golden age for the Russian peasants. In his poem "Inonia" (1918), dedicated to the prophet Jeremiah, he violently rejected Christ, in the grand tradition of Russian atheism, in favor of Man, the omnipotent Demiurge: "I shall fear neither death / Nor javelins, nor hail of darts, / Thus speaks according to the Bible, the prophet

Esenin, Sergei. / My hour is at hand, I fear not the scourge. /
I spit out of my mouth the Host, the body of Christ. / I will
not accept salvation through his torment and the Cross: /
I know another teaching which pierces the eternal stars. / I
behold another Coming / In which death doesn't dance on
truth. . . ."

This kind of inverted religious language was also characteristic of Mayakovsky's work at the time of the Revolution.
Already before it, in "Cloud in Trousers" (1915), he had proclaimed himself the John the Baptist of the Revolution: "at
the head of hungry hordes, / the year 1916 cometh / in the
thorny crown of revolutions. / In your midst, his precursor,
I am where pain is—everywhere; / on each drop of the tear-
flow / I have nailed myself on the cross. . . ." His first major
work in honor of the Revolution was a mock mystery play
(*Mystery Bouffe*, 1918) which is a brilliant farcical re-enact-
ment of the story of the Flood, with God, Methuselah, Beel-
zebub, and Lloyd George playing minor roles. Mayakovsky's
transposition of the revolutionary drama into biblical language was, of course, utterly lighthearted and frivolous
compared with Esenin's anguished blasphemy, but the un-
derlying emotion was much the same and he was thought of
by communist critics as a utopian visionary rather than as a
"proletarian" poet. As late as 1934 he could be described by
one such critic as "a peculiar kind of utopian socialist, a
spokesman of that petty-bourgeois humanistic intelligentsia
whose ideological development eventually led to their acceptance of the October Revolution." [1] Of *Mystery Bouffe*
the same writer said that it still contains "strong echoes of the
problems which exercised Mayakovsky in the prerevolu-
tionary period: abstract man and the socialist paradise."
Despite all his flamboyant self-identification with the cause,
it was only Stalin's offhanded canonization of him in 1935
which led to the creation of "proletarian" credentials for
him and his enthronement as the great tribune and drum-

---

[1] N. Plisko, *Literaturnaya Entsiklopedia.*

beater of the Revolution. This he certainly was in his own estimation, but he understood the true nature of the Revolution scarcely better than Blok or Esenin. The result was tragedy for all three of them and their last days, in the words of Pushkin's poem, were "without divinity, without inspiration, without tears, without life, and without love." Blok was the first to realize his mistake. When he died in 1921 he was already deaf to the "music of the Revolution" which only three years earlier had inspired him to write the first and greatest poem of the Soviet era. The unspeakable agony of his disillusionment is conveyed by Zoshchenko's portrait of him in "Before Sunrise."

For Esenin, who committed suicide in 1925, the years of disabusement were more productive. Unlike Blok he was able to rescue something from the wreck of his dreams and transmute his disenchantment into poetry, which perhaps better than anything else expresses the tragic alienation of the Russian intelligentsia in the twenties. Quickly understanding that October would not, as he fondly imagined, usher in a peasant paradise of which he would be the prophet, he reconciled himself with gentle submissiveness to the role of a stranger in his own land. He was not against the new way of things, but he could not be a part of it. In a poem written in 1920, he drew a picture of a poor little foal pathetically trying to race a steam engine; the image well expressed his belated recognition that October meant the advent of a harsh and ruthless machine age which would have no use for his "gentle songs." In "Soviet Russia," written shortly before his death, he accepts, in a mood of trusting patriotism, all that has happened in the country and offers up his soul to October and May. He could no more compete with the crude "proletarian" versifier Demyan Bedny than the poor foal could catch up with the locomotive, but in a pitiful gesture of defiance he refused to abandon his "beloved lyre" to the Revolution. He did not live to see the day when it would inevitably have been wrenched from his grasp.

The case of Mayakovsky is the most intriguing of all. The

self-appointed poet laureate of the Revolution, only too anxious to abandon not only himself but his lyre to the service of the Party ("I want the *Gosplan* to sweat / in debate, / assigning me / goals a year ahead. / I want / a commissar / with a decree / to lean over the thought of the age"), he seemed, on the surface, to be more in tune with the new age than any of his contemporaries.

In fact, however, he was one of those hypersensitive and introspective intellectuals for whom only total involvement in the turmoil and chaos of universal upheaval can offer any solution to hopeless inner agony. The Revolution, or rather his image of it, supplied a personal need which had nothing to do with his overt political convictions. When the image began to fade and when he could no longer hide the fact from himself, he put a bullet through his heart.

Boris Pasternak, the fourth great poet of the Soviet era and the only one to survive its worst rigors, was not spellbound by the Revolution. Judging from the evidence of *Dr. Zhivago*, he may have felt a momentary thrill of admiration at its "splendid surgery," but we may surmise that it was as short-lived as with the hero of his novel. Yet perhaps he understood the revolutionary temperament better than most of his contemporaries. The portrait of Antipov-Strelnikov in *Dr. Zhivago* is full of sympathetic insight into the character of a man who sacrifices life and love to an impersonal cause. The fragment "Without Love" shows that Pasternak was preoccupied with this problem as early as 1918. The title, which in Russian is an invented word (*bezlyubye*, meaning roughly "lovelessness"), evidently refers to the suppression of all personal feeling in the name of the Revolution, about which the young social-revolutionary conspirator Kovalevsky is thinking as he travels with his easygoing friend Goltsev to some industrial town in the Urals. The contrast between Goltsev and Kovalevsky foreshadows the relationship between Yuri Zhivago and Antipov-Strelnikov in the novel written some forty years later. While Goltsev is thinking of the woman he loves (who, like Lara in the novel, goes to the front as a nurse), Kovalevsky is entirely absorbed in his thoughts about the Revolution—thoughts which "meant more to him than his fur coat and his belongings, more than his wife and child, more than his own life and more than other people's lives. . . ." There is an obvious symbolism in the fact that, while dreaming his dreams of revolution, Kovalevsky imagines that his companion is asleep and that he himself is awake. In reality it is the other way round: it is Goltsev, with his more down-to-earth thoughts, who is awake. "Without Love" hence already contains in embryo one of the central themes of *Dr. Zhivago,* namely the trancelike state of those men who, like Kovalevsky and Antipov, attempt to apply "final" solutions to all the problems of humanity and who eventually wake up to the illusoriness of their efforts.

In the first decade after the Revolution it was possible for such moods as these to be expressed with more or less freedom. True, there was a fairly tight censorship, known as *Glavlit,* but its functions were mainly negative, i.e., to prevent the appearance in print of openly "counterrevolutionary" work. The Soviet prose of the period was, on the whole, remarkably objective in portraying the realities of the Revolution, the Civil War, and the period of N.E.P. The brutal naturalism of Isaac Babel (represented in this book by "The Journey") was accepted almost without criticism; Leonid Leonov was able to show, in *The Badgers* (1925), the hostility of the peasant masses to marauding Bolshevik requisitioners from the towns, and in *The Thief* (1927), the demoralization during N.E.P. of an idealistic communist who had fought in the Civil War; Sholokhov described in the first two volumes of *And Quiet Flows the Don* (1928), with an impartiality quite impermissible by later standards, the complicated clash of loyalties—by no means explicable only in terms of class warfare—which the Revolution produced among simple people. Almost all the human problems which arose in the aftermath of the great upheaval—the conflict between town and country, the collapse of utopian illusions, the inner doubts of the intellectuals, the material hardships of the population as a whole—all these and many other problems were presented truthfully, if not always sympathetically, in early Soviet literature. Most of the best writers of the period belonged to the category dubbed by Trotsky as the "fellow travelers." For the most part intellectuals by origin, they varied considerably in the degree of their loyalty to the new regime, but like "bourgeois specialists" in other fields, they were endowed with special skills which made them indispensable to it and they were, therefore, at first protected from excessive interference by the so-called "proletarian" writers. The latter were as vociferous as they were untalented, but their attempts to force the "fellow travelers" into absolute conformity were given little official encouragement until 1929. Until this year general Party supervision of literary and artistic affairs had been the responsibility of Anatoli Lunacharsky, one of the most cultivated of the Old Bolsheviks and himself a writer of standing, who exercised great tact in his handling of cultural problems. Under his aegis there was an uneasy coexistence between the "fellow travelers," grouped mainly in the All-Russian Union of Writers, and the "proletarians" of the Association of Proletarian Writers (RAPP). In another part of the memoirs excerpted in this book, Ilya Ehrenburg writes of Lunacharsky:

In their reminiscences of him people have spoken about his "enormous erudition" and his "many-sided culture." I was struck by something different: he was not a poet, he was absorbed in his political activities, but he had an extraordinary love for art and he always seemed to be tuned in to those elusive waves to which many others are deaf. On the rare occasions when we met we would argue. His views were alien to me. But he was very far from any desire to impose them on other people. The October Revolution put him in command of the People's Commissariat of Enlightenment and there is no denying that he was a good shepherd. "I have said dozens of times"—[wrote Lunacharsky]—"that the Commissariat of Enlightenment must be impartial in its attitude toward the various trends of artistic life. As regards questions of artistic form, the tastes of the People's Commissar and other persons in authority should not be taken into account. All individual artists and all groups of artists should be allowed to develop freely. No one trend, by virtue of its traditional renown or its fashionable success, should be allowed to oust another." It is a pity that various people who have been in charge of art, or who have been interested in it, have rarely remembered these wise words.[2]

The end of Lunacharsky's relatively mild stewardship spelled the end of freedom for literature in Russia and the beginning of an enforced state of "entropy" which went on for the next twenty-two years. The year 1929 was in general the "year of the great turning point," as Stalin aptly described it, and with the final defeat of all political opposition, whose fate was sealed by the capitulation of Bukharin at the Sixteenth Party Conference, the stage was set for the "revolution from above" which meant the violent transformation of all social and cultural life. In retrospect the N.E.P. period now seemed a golden age of liberalism and laissez faire. Side by side with the collectivization of the peasants went the so-called "bolshevization" of literature and the arts. This was done by encouraging RAPP to assert the hegemony of the "proletariat" in literature, that is, to allow them to do what Lunacharsky had so far managed to prevent. The leadership of RAPP, under its chairman, Leopold Averbakh, consisted of genuine fanatics who no doubt sincerely believed that only the "proletariat" could create an art that was in harmony with the new way of life and that hence "class warfare" must be fostered in cultural life just as was now being done in the countryside: the "fellow-traveling" goats must be separated from the "proletarian" sheep. To be a "proletarian" writer did not mean that one was necessarily a worker or a peasant by origin—indeed many of the "proletarian" writers were intellectuals—but one had to identify oneself body and soul with their supposed cause, and submit unquestioningly to their self-appointed and self-perpetuating "avant-garde,"

---

[2] *Novy Mir*, September 1960.

the Party. There was at this period a genuine mystique of communion with the "proletariat," and some intellectuals were indeed attracted by this possibility of a quasi-religious sublimation of personality. Like all religious processes it seems to offer a way of shedding the awful burden of individual responsibility, and RAPP was successfully able to exploit this appeal in a number of cases. But, like all fanatical proselytizers, they were too impatient to rest content with persuasion and in August 1929 they forced a showdown with the "fellow-traveling" writers. This was the first application to Soviet cultural life of the technique of the campaign against certain chosen scapegoats with the object of terrorizing a whole group into submission. The victims on this occasion were Boris Pilnyak, who was chairman of the All-Russian Union of Writers, and Evgeni Zamyatin, who headed the Leningrad branch of the Union. By later standards the campaign was clumsily handled and, as an attempt to compromise Pilnyak and Zamyatin morally, it was a failure. The original charge against them was that both had deliberately arranged for the publication abroad of works which had not been passed by the Soviet censorship: Pilnyak's fragment *Mahogany,* part of which is reproduced in this book, and Zamyatin's anti-utopian satire *We.* Both writers were able to demonstrate beyond any doubt that they were blameless on this score. In fact Zamyatin had done his best to prevent the publication of *We* abroad and the manuscript of Pilnyak's *Mahogany* had been sent to a Russian publisher in Berlin in accordance with what was then a legal procedure whereby Soviet writers obtained protection under the international copyright laws to which the Soviet Union was not a party. By arranging for the simultaneous publication of the original in Moscow and Berlin, it was possible for the author to retain control over translation and other rights abroad. Gorky, Sholokhov, Konstantin Fedin, and other Soviet writers regularly used this procedure. The Berlin firm Petropolis which published Pilnyak's *Mahogany* existed only to perform this service for Soviet writers. Such transactions went through Soviet lawyers and the official society for relations with foreign countries, VOKS. What happened in Pilnyak's case, however, was that Petropolis jumped the gun and published his manuscript prematurely, without waiting for it to be passed for publication in Moscow. When both authors were able to show that they were not guilty of deliberately evading Soviet censorship controls, the RAPP instigators of the campaign against them changed their tack, and concentrated on the alleged anti-Soviet nature of the works in question. They were said to be symptomatic of the work of many "fellow travelers," who were now bluntly told that they must either make manifest their solidarity with the "proletariat" and their complete loyalty to the Party, or forfeit the right to call themselves *Soviet* writers. The word "Soviet" in this context was henceforth to be interpreted, not as a mere territorial designation, but as a definition of the writer's political allegiance. After a series of rigged meetings in the various writers' organizations resolutions were adopted in accordance with which Pilnyak and Zamyatin, together with the whole of the old leadership of the All-Russian Union of Writers, were removed. At the same time the rank-and-file membership was "re-registered" and as many as one half were "purged." To mark the radical change in the literary situation the All-Russian Union of Writers now renamed itself the "All-Russian Union of *Soviet* Writers." All this happened in a society that was not yet entirely cowed—the Stalinist terror was only just beginning —and there were individual protests against the way in which the back of the "fellow-traveler" writers' organization had been broken. The most powerful came from Gorky, who wrote the following in *Izvestia:*

The punishment meted out to Pilnyak is far too severe. . . . All my life I have waged a struggle for care in dealing with people and I think that in our present conditions this struggle should be carried on even more intensively. . . . We have gotten into the stupid habit of raising people up into high positions, only to throw them down into the mud and the dust. I need not quote examples of this absurd and cruel practice, because such examples are known to everybody. I am reminded of the way in which thieves were lynched in 1917-1918. These dramas were generally the work of petty bourgeois elements, and one is reminded of them every time one sees with what delight people throw themselves on a man who has made a mistake in order to take his place.

This was perhaps the last publicly voiced protest in the Soviet Union against a literary frame-up. Later victims enjoyed neither the benefit of such support, however muted, from their colleagues, nor the luxury of being able to reply to their accusers. One cannot help wondering whether history might not have taken a somewhat different turn if more had been as courageous and uncompromising as Evgeni Zamyatin, who wrote in a letter to *Literary Gazette* on September 16, 1929:

When I returned to Moscow after a summer journey the whole affair of my book *We* was already over. It had been established that the appearance of fragments from *We* in *Volia Rossii* in Prague was a deliberate act on my part, and in regard to this "act" all the necessary resolutions had been adopted. But facts are stubborn. They are more stubborn than resolutions. Every one of them may be confirmed by documents or by people and I wish to make them known to my readers. . . . [He goes on to give conclusive proof that the publication of parts of *We* in the *émigré Volya Rosii* was none of his doing.] . . . Thus first there was a condemnation and only then an investigation. I imagine that no court in the world has ever heard of such a procedure. . . . A meeting of the Moscow branch of the All-Russian Union of Writers, without waiting for my explanations, or even expressing a desire to hear them, adopted a resolution condemning my "act." The general meeting of the Leningrad branch was called on September 22nd and I know of its results only through the newspapers. . . . From these it is evident that in Leningrad my explanations had been read and that here the opinion of those present was divided. A number of the writers, after hearing my explanations, considered the whole incident closed. But the majority found it more prudent to condemn my "act." Such was the act of the All-Russian Union of Writers and from this act I draw my conclusions: to belong to a literary organization which, even indirectly, takes part in the persecution of a co-member, is impossible for me, and I hereby announce my withdrawal from the All-Russian Union of Writers.

A year or so later, after being subjected to all kinds of petty humiliation and virtually having been excluded from the literary life of Russia (his stage version of Leskov's famous *conte*, "The Steel Flea," scheduled for production in a Leningrad theater, was withdrawn solely because of the "notoriety" of its author), Zamyatin wrote an astonishing letter to Stalin[3] in which he requested that his "condemnation to death" as a writer be commuted to exile from the Soviet Union, as provided for under the Soviet penal code, and even more astonishingly—owing perhaps to the intercession of Gorky—Stalin granted his request. Pilnyak on the other hand, made a groveling submission (in private—public recantations were not yet *de rigueur* in cases such as these) and he perished a few years later during the Yezhov terror.

The thirties were not the worst years for Soviet literature (these were to come after 1946) but they saw the establishment of those features of Soviet literature which distinguish it from all other literatures in the world. What makes it unique is that these features were imposed from without. It is obvious that literature need not necessarily suffer from purely negative limitations on the right of publication (nineteenth-century Russian literature and early Soviet literature flourished under censorship) or from the *voluntary* acceptance of a particular set of doctrinal terms of reference (as in the case of Catholic writers), but when matters of form and content are strictly regulated in accordance with extraliterary criteria, the result is very serious for creative effort. The way in which "socialist realism" was made binding on Soviet writers, the reasons for it, and the consequences of this imposition must be outlined.

---

[3] The full text is reproduced in *Litsa*, Chekhov Press, New York, 1955.

In April 1932 the Central Committee of the CPSU unexpectedly issued a decree ordering the disbandment of RAPP, the now cowed and emasculated All-Russian Union of Soviet Writers and other residual groups, and setting up in their place the Union of Soviet Writers which exists in the same form today. It was made clear that membership in this new unitary organization would be essential for anyone who wished to make writing his livelihood. One of Stalin's reasons for discarding the "proletarians" of RAPP (many of whom, including Averbakh, were later denounced and liquidated as "Trotskyists") was no doubt that, once they had performed their task of bringing to heel the "fellow travelers," their excessive zeal, which had been an advantage for this purpose, was now only an embarrassment to him. Stalin much preferred compliant "fellow travelers" to fanatical Marxist idealists, many of whom, like Akim and his uncle in Pilnyak's tale, were indeed temperamentally more in tune with the fervent intellectualism of Trotsky than with the humdrum empiricism of Stalin. In general the thirties are remarkable for the fact that genuine Marxists were gradually replaced in many fields by people with a "bourgeois" and even "counterrevolutionary" past who were willing to pay lip service to anything as the price of survival. Thus the bourgeois historians Tarle and Wipper were called in to glorify Kutuzov and Ivan the Terrible while the veteran Marxist, Pokrovsky, was denounced for "vulgar sociologism," i.e., for writing history as Marx and Engels had written it. In literature—with consummate skill, it must be admitted—the former count Alexei Tolstoy showed that his master had a not unworthy forerunner in Peter the Great.

To be a writer one now not only had to be a member of the Union of Soviet Writers but also had to subscribe to the "method" of socialist realism. This method—the question as to whether it is a "method" or a "theory" has never satisfactorily been resolved by the pundits—was elaborated in open debate during the two years between the Party decree of 1932 and the First Congress of Soviet writers in 1934 when the doctrine was promulgated by Zhdanov, who made his debut on this occasion as Stalin's great panjandrum in cultural matters. The theory appears to have been devised by Gorky in consultation with Stalin. For Gorky the principal intention was no doubt to keep Soviet literature in the mainstream of the classical realist tradition of which he himself was the last great representative, but for Stalin, as well as being in keeping with his own pedestrian tastes, it must have seemed an attractive way of subordinating literature and the arts to his purpose. Essentially an attempt to combine incompatible elements, it was from the first riddled with contradictions and was hence rarely satisfactorily applied from the official point of view. The inherent contradictoriness of the theory has best been described by Abram Tertz, the pseudonymous Soviet author of an essay on socialist realism first published in the French magazine *Esprit* in February 1959:

If many [Soviet] writers are going through a crisis at the moment . . . it is because they have to seek a compromise and unite what cannot be united: the "positive hero," who logically lends himself to schematized, allegorical treatment—with psychological character study; an elevated declamatory style—with description of prosaic, everyday life; a sublime ideal—with verisimilitude to reality. This results in a monstrous salad. The characters [of Soviet fiction] torment themselves almost à la Dostoevsky, grow sad almost à la Chekhov, arrange their family life almost à la Tolstoy, and yet at the same time vie with each other in shouting platitudes from the Soviet press: "Long live peace in the whole world" and "Down with the warmongers." This is neither classicism nor realism. It is semi-classical demi-art of a none too socialist demi-realism. [NOTE: The full text of this important essay was published by Pantheon Books in 1961, under the title *On Socialist Realism*.]

What it amounted to was that the Soviet writers were to model themselves on the nineteenth-century Russian classics (Gorky himself launched the slogan "Learn from the classics!") and adopt a kind of composite style based on the language of Turgenev, Tolstoy, and Chekhov (Dostoevsky was less favored as time went on). All the modernist movements of the beginning of the century and the early Soviet period (symbolism, imagism, futurism—of which Mayakovsky was a product—and the rich "ornamental" style which Pilnyak and others derived from Andrei Bely and Alexei Remizov) were declared to have been an aberration in the development of Russian literature and were henceforth denounced as "formalism." Strictly speaking, "formalism" had been nothing more than the name of a highly interesting and original method of literary criticism (its protagonists, such as Victor Shklovsky and Roman Jakobson, referred to it as "the formal method in literature" and its enemies called it "formalism") which had concentrated on the analysis of form in art and literature. It arose in the early twenties among a group of young critics and linguists who set themselves the task of restoring the balance in Russian literary criticism, which had always been almost exclusively concerned with matters of content. Readers may judge the true nature of formalism from the essay by Victor Shklovsky, extracts from which have been included in this book. In the era of socialist realism the word "formalism" was misappropriated, like many other terms, and came to cover a multitude of sins. It became a blanket term of abuse for the slightest deviation from the run-of-the-mill "realist" style and was freely applied to anyone, whatever the nature of his offense, who seemed to the now ubiquitous watchdogs to be in any way "offbeat."

But the greatest difficulty for the writers was that, in accordance with the formula laid down by Zhdanov, they were expected to employ the realist style of the nineteenth-century classics in a spirit which was quite alien to its creators. An essential feature of the new doctrine was the sharp distinction to be drawn between "socialist" realism and the "critical" realism of the classics. The latter, it was said, had used the realist method to *negate* the society in which they lived, whereas the Soviet writer was required by the same method to *affirm* the new socialist order, which was *ex hypothesi* the most benevolent and the most nearly perfect ever established on earth. It was therefore incumbent on the writers not only to describe it "realistically in its revolutionary development" (Zhdanov's phrase), but also to assist the Party in its task of completing the social transformation now in progress, of consolidating the gains already made, and of educating people in the ways of virtue. Since, in Marxist theory, consciousness always lags behind economic and social change, there were still admittedly many wayward citizens who were slow to realize the benefits of the new order, their minds being infected by "survivals of capitalism." One of the writers' principal duties was to expose and hold up to scorn these "survivals," and thus hasten the day when all would model themselves on the New Man. In the words of Stalin's famous *obiter dictum,* writers were to be "engineers of human souls." [4] A sanction for this total subjection of literature to the will of the Party was found in an essay of Lenin's, "Party Literature and the Party Organization," written in 1905. In it Lenin insisted that anybody who wrote for social-democrat journals should express the general line of the Party. At that time, when journals of different political complexions could be published more or less freely in Russia, this was a perfectly reasonable and legitimate demand to make, being designed to exclude interlopers from rival parties. It should be noted, furthermore, that in talking of "literature" in this connection, Lenin was not primarily referring to "belles-lettres." At the first Congress of Soviet writers in 1934 Zhdanov, however, quoted this article as his authority for making *partiinost* (roughly: complete submission to the Party line and acceptance of its guidance in all things) the cornerstone of socialist realism. Whether Lenin would have been displeased or not at this chicanery is open to question.

In these conditions, coupled with increasing terror which culminated in the *Yezhovshchina* of 1937, most Soviet writers

---

4 When and where he said this has never been revealed.

were faced with an agonizing choice: either to collaborate or to cease writing altogether. Some, like Pasternak and Babel, virtually ceased to publish. Some sought refuge in translation and in writing for children. The majority, however, collaborated to some degree or another. For the collaborators, willing or unwilling, various inner accommodations were necessary. It was no longer possible, as it had been during the twenties, to merge body and soul with the proletariat. Nobody merged with anybody any more. The alienation of man from man was more complete, in the name of collectivism, than it had ever been, possibly, in the whole of human history. Leonid Leonov, easily the most distinguished and subtle of the surviving Soviet novelists, and an avowed disciple of Dostoevsky, continued to write all through the worst period without unduly compromising his artistic integrity. But this was an isolated case. Leonov's rationalization of his position was based on the same sort of mystic nationalism, and probably combined with the same religious messianism, as one finds in Dostoevsky's *Diary of a Writer*. For Leonov bolshevism is only one episode in the eternal destinies of Russia. He may even have been intrigued by the special problems of writing within the cramped confines of socialist realism and he may well have regarded his work in these conditions as a kind of *podvig* (spiritual feat) in the Russian Orthodox tradition. His was the noblest type of collaboration and it was undoubtedly motivated by a feeling of duty towards his generation. Not everybody could enjoy the relative luxury of silence and he felt it necessary to convey to his readers—through all the almost insuperable barriers—something of the truth about man and Russia. In this, for all those capable of interpreting his subtle ambiguities, he succeeded well. His most impressive "feat" was the novel *Russian Forest*, written in the most difficult years preceding Stalin's death and published in 1953. Impeccably "socialist realist" in tone and structure, this novel yet manages to suggest by devious symbolism that human affairs and the fate of Russia are much more complex than the crude oversimplifications of official thought would ever follow. Ilya Ehrenburg adapted himself to circumstances, but with far less success from a literary point of view, for very different reasons from those of Leonid Leonov. Essentially an internationalist in outlook, he adopted the "lesser evil" fallacy that since fascism, of the two competing totalitarian systems which threatened to dominate the world, was palpably the more evil, an intellectual who wished to work for its defeat could not logically refuse support to Soviet communism, even in its rapidly degenerating Stalinist form. Judging from his work after Stalin's death he has considerably modified his previous attitude and he now appears as a strong champion of greater independence for Soviet writers.

Leonov and Ehrenburg are the best examples of the two main types of adaptation to the exigencies of socialist realism and stringent Party control over literary life. There were, of course, other categories. A small minority, including Alexander Fadeyev who committed suicide in 1956, fanatically believed in socialist realism, and by virtue of their sincerity, they were able to use the method with somewhat greater effect than those, like Alexei Surkov (a former RAPPist and Fadeyev's successor as secretary of the Union of Soviet Writers), in whom one may suspect a considerable element of cynical opportunism. Sholokhov stood apart, apparently not caring, writing scarcely anything and basking complacently in his officially sponsored and quite incongruous reputation as the greatest socialist realist of them all. This judgment, together with Stalin's canonization of Mayakovsky, made the work of the literary theorists even more difficult. *And Quiet Flows the Don,* written well before the promulgation of the new doctrine, offends many of the canons of socialist realism, not least by the comparative objectivity of its treatment of history, its naturalistic language in scenes involving violence or sex, and the moral ambiguity of its hero. A year or two ago, addressing a group of Czech writers in Prague, Sholokhov said that he had not the faintest idea of what was meant by socialist realism.

What it meant in practice, particularly in the postwar
years, was an extreme schematism in the presentation of
character which would scarcely be tolerated in even the
most fourth-rate cowboy film, a falsification, blatant beyond
belief, of native and foreign realities, both past and present,
and a drab emasculated language reminiscent of Tolstoy and
Gorky at their worst. The latter conducted a campaign in
the middle thirties for the "purity" of the Russian language,
and Soviet writers, in their anxiety to avoid being charged
with "naturalism" (a cardinal offense against "realism")
began to use a sterilized language carefully shorn of all the
expressive slang and dialect which had been characteristic
of Russian writing in the twenties. Plots became more and
more simple and their outcome more and more predictable.
Optimism reigned supreme and all endings were happy—
except, of course, in capitalist countries.[5]

The outbreak of war in 1941 made an immense difference.
In a memorable passage at the end of *Dr. Zhivago* Pasternak
has described how the war "broke the spell of the dead
letter." The almost universal sense of liberation from the
unbearable terrors and shams of peacetime is also conveyed
in the poem by Julia Neiman in this book. The Stalinist
terror—and this may well have been one of its principal
aims—had so atomized society, mistrust among people (even
among members of the same family) was so intense, and the
public obligation, again in Pasternak's words, "to praise what
you hate most and to grovel before what makes you unhappy" had become so intolerable that the ordeal of the war
came as a blissful release.

In that year of "camouflage," as Julia Neiman says in her
poem, people saw each other without masks. Human bonds
were restored in the face of death and suffering, and in the
camaraderie of war people began to trust each other again.
Most Soviet writers served at the front as war correspondents
and many were killed. Freed of the enforced hypocrisies of

---

[5] Frightened editors were often as much to blame as the writers for this state
of affairs, as readers may judge from Polyakov's "Fireman Prokhorchuk."

peacetime, they wrote about people and things with relative truth and sincerity. Apart from excellent war reportage there was a number of novels and poems of high quality which will survive. Konstantin Simonov's *Days and Nights* and *Russian People*, Alexander Korneichuk's *Front*, Vasili Grossman's *The People Is Immortal*, Alexander Fadeyev's *Young Guard* (before he rewrote it on the instructions of the Party) and particularly Petro Vershigora's unfinished *Men with a Clear Conscience*, a remarkable account of partisan warfare in the Ukraine, are real works of literature. Surkov and Simonov will be remembered for their wartime lyrics. The new-found feeling of solidarity and relative freedom from fear made it possible for editors to publish works which could scarcely have appeared in print before the war. Perhaps the most extraordinary example is Mikhail Zoshchenko's "Before Sunrise," extracts from which appear in this volume. Poets who had long been silent, such as Boris Pasternak and Anna Akhmatova, were published again.

The wartime solidarity which had sprung up among Russians was intolerable to Stalin. He regarded mutual trust among people as tantamount to a conspiracy against himself and he hastened to bring it to an end. The greater freedoms which the writers had enjoyed during the war were abruptly destroyed in August 1946. The technique was very much the same as in the case of Pilnyak and Zamyatin eighteen years before. This time the chosen scapegoats were Zoshchenko, Akhmatova, and Pasternak. In a denunciatory speech of unparalleled scurrility Zhdanov accused Zoshchenko and Akhmatova (whom he described as "half nun and half whore") of disarming the Soviet people in their struggle to build communism, of disorienting and demoralizing Soviet youth, and of undermining the principles of socialist realism by writing in a subjective and pessimistic way without regard for the great political ideas from which the people drew its inspiration. Zhdanov's speech was followed by a decree of the Central Committee which ordained the strict observance of socialist realism and announced cer-

tain practical measures to insure that there would be no
backsliding from it in the future. *Leningrad,* one of the
journals which had published offending work, was abolished
altogether and the other, *Zvezda,* was put under the charge
of a member of the Central Committee. The easygoing
Tikhonov, whose "fellow-traveling" past had been anything
but orthodox, was replaced as secretary of the Union of
Soviet Writers by the fanatical Fadeyev. The orgy of denunciation in the press after this decree was as bad as anything before the war. The atmosphere of terror was re-
established and all the gains made during the war were
wiped out. The years that followed were unimaginable.
Literature and the arts ceased to exist in any recognizable
form. The cinema was almost completely destroyed. After
the Central Committee's decree denouncing, among other
films, the second part of Eisenstein's *Ivan the Terrible,*[6]
most of the studios were closed down and there was consequently such a shortage of material for the movie houses
that several captured Nazi films, dubbed in Russian and
billed as "new foreign films," were shown to Soviet audiences.
One was the anti-British *School of Hatred,* which had its
première in Berlin in 1941. It shows the revolt of some Irish
schoolboys against their sadistic English master and it ends
with the burning of the Union Jack. Another such film, *The
Last Round,* is anti-American and it concerns the fixing of
boxing matches in New York; the hero is a blond member
of the master race. The showing of these films occurred at a
time when the West was frequently accused in the Soviet
press of borrowing its propaganda techniques "from the
kitchen of the late Dr. Goebbels." The whole atmosphere of
the period is suggested in Lev Kassil's allegory "The Tale of
the Three Master Craftsmen." Its reference to the terroriza-
tion of creative artists by Stalin ("King Vainglorious") is so
obvious that one may ask how it ever got into print. It seems

---

[6] Eisenstein was accused of having depicted the "progressive" praetorian
guard (*oprichnina*) of Ivan the Terrible as a band of fascist hooligans like
the Ku Klux Klan.

likely that the censor who dealt with it was not overanxious to admit that he saw any resemblance between the unhappy kingdom of Sinegoriya and postwar Russia. It is probably unique as an anti-Stalinist satire published while Stalin was still alive.

The death of "King Vainglorious" in March 1953 had a liberating effect far greater even than that of the war. In the last eight years, though sudden advances have often been succeeded by alarming setbacks, there has been a constant and cumulative improvement in nearly all spheres. Though ultimate Party control of literature and the arts has never been abandoned (and could of course at any moment be restored in all its vigor) it has nevertheless been exercised, on the whole, with restraint and intelligence and has even, for brief periods, been relaxed to a degree which would have been quite inconceivable in Stalin's day. The paraphernalia of socialist realism and particularly the basic concept of *partiinost* have been firmly maintained in theory, but in practice there has often been considerable latitude in the interpretation of them. Outright questioning of the Party's right to control literature has always provoked a strong reaction, but that its wisdom may sometimes be doubted by implication is shown by the passage from Ehrenburg's memoirs quoted above. Altogether one has the impression that censorship controls have gradually been relaxed to some extent, much more being left to the discretion of editors. Since "mistakes" are no longer automatically denounced as crimes, editors have become increasingly ready to take risks. This new confidence is well expressed by the editor of *Novy Mir*, Alexander Tvardovsky, who wrote in one of his poems a few years ago: "In future, too, things may be hard, but we shall never again be afraid." The course of events since Stalin's death may be summarized as follows:

At the end of 1953 two articles published in *Novy Mir* cast doubt on socialist realism and the Party's guidance of literature. In his article "On Sincerity in Literature" V. Pomerantsev suggested that the only criterion for a writer should be his own inner convictions. Mark Shcheglov, in a review of Leonov's *Russian Forest,* said that the novel's only major defect was that the "negative hero" was not clearly shown to be a product of the Soviet system. Leonov had of course covered himself (or "re-insured" in the writers' argot of those days) by tracing the villain's original sin to the pre-revolutionary conditions in which he grew up. One of the particularly constricting demands of socialist realism is that there can never be the slightest implication that Soviet society might generate its own specific defects. It always had to be made plain that such shortcomings as exist are untypical "survivals of capitalism." Early in 1954 there was a crop of stories and plays which for the first time dealt with certain ugly phenomena in Soviet life. Ehrenburg's *Thaw* hinted at the true nature of the prewar purges and openly referred to the officially inspired anti-Semitism of the last years of Stalin's life. Leonid Zorin in his play *The Guests* described a police frame-up, on the lines of the "doctors' plot," and the degeneration of the cynical Soviet bureaucrat responsible for it. Korneichuk's *Wings* was similarly concerned with a deliberate perversion of justice, this time involving the wife of a high Party functionary who had been left behind in enemy-occupied territory during the war and who was consequently, like so many others in this category, regarded as a traitor. The play is remarkable for the first use in print of the term "concentration camp" instead of the usual euphemistic "corrective labor camp" and for a highly artificial "optimistic" ending (strikingly different from the denouement of Zorin's play). In *Wings* the victim of the outrage renders impassioned thanks to the Central Committee (at this time headed by Malenkov, who, in the pursuance of power after Stalin's death, was vying with his colleagues for the popular support which would accrue to the one who would first reveal the scope and nature of their late master's misdeeds) for its timely intercession and its determination never to permit such things to happen again. Significantly this play was never attacked during the "freeze-up" of 1954, and it was the first in a genre which should be approached with caution. In the first few years after Stalin's death the Party undoubtedly indulged in what might be called "literary zubatovism" [7] as one of its more intelligent efforts to combat opposition without recourse to brutal repression. By allowing certain writers to outbid genuine protest (it is noteworthy that their "revelations" are always more "sensational" than those of genuine oppositionists who are naturally more cautious) it evidently hoped that the true writers of the "thaw" might be thereby disarmed and their effect on Soviet readers neutralized. Another patently "zubatovist" work was Galina Nikolayeva's *Battle on the Way* with its interesting description of Stalin's funeral. This policy was probably associated with such members of the "anti-Party group" as Malenkov, and appears to have been abandoned now.

The reaction against the first phase of "thaw" literature came during 1954. Simonov attacked Ehrenburg's novel. Pomerantsev's article and Zorin's play were officially condemned in a statement from the Ministry of Culture, and Tvardovsky (as well as Feodor Panferov, the editor of another literary monthly, *Oktyabr*) were dismissed from their posts following a public denunciation by Surkov. On the face of it, this looked like a total reversal to Stalinist methods, but in fact it was not. There was no general campaign of intimidation and no gross interference by the Party, which was now already committed to the creation of a somewhat better public image for itself in the eyes of both Russia and the West. There was much to live down and a repetition of the Zhdanov scandal of 1946 would have been inconvenient at this moment. So the covert campaign for freedom went on, and at the second Congress of the Union of Soviet Writers in December 1954 there were some notable, albeit cautiously-

---

[7] Zubatov was a Czarist police official in the early years of the century who with the connivance of his superiors set up trade unions which attempted, with some success, to canalize the workers' revolutionary energies into the comparatively innocuous struggle for economic improvement. It was difficult to tell, in the case of many people associated with this unprecedented experiment in "police socialism," who was genuine and who was not.

worded, pleas—particularly from Alexander Yashin, Benjamin Kaverin, and Ehrenburg—for a more reasonable approach to the problems of literature. It was clear, however, that the diehards were still overwhelmingly strong and could count on decisive political support, even though they were not allowed to destroy their opponents as they would have done in former days. In the next two years there was an uneasy truce between both camps, neither side going out of its way to be unduly provocative. After Khrushchev's "secret speech" at the Twentieth Party Congress in 1956, there was a renewed outburst of "oppositional" writing, similar to the one after Stalin's death. In fact 1956 was the *annus mirabilis* of postwar Soviet literature. Apart from Dudintsev's *Not by Bread Alone,* with its indictment of the Soviet bureaucracy and, even more important, its emphasis on the need for intellectual independence, there was the second volume of the almanac *Literary Moscow,*[8] from which we have taken Julia Neiman's poem. What she says in this about 1941 applied with even greater force to 1956, but unfortunately *Literary Moscow* was published only a few weeks before the outbreak of the Hungarian Revolution. The Party's fear of "revisionism" and the neo-Stalinist exploitation of this fear—they could now say in triumph "We told you so!"—led to a setback which at first looked even worse than in 1954. Khrushchev himself, at a famous meeting in a country villa near Moscow, gathered the writers together and admonished them to adhere more strictly to the principles of socialist realism and never to forget that they were the servants of the Party. A hitherto little-known writer from Leningrad, Vsevolod Kochetov, wrote an "anti-revisionist" novel, *The Brothers Ershov,* which was in effect a denunciation of those Soviet writers responsible for the "thaw." It has an undercurrent of hostility to the intelligentsia as a whole and contrasts it with the right-minded and loyal "proletariat." There are ugly insinuations about Ilya Ehren-

---

[8] The best and most revealing story in this collection, "The Levers," by A. Yashin, was published in the Summer 1958 issue of *Partisan Review.*

burg, the journal *Novy Mir* (which has consistently in the
last few years been the main forum of the more independent-
minded intellectuals) and the second volume of *Literary
Moscow*. The latter, incidentally, was produced by a group
of Moscow writers who evidently tried, some time in 1956,
to set up a semi-autonomous writers' organization outside
the rigidly controlled Union of Soviet Writers. This could
easily have led to the creation of a center of intellectual dis-
affection on the lines of the Petoeffi Circle in Budapest.
Although it would hardly have been allowed to develop this
far, and would certainly not have made the explosive contact
with the workers which was so remarkable in Hungary,
it is nevertheless fair to say that anything seemed possible in the hectic atmosphere after Khrushchev's revelations
about Stalin. In his novel Kochetov made the ominous point
that there could indeed have been a "Hungarian" crisis in
Russia itself and that the Soviet intellectuals—he sometimes
puts the word in a pejorative diminutive form: *intelligentiki*
—of the type of Ehrenburg (who though not mentioned
by name is clearly alluded to) would have been morally
responsible for it. The lesson of the book is that "revisionism"
is potential treachery and that hence the intellectuals must
be kept firmly under the control of the "proletariat," i.e. the
Party leadership.

For several months after Hungary there was a violent
campaign against "revisionism"; for a short time in 1957
Kochetov was editor of the strategic and hitherto on the
whole "liberal" *Literary Gazette* and there was scarcely any
interesting new literature. In general things looked black.
But as in the reaction of 1954, the situation looked more
serious than it really was. The Party got over its panic about
Hungary and, its confidence restored—probably not least
owing to the Soviet triumph in outer space—it decided not
to use Kochetov, Surkov, and the other neo-Stalinists (by
now a thoroughly discredited and very small group utterly
despised by the majority of Soviet intellectuals) as an in-
strument against the "opposition." Early in 1958 Kochetov

was removed from the editorship of *Literary Gazette* and replaced by S. Smirnov, the author of a "decent" (i.e. "non-zubatovist") novel, *The Brest Fortress,* which describes without the usual embellishments the military debacle of the beginning of the war. The Third Congress of the Union of Soviet Writers, which took place in May 1959, marked a very important stage of development in Soviet literary affairs. In a good-humored and conciliatory speech Khrushchev called upon the writers to settle their squabbles among themselves and not come running to the "government" for the solution of their problems and to show more tolerance for writers who had "erred" (there was a specific reference to Vladimir Dudintsev). Despite the usual ritualistic mention of the dangers of "revisionism" and the cardinal importance of *partiinost,* the effect of this speech was remarkably beneficial and developments since the Third Congress have on the whole been encouraging.[9] By failing to give them the decisive support for which they evidently hoped, Khrushchev in fact disarmed the neo-Stalinists, who as a consequence have clearly been on the defensive ever since. After the Congress the writers immediately took advantage of Khrushchev's invitation to set their own house in order and ousted Surkov as secretary of the Union of Soviet Writers, appointing the moderate Konstantin Fedin in his place. Further-

---

[9] An interesting sidelight at this Congress was the speech of Boris Polevoi in which he settled accounts with his old friend Howard Fast. One of Fast's reasons for breaking with the Communist Party was that Polevoi, on one of his visits to America, had lied to him about the fate of Kvitko, one of the twenty or so Soviet Yiddish writers who were shot in 1952—a fact which was revealed in the Warsaw *Folkshtimme* in 1956, but which has still not publicly been admitted in the Soviet Union, where Itzik Feffer, Bergelson, and some of the other dead Yiddish writers are occasionally referred to as having "died tragically." Polevoi said in his speech that the defection of Fast from the ranks of "progressive" literature was more than compensated for by the acquisition of Curzio Malaparte who, according to Polevoi, had applied for membership in the Italian Communist Party on his deathbed. Malaparte, a former Fascist and a correspondent with the Italian division fighting the Russians during the war, is the author of *The Skin,* a novel in which it is suggested, among other things, that all communists are homosexuals.

more, two former victims of Surkov, Tvardovsky and Panferov, were adopted onto the board of the Union.

   In the improved atmosphere of the last three years a considerable amount of interesting work, some specimens of
which are given in our collection, has appeared in the literary
journals. What is striking about much recent writing is its
unorthodoxy, in formal rather than political terms, by the
traditional standards of socialist realism. "Three, Seven, Ace"
by the gifted young writer Vladimir Tendryakov is a case in
point. It would have been unthinkable a few years ago to
suggest, however obliquely, that it would be possible for a
whole collective of honest Soviet working men to be cor-
rupted by one evil man. Even more striking is the ending
which leaves the reader in doubt as to whether justice—even
"socialist justice"—will be done or not. Yuri Kazakov's "Outsider" is equally impressive for its sympathetic approach
to the frailties of human nature. Evtushenko's poem "Babi
Yar" speaks for itself as an example of the extent to which
Soviet writers may now express their commitment to radical
change. There is a new style in prose of almost Chekhovian
objectivity, and the once obligatory distortion of Soviet
reality, with the presentation of shortcomings in human nature as transitory "survivals of capitalism" untypical of Soviet
society, is much less common than it was. The extent to
which some Soviet writers would certainly go in dismantling
the literary and political orthodoxies of the past, if all barriers
to free publication were removed, is indicated by the "clan-
destine" tale of the writer who calls himself Nikolai Arzak.
A striking characteristic of this underground fiction is the
extent to which it relies on macabre fantasy and eroticism.
Like Abram Tertz, Arzak revolts against the humdrum realism and the sexual prudery so characteristic of the last three
decades.

   In 1960 there were ominous signs of a comeback on the
part of the neo-Stalinists. In July 1960 Kochetov, writing
in the popular illustrated weekly *Ogonyok*, described *Novy*

Mir as "that paltry little journal which spreads its nihilistic poison among our intelligentsia," and his friend in Leningrad, V. Arkhipov, writing in the neo-Stalinist *Neva*, attacked Ilya Ehrenburg for undermining the principle of *partiinost* and denounced *Literary Gazette* for publishing an article by Norman Cousins, described as "cosmopolitan balderdash." At the end of the year, though probably not as a result of this attack, S. Smirnov was dismissed as the editor of *Literary Gazette* and replaced by his deputy, V. A. Kosolapov. Worst of all, Kochetov was appointed at the beginning of 1961 as the editor of one of the leading literary monthlies, *Oktyabr*, in succession to Feodor Panferov, who died in 1960.[10]

It is unlikely that the re-emergence of Kochetov, which could scarcely have happened without strong official support, is a sign of some impending regression in Soviet literature. The most likely explanation is that the Party wishes to restore some balance between the two camps which now for the first time since the twenties almost openly exist among Soviet writers. There is even a clear identification of certain journals with both sides: the monthlies *Novy Mir* and *Yunost* and the bi-weekly *Literary Gazette* are on the whole "progressive," while *Neva* (and now *Oktyabr*) and the bi-weekly *Literatura i Zhizn* are "reactionary." The progressives, now overwhelmingly strong in numbers, are, it is no doubt considered, best kept in check by having the threat of total reaction always hanging over them. This is a better and more intelligent way of imposing restraint on them than by gross administrative interference.

If anybody should doubt that there are indeed "two camps" among Soviet writers (and this is insistently denied by Soviet publicists), then he has only to read the speeches of Alexander Tvardovsky, and Vsevolod Kochetov, at the Twenty-

---

10 Just before his death Panferov completed a novel, *In the Name of the Young*, which was attacked for its near-pornographical elements. The writer of these lines, who was Panferov's host during his month's visit to England in 1958, is introduced at one stage, under the thinly disguised name of "Mister Wood," in the role of an unsuccessful pimp.

second Party Congress.[11] Kochetov, needless to say, was the
spokesman for the "reactionaries",[12] and his nostalgia for the
clear-cut situation of Stalin's day was only too apparent. He
spoke on the last day of the Congress, evidently having requested permission to reply to Tvardovsky's eloquent appeal
on behalf of the "liberals." It is significant that Kochetov was
the only speaker on this last day who did not welcome in the
prescribed ritualistic fashion the decision, announced the
previous day, to remove Stalin's body from the mausoleum.
Although he never mentions him by name, his speech is
almost a point-by-point reply to Tvardovsky.

Tvardovsky had begun by welcoming what he called the
"spiritual regeneration and liberation from certain con-
straints" which had taken place in "the period after the
Twentieth Congress." As a token of this liberation he mentioned the rehabilitation and restoration to Soviet literature
of those many writers whose names had been erased from
the record as a result of the "cult of personality." But, he
said, none of this was achieved without a struggle, and not
everybody understood the "serious and highly complicated
ideological changes" which resulted from the Twentieth
Congress, and, in a clear reference to such people as Kochetov, he warned his listeners that "we still encounter certain
residual forms of . . . former habits of thought and of
literary practice in the way in which our realities are depicted." Despite all improvements since the Twentieth Congress, literature had not yet been able to take full advantage
of the favorable conditions created by it, and had often not
followed the Party in being bold and truthful. There was
still too much "reticence" and a lack of "living depth and

---

[11] Both speeches appeared in *Pravda*, Tvardovsky's on October 25 and
Kochetov's on October 31, 1961.

[12] It is interesting that a current term among Soviet intellectuals for the
"reactionaries" is *chernosotentsy*, intended to indicate their spiritual kinship with the extreme right-wing, anti-intellectual, and anti-Semitic groups
("Black Hundreds") under Nicholas II. The main appeal, as it was then,
is to "working-class" chauvinism. Concomitantly, more progressive trends in
art and literature are often colloquially described as "left-wing."

truth." Here he reminded his audience of Tolstoy's words: "The hero of my tale, whom I love with all my soul, . . . is *truth*." This continuing lack of truth, according to Tvardovsky, implied lack of trust in the reader, and went back to that period of universal suspiciousness which was so "fatal to art." Tvardovsky then cleverly suggested that, since one of the functions of literature was to assist the Party in educating the New Man, those writers who persisted in trying to deceive their readers about the facts of life in the Soviet Union were in effect cheating the Party as well. Suvorov had said that a soldier is proud not only of his exploits but also of his hardships, and it was therefore incumbent on Soviet literature to describe such hardships "without varnishing reality" (*bez lakirovki*). In literature and "in our press in general" there was still too much immoderate boastfulness in the spirit of the cult of personality, too much concentration on red-letter days, and a corresponding neglect of everyday life with all its work, cares, and needs. There were still some writers who believed that reality should be "embellished," and who never went further than the latest Party decree in their treatment of shortcomings. Writers who just took their materials from the newspapers and from Party documents were, he said, to be compared only with *kolkhozniks* who met their compulsory state deliveries of meat by buying it in the shops. It is noteworthy that not once in his speech did Tvardovsky use the terms "socialist realism" or *partiinost*.

In his reply to Tvardovsky, Kochetov, employing a device which is now characteristic of the literary diehards, quoted some of those remarks in Khrushchev's ambiguous speech to the Third Writer's Congress, in May 1959, which appeared to be favorable to the Zhdanovist treatment of literary problems. He quoted, for instance, Khrushchev's remark that the writers should educate people "primarily by *positive* examples in life." He noted with satisfaction that there had indeed been some books in recent years which laid the main emphasis on "positive heroes," and he picked out for special mention only such writers as Mikhail Bubennov, Anna Kara-

vayeva, and Oles Gonchar, who were notorious under Stalin
for their abject conformity and whom Tvardovsky certainly
had in mind in speaking of those who have failed to draw
any consequences from the Twentieth Congress. Later on,
Kochetov gave a list of approved poets, such as Mikola
Bazhan and Maxim Rylski, who are also distinguished only
by their resistance to the wind of change.

Having noted these "successes," Kochetov went on to de-
nounce those who have attempted in recent years to intro-
duce into Soviet literature the "truth" for which Tvardovsky
appealed in his address to the Congress. Although he mentioned no names, he was clearly referring to Ehrenburg, one
of the main spokesmen of the liberals, in the following passage, which is also a reply to Tvardovsky's remark about the
rehabilitation of writers liquidated under Stalin: ". . . there
are still . . . morose compilers of memoirs who look to the
past rather than to the present day or to the future and who
because of their distorted vision, with zeal worthy of a better
cause, rake around in the rubbish dump of their very fuddled
memories in order to drag out into the light of day moldering
literary corpses and present them as something still capable
of living . . ." He then referred to the young poets of the
type of Evtushenko in the following terms: ". . . we also
have some poetic, and also prosaic, chickens who have still
scarcely lost their yellow down, but who are desperately
anxious to be thought of as fierce fighting cocks . . ." But the
most astonishing passage in Kochetov's speech was one in
which, in total contradiction to the spirit of the Congress, he
virtually called for a purge of the leadership of the Union
of Writers, which the "liberals" have dominated since the re-
moval of Alexei Surkov as General Secretary three years ago:
"It should be said in all frankness that the Congress should
have been told about the state of our literary affairs by the
leadership of the Union of Writers, but this leadership . . .
to put it in military language, has, as you can see yourselves,
lost its combative spirit and is in need of a radical regroup-
ing. Yet it would have a lot to report, if it had not consigned

to oblivion the main questions of our ideological and creative life."

Finally, again clearly replying to Tvardovsky, Kochetov hotly defended the concept of *lakirovka,* i.e. the typically Zhdanovist practice of emphasizing only the positive features of Soviet life. In this connection, too, he appealed to some remarks made by Khrushchev at the third Writer's Congress in defense of the "embellishers," who at that time were less discredited, and were more able to command some political support than is now the case.

To sum up, it must be said that the Twenty-second Congress brought further encouragement for the "liberals." Kochetov was patently out of tune with the general mood and indeed, according to a number of reliable reports, he was constantly interrupted and heckled from the floor with shouts of "Enough!" and "Shut up!" For the time being at any rate, it is clear that the liberals, as represented by Tvardovsky (who is now a candidate member of the Central Committee), have greater political influence, and have little to fear from the desperate rear-guard action of the neo-Stalinists. The latter, however, evidently still have their powerful protectors. Kochetov was given the Order of Lenin on his fiftieth birthday, and his new novel, *The Obkom Secretary,* has received some support, even though it has enraged the liberals by its clearly neo-Stalinist tone. There is the passage, for instance, in which the hero of the novel returns home after attending the secret session on Stalin at the Twentieth Congress and has the following conversation with his wife: " 'Sonya, Sonya,' he said, 'all our life we spent with him, life was unthinkable without him. We thought: We will die but he will live on and on, because in him we loved Lenin. Do you remember how he taught us to love Lenin? Do you remember *Questions of Leninism?'* Then they took out *Questions of Leninism* and read again the inspired chapters of Vladimir Ilich. 'Sonya, Sonya,' he said, 'in him we loved the Party, our dear Party which brought us up, which taught us, which armed us with an idea which made life three times

more sensible and more contented. Sonya!'" The novel was
scathingly attacked in the *Literary Gazette* of December 16,
1961, by Y. Surkov (no connection with Alexei Surkov) for,
in effect, apologizing for Stalin: "[Kochetov] confines criticism of the cult of personality . . . only to the admission
that 'there was a time when Lenin's name was overshadowed
by the name of Stalin,' and then, having admitted this, he
returns to the old song: 'Then came years of struggle against
the deviationists, then the war years. During our common
ordeals Stalin's name rose to untouchable heights.'" Soon
after this, however, Kochetov was defended in *Sovietskaya
Rossiya* (December 22, 1961) and by a Party secretary writing in *Partiinaya Zhizn* (February, 1962). It is quite evident
from the latter that Kochetov has a considerable following,
among all the innumerable jacks-in-office who cannot accept
the implications of the exposure of Stalin, because of their
own past involvement in his crimes.

The affair of Evtushenko's poem "Babi Yar," published in the
Literary Gazette of September 19, 1961, was an even clearer
indication of the division in the ranks of Soviet writers. The
reactions to Evtushenko's vehement denunciation of Russian
anti-Semitism were an ominous expression of the Great Russian chauvinism which characterizes the neo-Stalinists. It was
wrongly assumed in the West at the time that these reactions
were officially inspired. In fact, however, it seems as though
the authorities were far less distressed by Evtushenko's poem
than by the embarrassing display of scarcely veiled anti-
Semitism which it provoked. It is an encouraging sign of the
relative lack of influence of the neo-Stalinists that, while no
sanctions appear to have been applied to Evtushenko, the
editor of *Literatura i Zhizn* was dismissed for having published the disgraceful outbursts of Markov and Starikov.
From all this and much similar evidence it would seem that
Khrushchev, if not the Party as a whole, continues to lean
toward a neutrality which is favorable to the "progressives."
It is of course impossible to say how long this state of affairs
will continue, since it obviously depends on obscure group-

ings at the center of power, of which we can have no real knowledge.

In a passage at the end of *Dr. Zhivago*, Pasternak says: "Although the enlightenment and liberation which had been expected to come after the war had not come with victory, the presage of freedom was in the air throughout these post-war years, and it was their only historical meaning."

We have seen that there has indeed been a growth of freedom in the years since Stalin's death. The writers have played a great part in this. In this brief and necessarily inadequate survey I have dwelt on some of the more unsavory aspects of Soviet literary history, but I should like to end by saying that the majority of Soviet writers have acquitted themselves with honor in a situation which required more courage, patience, intelligence, and fortitude than could ever be imagined by people who live in more fortunate circumstances. One day it will perhaps be shown that not only Russia, but the whole world, is indebted to Soviet literature for keeping alive, in unimaginable conditions, that indefinable sense of freedom which is common to all men.

DISSONANT VOICES
IN SOVIET LITERATURE

This early prose fragment was originally published in an obscure and ephemeral Social-Revolutionary newspaper Liberty of Labor (Volya Truda), *on November 20, 1918, and has only recently come to light. It will be of interest to readers of Dr.* Zhivago *since it shows that already in 1918 Pasternak had arrived at the central conception of his novel, published forty years later. Moreover, it contains three names (Galliula, Gimazetdin, and Mekhanoshin) which later appeared in Dr. Zhivago, and the episode of the accident foreshadows three important events in the novel: the death of the hero's father, the interruption of a concert because of an accident to one of the performers, and the death of Zhivago himself. But most interesting of all is the attitude to the Revolution and revolutionaries suggested by Kovalevsky's reflections as he travels with his Zhivago-like companion to Moscow, presumably after having heard the news of the abdication of the Czar and of the February Revolution. This aspect of the fragment is discussed at greater length in Mr. Hayward's introduction. The editors are indebted to George Katkov for the discovery and interpretation of this fragment.* Translation by Max Hayward.

BORIS PASTERNAK

Without Love

A Chapter from a Novel

He had a brother and it was the brother who walked around the house, his feet crunching in the snow, and on the frozen steps as he went up them to knock on the door, to knock as one does on the door of a blizzard-swept house when the

wind turns your fingers to ice and, whistling and howling,
roars into your ears that you should knock even louder, if you
know what's good for you . . . and all the time the same
wind hammers on the shutters to drown your knocking and
confuse the people inside.

They heard him and opened. The house stood on a hill.
The door was torn from his grasp together with one of his
gloves, and, as the door flew to and fro and they tried to
catch it, the gray snow-swept countryside rushed into the
hall and breathed on the lamps, bringing with it the distant
tinkle of a sleigh bell. The sound sank in the vast snow field
and, gasping for breath, called to the rescue. It was carried
to the house by the overwhelming onrush of the blizzard,
which had gripped the door in its clutches, and by the dips
in the sleigh track which had been caught up in some demo-
niac movement and was slithering under the runners, throwing up swirling columns of choking snow for all to see for
miles around.

When the door had been caught and shut they all got up
to meet the specter in the hall; in his high boots of reindeer
skin he was like a wild animal standing on its hind legs.

"Is it coming?" Kovalevsky asked.

"Yes, they're on the way. You must get ready." He licked
his lips and wiped his nose. There was pandemonium as
bundles and baskets were brought out; the children had
sulked since nightfall—till then, for want of something better to do and on learning that everything was packed, and
that there would still be a long wait and nothing to talk about,
they had pointlessly weighed out raisins on the bare table—
and now they set up a great wail, putting the blame on each
other—"It's not me, it's Petya who's howling because papa's
going away"—and, seeking fair play and a refuge from the
night, the raisins, the blizzard, the chaos, their papas about to
depart, the traveling baskets, the oil lamps, and the fur coats,
they tried to bury their heads in their mothers' aprons.

But instead they were snatched up, as though on a signal,
by their nurses and mothers and carried with a sudden gust

of feeling into the passage, and in the hall, which echoed the voices of the coachmen through the folding door, they were held up to their fathers. They all stood bare-headed and, crossing themselves with emotion, exchanged hurried kisses and said it was time to go.

Meanwhile the Tartar coachmen (they were three in number, but there seemed to be ten), carrying lights which splashed the snow without spilling into it altogether, dashed up to the horses harnessed in file and, ducking down to look at the girths and fetlocks, jumped up again at once and began to race around like madmen, brandishing their flares and lighting up in turn the trunks standing around the sleigh, the snow, the underbellies and flanks of the horses and their muzzles which together formed a slender garland, borne aloft, as it seemed, by the wind. The moment of departure depended on the Tartars. Round about the snow sang in the forest and raved in the open country, and it seemed as though the surging sound of the night knew Tartar and was arguing with Mininbay, who had climbed onto the roof of the sleigh and, clutching at his hands, was telling him to fasten down the trunks not in the way Gimazetdin was shouting, nor in the way suggested by Galliula, who was hardly able to keep his feet because of the storm and had gone quite hoarse. . . . The moment of departure depended on the Tartars. They could hardly wait to take up their whips, whistle at the horses, and abandon themselves to the final devil-may-care *aida*.[1] After this no power on earth would hold the horses back. Like drunkards to the bottle the Tartars were drawn irresistibly, more and more eagerly with each passing minute, to the mournful whoops and cajolery of their trade. Hence the feverish movements of their frenzied alcoholic hands as they rushed to help their masters into their heavy fur coats.

And now the flares sent a last farewell kiss to those who were being left behind. Goltsev had already stumbled into the depths of the sleigh and Kovalevsky, floundering in the

---

[1] A Tartar word meaning, roughly "let's go!"

tails of his three coats, climbed after him under the heavy
traveling rug. Unable to feel the floor through their broad
felt boots, they nestled down in the straw, the cushions, and
the sheepskins. A flare appeared on the far side of the sleigh
but suddenly bobbed down out of sight.

The sleigh shuddered and heaved. It slithered forward,
lurched over, and began to turn on its side. A low whistle
came from the depths of an Asian soul, and after righting the
sleigh with their shoulders, Mininbay and Gimazetdin leaped
into their seats. The sleigh shot forward as though borne on
wings and plunged into the nearby forest. The open country,
disheveled and moaning, rose up behind it. It was glad to see
the end of the sleigh which disappeared without a trace
among the trees with branches like carpet slippers, at the
junction with the main road to Chistopole and Kazan. Mininbay got off here and, wishing his master a good journey,
vanished in the storm like a flurry of powdered snow. They
sped on and on over the arrow-straight highway.

"I asked her to come here with me," one of them thought,
breathing in the dampness of thawing fur. "I remember how
it was." A lot of streetcars had got stuck in front of the theater
and an anxious crowd was milling around the first one. . . .
"The performance has begun," the usher said in a confidential
whisper and, gray in his cloth uniform, he drew back the
cloth curtain separating the stalls from the lighted cloakroom
with its benches, galoshes, and posters. In the intermission
(it went on longer than usual) they walked around the foyer,
peering sideways at the mirrors, and neither of them knew
what to do with their hands which were hot and red. "So
there now; thinking it all over," she took a sip of seltzer
water, "I just don't know what to do or how I should decide.
So please don't be surprised if you hear that I've gone to the
front as a nurse. I shall enroll in a few days' time. . . ." "Why
don't you come with me to the Kama?" he said. She laughed.

The intermission had gone on so long because of the musical item at the beginning of the second act. It could not be
played without an oboe, and the oboist was the unfortunate

cause of the streetcar stoppage in front of the theater. "He's badly hurt," people whispered to each other, taking their places when the painted hem of the curtain began to glow. "He was unconscious when they pulled him from under the wheels," their friends told them, as they padded over the cloth-covered carpet in heavy galoshes, trailing the ends of kerchiefs and shawls.

"And now they'll be surprised," he thought, trying to synchronize the flow of his thoughts with the movement of the sleigh and lull himself to sleep.

The other man was thinking about the purpose of their sudden departure, about the reception awaiting them at the other end, and about what should be done in the first instance. He also thought that Goltsev was asleep, not suspecting that Goltsev was wide-awake and that it was he himself who was asleep, plunging in his dreams from pothole to pothole together with his thoughts about revolution, which now, as once before, meant more to him than his fur coat and his belongings, more than his wife and child, more than his own life and more than other peoples' lives, and with which he would not part for anything in the world—even in his sleep—once he had laid hold of them and kindled them within himself.

Their eyes opened languidly, of their own accord. They could not help their surprise. A village lay in a deep otherworldly trance. The snow glittered. The three horses had broken file, they had left the road and stood huddled together. The night was bright and still. The front horse, its head raised, was gazing over a snowdrift at something left far behind. The moon shone black and mysterious behind a house tightly swathed in frosty air. After the solemnity of the forest and the blizzard-swept loneliness of the open country a human dwelling was like an apparition in a fairy tale. The house seemed conscious of its awesome magic and was in no hurry to answer the coachman's knock. It stood silent, unwilling to break its own oppressive spell. The snow glittered. But soon two voices, unseen to each other, spoke loudly through

the gate. They divided the whole world between them, these
two, as they talked to each other through the timbers, in the
midst of infinite stillness. The man who was opening the gate
took the half which looked north, unfolding beyond the roof
of the house, and the other man, who was waiting for him,
took the half which the horse could see over the edge of the
snowdrift.

At the previous station Gimazetdin had wakened only
Kovalevsky, and the coachman who had driven them to this
point was a stranger to Goltsev. But now he immediately recognized Dementi Mekhanoshin to whom he had once issued
a certificate in his office—a good sixty miles from here—to
the effect that, being the owner of a troika and plying the last
stage between Bilyar and Syuginsk, he was working for
defense.

It was odd to think that he had certified this house and its
coachyard and that, knowing nothing at all of them, he had
underwritten this magic village and the starry night above it.
Later, while the horses were being reharnessed and the
sleepy wife of the coachman gave them tea; while the clock
ticked and they tried to make conversation, and bugs crawled
sultrily over calendars and portraits of crowned persons;
while bodies sleeping on the benches snored and wheezed
fitfully like clockwork devices of different systems, Dementi
kept going out and returning, and each time his appearance
changed, depending on what he had taken down from a nail
or dragged from under his bed. When he came in the first
time to tell his wife to give the gentlemen sugar and to get
out the white bread for them, he was wearing a smock and
looked like a hospitable peasant; the second time, coming in
for the reins, he was a laborer dressed in a short Siberian
jacket, and finally he appeared as a coachman in a heavy fur
coat. Without coming in, he leaned through the doorway and
said that the horses were ready, that it was past three in the
morning and time for them to leave. Then, pushing open the
door with the stock of his whip, he went into the dark world
outside which reverberated loudly at his first steps.

The rest of the journey left no trace in their memories. It was getting light when Goltsev woke and his countryside was covered in a haze. An endless, straggling convoy of sleighs was lumbering by in a cloud of steam. They were overtaking it, and it looked therefore as though the timber-loaded sleighs were creaking and swaying without moving forward and that the drivers were just marking time, stomping their feet on the ground to keep warm. The broad cart road ran to one side of the track over which they were racing and it was a much higher level. Legs rose and fell, trampling the still, lit stars, and there was a movement of hands, horses' muzzles, cowled heads, and sleighs. It seemed as though the gray and weary suburban morning was itself drifting over the clear sky in great damp patches toward the place where it sensed the railroad, the brick walls of factory buildings, heaps of damp coal, and the drudgery of fumes and smoke. The sleigh raced on, flying over ruts and potholes, its bell jingling frantically. There was still no end to the convoy and it was high time for the sun to rise, but the sun was still far away.

The sun was still far away. They would see it only after another five versts, after a short stop at the inn, after the message from the factory director and the long restless wait in his anteroom.

Then it appeared. It entered the manager's office with them, flooded rapidly over the carpet, settled behind the flowerpots, and smiled at the caged chaffinches by the window, at the fir trees outside, at the stove, and at all forty-four volumes of the leather-bound Brockhaus encyclopedia.

After this, during Kovalevsky's conversation with the manager, the yard outside was alive and at play, tirelessly scattering turquoise and amber, wafts of pungent resin from the sweating pines and beads of molten hoarfrost.

The manager glanced toward Goltsev. "He's my friend," said Kovalevsky quickly. "Don't worry, you can talk freely. . . . So you knew Breshkovskaya?" [2]

---

[2] One of the founders of the Social Revolutionary party.

Suddenly Kovalevsky got up and, turning to Goltsev, shouted in panic: "And what about my papers? Just as I said! Kostya, now what shall I do?"

Goltsev didn't at first understand: "I've got our passports. . . ."

"That bundle of papers!" Kovalevsky interrupted him angrily. "I asked you to remind me."

"Oh, I'm sorry, Yura. We left them behind. It really is too bad of me. I can't think how I . . ."

Their host, a short thickset man who had difficulty with his breathing, attended in the meantime to his managerial business. He kept looking at his watch and, puffing and blowing, stirred the logs in the stove with a poker. Sometimes, as though changing his mind about something, he would suddenly stop in his tracks halfway across the room, swivel around, and dart over to the desk at which Kovalevsky was writing to his brother: . . . "in other words, all is well. I only hope it goes on like this. Now for the most important thing. Do exactly as I tell you. Kostya says that we left a bundle with all my illegal stuff lying on Masha's suitcase in the hall. Open it up and if there are any manuscripts among the pamphlets (memoirs, notes on the scope of the organization, letters in code relating to the secret rendezvous in our house, to the period of Kulisher's escape, etc.) wrap it all up, seal it, and send it to me in Moscow at the office in Teploryadnaya with the first reliable person—depending of course on how things work out. But you know what to do as well as I do and if there is a change of . . ."

"Do come and have some coffee," whispered the manager with a shuffle and a click of the heels. "I mean you, young man," he explained to Goltsev with even greater care and paused respectfully at the sight of Kovalevsky's cuff which was poised over the paper, waiting to pounce on the needed word.

Three Austrian prisoners of war went past the window, talking and blowing their noses. They carefully walked around the puddles which had formed.

". . . if there is a change of climate," Kovalevsky found the word he needed, "don't send the papers to Moscow, but hide them in a safe place. I'm counting on you for this and all other things we agreed on. We have to catch the train soon. I'm dead tired. We hope to have a good sleep in the train. I'm writing to Masha separately. Well, all the best. P.S. Just imagine, it turns out that R., the manager, is an old Social-Revolutionary. What do you make of that?"

At this moment Goltsev looked into the office with a slice of buttered bread in his hand. Swallowing the half-chewed piece he had just bitten off, he said: "You're writing to Misha, are you? Tell him to send," he took another bite at his bread and butter and continued chewing and swallowing, "my papers as well. I've changed my mind. Don't forget, Yura. And come and have some coffee."

Zamyatin was one of those few Soviet writers who refused to make compromises or rationalizations in the face of the inherent moral evil of the Soviet dictatorship. Had other Soviet intellectuals followed his (and Pasternak's) example it is possible that Stalin would not have obtained his ascendancy over the nation in 1929.

Before the revolution Zamyatin was a member of the Bolshevik faction of the Social Democratic Party. In a short autobiographical sketch published in 1925, he ended with the words: "Then I was a Bolshevik, now I am not a Bolshevik." Like Gorky he had recoiled from Lenin's premature assumption of supreme power; but unlike Gorky, Zamyatin did not subsequently come to terms with the fait accompli. *His novel* We, *published in Prague in 1924, a forerunner of Orwell's* 1984, *foresaw the horrors to come. In "On Literature, Revolution, and Entropy," published in Moscow in 1924 and again in 1926, he defiantly asserted the need for heresy in literature as the very condition of its existence. When, in 1929, he was framed together with Pilnyak, he refused to submit, and, apparently with the assistance of Gorky, was able to emigrate to Paris where he died in 1937.* Translation by Walter N. Vickery.

EVGENI ZAMYATIN

On Literature, Revolution, and Entropy

Tell me what is the final integer, the one at the very top, the biggest of all.

But that's ridiculous! Since the number of integers is infinite, how can you have a final integer?

Well then how can you have a final revolution? There is
no final revolution. Revolutions are infinite.

—Evgeni Zamyatin, *We*

Ask the question point-blank: What is revolution? You get a
variety of replies. Some people will answer in the style of
Louis XIV: *La révolution, c'est nous.* Others turn to the
calendar, giving you the day and the month. Still others spell
it out letter by letter. But if we go one stage beyond the al-
phabet and articulate our answer, this is what we get:

Two dead, dark stars collide with a deafening but unheard
crash and spark into life a new star: that's revolution. A mole-
cule breaks loose from its orbit, invades a neighboring atomic
universe, and gives birth to a new chemical element: that's
revolution. With one book Lobachevsky[1] cleaves the cen-
turies-old walls of the Euclidean world and opens the way
to the infinities of non-Euclidean space: that's revolution.

Revolution is everywhere and in all things; it is infinite,
there is no final revolution, no end to the sequence of integers.
Social revolution is only one in the infinite sequence of integers. The law of revolution is not a social law, it is immeasurably greater, it is a cosmic, universal law—such as the law
of the conservation of energy and the law of the loss of energy
(entropy). Some day an exact formula will be established
for the law of revolution. And in this formula nations, classes,
stars—and books will be expressed as numerical values.

Red, fiery, death-dealing is the law of revolution; but that
death is the birth of a new life, of a new star. And cold, blue
as ice, as the icy interplanetary infinities, is the law of entropy. The flame turns from fiery red to an even, warm pink,
no longer death-dealing but comfort-producing; the sun ages
and becomes a planet suitable for highways, shops, beds,
prostitutes, prisons: that is a law. And in order to make the

---

[1] Nikolai Lobachevsky (1793-1856), Russian mathematician who pioneered
non-Euclidean geometry.

planet young again, we must set it afire, we must thrust it off the smooth highway of evolution: that is a law.

The flame, true enough, will grow cold tomorrow or the day after tomorrow (in the Book of Genesis days are years and even aeons). But already today there should be somebody who can foresee that; there should be somebody today to speak heretically of tomorrow. Heretics are the only (bitter-tasting) remedy for the entropy of human thought.

When (in science, religion, social life, art) a flaming, seething sphere grows cold, the fiery molten rock becomes covered with dogma—with a hard, ossified, immovable crust. In science, religion, social life, and art, dogmatization is the entropy of thought; what has been dogmatized no longer inflames, it is merely warm—and soon it is to be cool. The sermon on the Mount, delivered beneath the scorching sun to upstretched arms and rending sobs, gives way to slumberous prayer in some well-appointed abbey. Galileo's tragic *"E pur si muove"* gives way to calm calculations in some well-heated office in an observatory. On the Galileos the epigones build —slowly, coral upon coral, forming a reef: this is the path of evolution. Till one day a new heresy explodes and blows up the dogma's crust, together with all the ever so stable, rock-like structures that had been erected on it.

Explosions are not comfortable things. That is why the exploders, the heretics, are quite rightly annihilated by fire, by axes, and by words. Heretics are harmful to everybody today, to every evolution, to the difficult, slow, useful, so very useful, constructive process of coral reef building; imprudently and foolishly they leap into today from tomorrow. They are romantics. It was right and proper that in 1797 Babeuf[2] had his head cut off: he had leaped into 1797, skipping one hundred and fifty years. It is equally right and proper that heretical literature, literature that is damaging to dogma,

---

[2] François Babeuf (1760-1797), French revolutionary who demanded a program of egalitarianism and practical socialism after the Thermidorian reaction. He was executed for plotting to overthrow the government by force.

should also have its head cut off: such literature is harmful.

But harmful literature is more useful than useful literature: because it is anti-entropic, it militates against calcification, sclerosis, encrustedness, moss, peace. It is utopian and ridiculous. Like Babeuf in 1797 it is right one hundred and fifty years later.

We know Darwin, we know that after Darwin came mutations, Weismannism, neo-Lamarckism. But these are only penthouses and balconies while Darwin is the building itself. And the building contains not only tadpoles and toadstools, it also contains man. Fangs grow sharp only if there is someone to gnaw on; the domestic hen's wings serve only to flap with. Ideas and hens obey the same law: ideas which feed on minced meat lose their teeth just as civilized men do. Heretics are necessary to health. If there are no heretics, they have to be invented.

Live literature does not set its watch by yesterday's time, nor by today's, but by tomorrow's. Live literature is like a sailor who is sent aloft; from the masthead he can descry sinking vessels, icebergs, and maelstroms which are not yet visible from the deck. You can drag him down from the mast and put him to work in the boiler room or on the capstan, but that won't change a thing: the mast is still there and from the masthead another sailor will be able to see what the first sailor has seen.

In stormy weather you need a man aloft. And right now the weather is stormy. SOS signals are coming in from all directions. Only yesterday the writer was able to stroll calmly on deck, taking snapshots of "real life"; but who wants to look at pictures of landscapes and scenes from daily life when the world has taken on a forty-five-degree list, when the green waves are threatening to swallow us and the ship is breaking up? Right now we can look and think only as men do in the face of death: we shall die—and what then? How have we lived? If we are to live all over again in some new way, then

by what shall we live, and for what? Right now we need in
literature the vast philosophical horizon, the vast sweep from
the masthead, from the sky above, we need the most ultimate,
the most fearsome, the most fearless "Whys?" and "What
nexts?"

Those are the questions that children ask. But children are
after all the boldest of philosophers; they come into life
naked, not covered by one single small leaf of dogma or
creed. That is why their questions are always so ridiculously
naïve and so frighteningly complicated. The new people,
who are right now coming into life, are naked and fearless
as children, and they too, like children, like Schopenhauer,
Dostoevsky, Nietzsche, are asking their "whys" and "what
nexts." Philosophers of genius, children, and ordinary people
are equally wise, because they ask equally stupid questions—
stupid for civilized man who possesses a well-furnished apartment, with a magnificent bathroom, and a well-furnished
dogma.

Organic chemistry has blurred the dividing line between
living and dead matter. It is a mistake to divide people into
the living and the dead: there are live-dead people and live-
live people. The live-dead people also write, walk, talk, act.
But they do not make mistakes; only machines produce without mistakes, but they produce only dead things. The live-
live people are all mistakes, searchings, questions, torments.
So too what we write also walks and talks, but it can be
live-dead or live-live. The genuinely live, stopping at nothing,
brooking no obstacle or hindrance, searches for the answers
to foolish, "childish" questions. The answers may be wrong,
the philosophy erroneous—but errors are of greater value
than truths: truth is machinelike, error is alive, truth re-
assures, error unsettles. And even if the answers are quite
impossible, so much the better: to ask answered questions
is the privilege of minds constructed on the same principle

as the cow's stomach, which is ideally suited, as well we know, to chewing the cud.

If there were in nature something fixed, if there were truths, all this would, of course, be wrong. But happily all truths are erroneous. This is precisely the significance of the dialectic process: today's truths become tomorrow's errors; there is no final integer.

This (one and only) truth is only for the strong: weak-nerved minds unfailingly require a finite universe, a final integer; they require, as Nietzsche said, "the crutches of as-surance." The weak-nerved do not have the strength to in-clude themselves in the dialectic syllogism. True, this is difficult. But it is the very thing that Einstein did succeed in doing: he managed to remember that he, Einstein, with watch in hand observing motion, was also moving; he suc-ceeded in looking at the earth's movements *from outside.*

That is precisely how great literature—literature that knows no final integer—looks at the earth's movements.

The formal characteristic of live literature is the same as its inner characteristic: the negation of truth, that is, the negation of what everyone knows and what I knew up to this moment. Live literature leaves the canonical rails, leaves the broad highway.

The broad highway of Russian literature, worn shiny by the giant wheels of Tolstoy, Gorky, Chekhov, is realism, real life: consequently we must turn away from real life. The rails, sanctified and canonized by Blok, Sologub, Bely, are the rails of symbolism— symbolism which turned away from real life: consequently we must turn toward real life.

Absurd, isn't it? The intersection of parallel lines is also absurd. But it's absurd only in the canonical, plane geometry of Euclid; in non-Euclidian geometry it's an axiom. The one essential is to cease to be flat, to rise above the plane. Today's literature has the same relation to the plane surface of real

life as an aircraft has to the earth: it is nothing more than a
runway from which to take off and soar aloft from real life
to reality, to philosophy, to the realm of the fantastic. Leave
the carts of yesterday to creak along the great highways. The
living have strength enough to cut off their yesterdays.

We can put a police officer or a commissar in the cart, but
the cart will still remain a cart. And literature will still remain the literature of yesterday, if we drive real life—even
"revolutionary real life"—along the well-traveled highway—
even if we drive it in a fast troika with bells. What we need
today are automobiles, airplanes, winged flight, seconds, dot-
ted lines.

The old, slow, soporific descriptions are no more. The order
of the day is laconicism—but every word must be super-
charged, high-voltage. Into one second must be compressed
what formerly went into a sixty-second minute. Syntax becomes elliptical, volatile; complicated pyramids of periods
are dismantled and broken down into the single stones of
independent clauses. In swift movement the canonical, the
habitual eludes the eye: hence the unusual, often strange
symbolism and choice of words. The image is sharp, syn-
thetic, it contains only the one basic trait which one has time
to seize upon from a moving automobile. The lexicon hallowed by custom has been invaded by dialect, neologisms,
science, mathematics, technology.

There is a rule, if you can call it a rule, that the writer's
talent consists in making the rule the exception; but there
are far more writers who turn the exception into the rule.

The business of science and art alike is the projection of
the world onto co-ordinates. Differences in form are due to
differences in the co-ordinates. All realist forms involve projection onto the fixed, plane co-ordinates of the Euclidian
world. These co-ordinates have no existence in nature. This
finite, fixed world does not exist; it is a convention, an ab-
straction, an unreality. And therefore realism—be it "so-

cialist" or "bourgeois"—is unreal; immeasurably closer to reality is projection onto fast-moving, curved surfaces—as in the new mathematics and the new art. Realism which is not primitive, not *realia* but *realiora*, consists in displacement, distortion, curvature, nonobjectivity. The lens of the camera is objective.

A new form is not intelligible to all; for many it is difficult. Maybe. The habitual, the banal is of course simpler, pleasanter, more comfortable. Euclid's world is very simple and Einstein's world is very difficult; nevertheless it is now impossible to return to Euclid's. No revolution, no heresy is comfortable and easy. Because it is a leap, it is a rupture of the smooth evolutionary curve, and a rupture is a wound, a pain. But it is a necessary wound: most people suffer from hereditary sleeping sickness, and those who are sick with this ailment (entropy) must not be allowed to sleep, or they will go to their last sleep, the sleep of death.

This same sickness is common to artists and writers: they go contentedly to sleep in their favorite artistic form which they have devised, then twice revised. They do not have the strength to wound themselves, to cease to love what has become dear to them. They do not have the strength to come out from their lived-in, laurel-scented rooms, to come out into the open air and start anew.

To wound oneself, it is true, is difficult, even dangerous. But to live today as yesterday and yesterday as today is even more difficult for the living.

Victor Shklovsky (b. 1893), together with Roman Jakobson, was the leader of the formalist movement, the most significant Russian contribution to the theory of literature. Formalism continues to have considerable influence abroad, although, in Russia from the early thirties onwards, the very word "formalism" became a highly elastic term of abuse, and has often been wrongfully applied to deviations from socialist realism.

This excerpt from Shklovsky's pamphlet Literature and Cinema, published in Berlin in 1923, is a concise expression of the formalist position. Translation by Charles A. Moser and Patricia Blake.

VICTOR SHKLOVSKY

Form and Material in Art

It is usually thought to be obvious that every artist wishes to express something, to recount something, and that this "something" is called the content of a work. And the means by which this "something" is expressed—words, images, meter in verse, color and line in a painting—are called the form of the work.

Nearly everybody distinguishes between these two aspects of every work of art. People who want art to be of direct benefit to humanity usually say that in art the most important thing is content, i.e. what is said in it.

The so-called aesthetes, lovers of the beautiful, say that for them the important thing in art is "not what, but how," i.e. the main thing is form. Now let us calmly attempt, with-

out becoming involved in this dispute, to look detachedly
upon the object of the dispute.

The problem concerns works of art.

Let us begin with an analysis of musical compositions.

Music

A musical composition consists of a series of sounds of different pitch and different timbre, i.e. of sounds high and
low following one after the other. These sounds are combined
into groups; the groups bear a certain relationship to one
another. Besides this, there is nothing in a musical composition. Now what have we found in it? We have found, not
form and content, but rather material and form, i.e. sounds
and the disposition of sounds. Of course there may be people
who say that in music there is also content, namely a sad or
a gay mood. But there are facts which show that there is
contained in a musical composition neither sadness nor joy,
that such feelings are not the essence of music, and that its
creators set no store by them. Hanslick, a famous student of
the theory of music, cites the example of how Bach wrote
indecent couplets to music which he had composed for
psalms; the music was just as suitable for the couplets. On
the other hand, it is by no means rare for many sects to use
dance tunes for their hymns. Moreover, to do this they had
to overcome the traditional connection of these tunes with
the normal circumstances of their performances.

This is why Kant defined music as pure form, i.e. denied
the existence of so-called content in it.

Painting

Now let us look at the so-called graphic arts. This name is
inaccurate and does not cover all phenomena involved. Decorative art obviously depicts nothing. But in European art
at least the graphic arts usually depict the so-called external
world, scenes of work, pictures of men and wild animals.

Scarcely anyone will dispute this, and moreover, we know
from the artists themselves that when they paint flowers or
grass or a cow, they are not interested in whether these have
any practical use, but only in how they appear, i.e. in color
and line. For the artist the external world is not the content
of a picture, but material for a picture. The famous Renaissance artist Giotto says: "A picture is—primarily—a con-
junction of colored planes." The Impressionists painted things
as though they saw them without understanding—only as
spots of color. They perceived the world as if they had just
suddenly awakened. This is how the Russian "Itinerant"
artist Kramskoy[1] defined the effect made on him by the
Impressionists' pictures.

Another realistic painter, Surikov,[2] used to say that the
"idea" of his famous picture "The Boyar's Wife, Morozova"
occurred to him when he saw a jackdaw on the snow. For
him this picture was primarily "black on white." To anticipate
a little, I will say that Surikov's picture is not merely the
development of his impression of a color contrast; in this
picture we encounter a great many heterogeneous elements,
particularly in relation to meaning, but even meanings are
used as material for artistic construction.

Thanks to such an attitude toward "representation," there
is in art an inclination to transform depiction, so-called organic forms, e.g. the outlines of a flower, a wild animal, grass,
a ram's horn (as in Buryat designs), into an ornament—a
design which no longer represents anything. . . . All rug designs, in particular the designs on Persian rugs, are the result
of just such a transformation of organic form into purely
artistic form.

This transformation cannot be explained by religious pro-
hibition (Islam avoids depiction out of "dread of idolatry"),
since there exist, during all stages in the development of Persian tapestry, rugs depicting entire scenes involving people
and animals. This shocks nobody. We have Persian miniatures

---

[1] Ivan Kramskoy (1837-1887), Russian painter of realistic portraits.
[2] Vasili Surikov (1848-1916), Russian realist painter.

which, it would seem, were influenced just as much by religious prohibitions as tapestry. On the other hand, we know that in Greece, where there were no religious prohibitions of this kind, a geometrical style developed (there is a vase in this style in the Petersburg Hermitage), and during this phase the way the human body was depicted vividly recalls the rendering of stylized deer in tapestry.

The entire history of written languages illustrates the struggle between the ornamental principle and the representative principle.

It is, moreover, curious to note that written languages at the first stages of their existence, and among many peoples, even to the present day (Turks, Persians), fulfilled decorative purposes.

The divorce of the letter or ideograph from its conventional function is a result not only of the technique, but also of the stylization of writing. . . . The letter is an ornament.

The artist clings to depiction, to the world, not in order to create a world, but rather to utilize complex and rewarding material in his art. This break with representation, this transformation of picture into calligraphy, occurs more than once in the history of art, but artists have always returned to representation.

But the artist needs the world for his picture. There is a Greek anecdote about an artist: people came up to him at an exhibition and asked him to remove the cloth from his painting. "I cannot do that," said the artist. "My painting depicts a painting covered with a cloth." In analyzing a painting, people who wish to go beyond its limits, who talk about demons in connection with Picasso, about war in connection with all of cubism, who wish to decipher paintings like a rebus, want to deprive a painting of its form in order to see it better.

Paintings are not at all windows onto another world—they are things.

Literature

It is in literature that the view of the separation between form and content seems most plausible.

And in fact, a great many people suppose that the poet possesses a specific thought, a thought about God, for example, and expounds this thought in words.

These words may be beautiful, and then we say that the work's form, sound-form or image-form, is beautiful. This is what most people think about form and content in literature.

But first of all it cannot be affirmed that there is content in every work of art, since we know that in the first stages of its development poetry possessed no precise content.

For instance, the songs of the Indians in British Guiana consist of the exclamation: "Heya, heya." The songs of the Patagonians, the Papuans, and certain North American tribes are also senseless. Poetry appeared before content.

The singer's task was not to render in words some thought or other, but to devise a series of sounds possessing a definite relationship one to another, which is called form. These sounds should not be confused with sounds in music. They have not only an acoustic but also an articulated form: they are produced by the singer's vocal organs. Perhaps in a primitive poem we are dealing not so much with an ejaculation as with an articulated gesture, a sort of ballet of the speech organs. Even in modern poetry, the act of speaking it may have, in varying degrees, the same sensuous effect on us— "the sweetness of verses on the lips.". . .

A line of verse quite often appears in the poet's mind as a definite patch of sound not yet verbalized. . . .

Alexander Blok used to tell me about this phenomenon as he had observed it in himself.

Victor Hugo used to say that what was difficult was not finding a rhyme, but "filling the spaces between rhymes with poetry," i.e. fitting the "image" aspect to the already existing sound aspect.

In short, the deeper we go into the study of verse, the more complex become the phenomena of form which we discover within it.

But poems are formal throughout and it is unnecessary for us to change our methods of investigation. What is called the image aspect is also not intended to be depictive or explanatory.

Potebnya's notion that the image is always simpler than the concept it replaces is absolutely incorrect.

There is a line in one of Tyutchev's poems saying that flashes of heat lightning are "like deaf and dumb demons conversing with each other." Why is the image of the deaf and dumb demons simpler or more obvious than the lightning flashes?

In erotic poetry we generally find that erotic objects are designated by various "image" names. The "Song of Songs" is an extended series of such comparisons. Here we are dealing not so much with imagery as with what I call "estrangement," in the sense of making things strange.

We live in a poor and enclosed world. We no more feel the world in which we live than we feel the clothes we wear. We fly through the world like Jules Verne characters, "through outer space in a capsule." But in our capsule there are no windows.

The Pythagoreans used to say that we do not hear the music of the spheres because it goes on uninterruptedly. In the same way those who live by the sea do not hear the noise of the waves. We do not hear even the words we speak. We speak a pitiful language of incompletely uttered words. We look one another in the face but do not see one another.

The Renovation of Form

In his diary, Tolstoy wrote ". . . I dusted off the sofa and couldn't remember doing it. . . . So if I did dust it off, I did it unconsciously. . . . If someone had seen it consciously he could have reconstructed my action. . . . And our entire life, lived through unconsciously, is all as if it had never been."

Perhaps mankind began using reason too early. With its reason it jumped forward out of turn, like a soldier from the ranks, and began running amok.

We live as if coated with rubber. We must recover the world. Perhaps all the horror (which is little felt) of our days, the Entente, the war, Russia, can be explained by our lack of feeling for the world, by the absence of an extensive art. The purpose of the image is to call an object by a new name. To do this, to make the object an artistic fact, it must be abstracted from among the facts of life.

To do this, we must first of all "shake up" things. . . . We must rip things from their ordinary sequence of associations. Things must be turned over like logs in a fire. . . .

The poet removes the labels from things. . . . Things rebel, casting off their old names and taking on a new aspect together with their new names. The poet brings about a semantic dislocation, he snatches the concept out of the sequence in which it is usually found and transfers it with the aid of the word (the trope) to another meaning-sequence. And now we have a sense of novelty at finding the object in a fresh sequence.

This is one of the ways of making things tangible. In the image we have the object, the recollection of its former name, its new name, and the associations connected with the new name. . . .

One device in modern artistic prose is very curious. To create an unusual perception of things in modern prose there

is a widely used device which has never been described and
which I would define as the "recurrent image." In Russian
literature it is represented by Dostoevsky, Rozanov, Andrei
Bely, Zamyatin and also by the Serapion brothers. It consists
in using a certain word (usually such a word is "orchestrated"
by means of repetition or else an exotic word is chosen) and
then equating all the other matter in the work of art to
this word. . . .

Andrei Bely in his reminiscènces of Blok (*Epopeya*, book
2) notes that Merezhkovsky wore shoes with pompons on
them. These "pompons" rapidly come to define Merezhkovsky's entire life. He speaks with pompons, he thinks with
pompons, etc. In this case we seem to have a certain mech-
anization of the imagery device.

The word deprived of sense is constantly associated with
a number of other words, which are thus removed from the
way they are usually perceived. I cannot trace the history of
this device outside Russian literature, but I think that perhaps Dostoevsky borrowed it from Dickens, who was a great
devotee of it.

In *Little Dorrit* the governess Mrs. General advises the
young ladies in her charge, to give a pretty shape to their
lips, to constantly pronounce "prunes and prisms."

For Dickens these "prunes and prisms" soon become a dis-
tinct condition of the newly rich Dorrits' life.

Dickens writes of "the heaps of prunes and prisms" which
had filled the Dorrits' life to overflowing. In *Our Mutual
Friend* the same use is made of the conversations about lime,
with which at first the detectives concealed their real inten-
tions, but which later became for them a sort of game. . . .

It seems clear to me that for a writer words are not at all
a sad necessity, not just a means by which something is said,
but are rather the very material of the work. Literature is
created from words and takes advantage of the laws by
which they are governed.

It is true that in a work of literature we also have the expression of ideas, but it is not a question of ideas clothed in artistic form, but rather artistic form created from ideas as its material.

In verse, rhyme is opposed to rhyme, the sounds of one word are connected by repetitions with the sounds of another word and form the sound-aspect of the poem.

In parallelism, image is opposed to image and forms the image-aspect of the work.

In the novel, thought is opposed to thought, or one group of characters to another, and this constitutes the meaning-form of the work.

Thus in Leo Tolstoy's *Anna Karenina* the Karenin-Vronsky group is opposed to the Kitty-Levin group.

It was this that entitled Tolstoy to say that he had no use for "those sweet and clever little fellows who fish out individual ideas from a work," and that "if I had wanted to say in one word everything that the novel was intended to express, then I should have had to write the novel all over again, and if my critics understand it and can put down in a review everything I meant, then I congratulate them and can say without hesitation that they are capable of much more than I."

In a work of literature it is not the idea that is important but the way ideas are combined. Again I quote from Tolstoy: "the combination itself is made not by means of thought (I think), but by something else, and it is impossible to express directly the basis for this combination. It can, however, be expressed indirectly by the description of images, actions, situations in words."

Consequently, the ideas in a literary work do not constitute its content but rather its material, and in their combination and interrelations with other aspects of the work they create its form.

A *peasant's son and former shepherd, Esenin was at first an enthusiast of the Bolshevik Revolution. He saw in it the coming of the bucolic, democratic utopia of which he dreamed in his early lyrics. But the terrible reality of the Civil War and industrialization in Soviet Russia soon bewildered the "peasant poet." Profoundly self-destructive in temperament, Esenin yielded to an almost continuous orgy of liquor and high living. His love affairs, his broken marriages—to Isadora Duncan, among others—and his extravagant escapades made headlines in Berlin, Paris, and New York. In 1924, he made a final attempt to accommodate himself to the Soviet world; he returned from abroad to his native village. The experience was hardly a success, as "Soviet Russia," the poem he wrote after his trip, suggests. A year later, the thirty-year-old Esenin cut his wrists and hanged himself.*

Although Esenin's verse was scarcely published during the Stalin era, he remains one of the most popular poets among Russians of all ages. Translation by George Reavey.

SERGEI ESENIN

Soviet Russia

That hurricane swept past. But few of us survived.
Renewing friendship's ties, we found many missing.
Again I turned my steps toward my orphaned birthplace,
Where I had set no foot for some eight years.

Whom shall I call? Share now with whom
The grievous joy of being still alive?
Here even the windmill—a bird of wooden beams
With just one wing—still stands, cross-eyed.

. . .

To everyone here I am a stranger,
And those who knew me once have now forgotten.
A heap of ashes layered with roadside dust
Lies where my father's house once stood.

Yet life is seething.
Faces throng
Around me, young and old.
But no one's here to whom I'd raise my hat,
Not one whose eyes would give me refuge.

A swarm of thoughts sweeps through my mind:
My native land—yes, what is that?
Is it just a dream?
For here I'm merely a frowning pilgrim,
Issued God knows whence . . .
So this is I!
I, citizen of this village,
Whose only claim to fame will be
That, in this place, a peasant woman bore
A rowdy Russian poet.

But the voice of thought enjoins the heart:
"Think twice! Why feel the hurt?
It is the new light burning
Of another generation in the huts.

You're past your prime already:
Other youths sing other songs.
They may be more interesting—
The earth, not just this village, is their mother."

Ah, native place! What a misfit I've become.
A dry flush colors my sunken cheeks.
My fellows' idiom sounds so alien,
And I feel a foreigner in my land.

. . .

I see before me
Villagers in Sunday best
Transact a meeting as if attending church.
In clumsy, unwashed speeches
They debate their "life."

Evening's here. The sunset sprayed
The graying fields with thin veneer of gilt.
Like calves that huddle beneath a gate,
The poplars thrust bare feet into the ditches.
Wrinkling his reminiscent forehead,
A lame Red Army man with drowsy face
Grandly expatiates upon Budyonny
And the Reds who captured Perekop[1] by storm.

"We gave them hell, we did—this way and that—
That bourgeois . . . the one . . . in the Crimea . . ."
The maples wrinkle the ears of their long branches,
While the peasant women groan into the silent dusk.

Then a band of peasant Komsomols descends the hill
And, bawling furiously to the accordion,
Sing Demyan Bedny's agit-verse,[2]
Drowning the valley with their lusty shouts.

What a land!
Whatever made me shout
In verse that I was the people's friend?
My poetry is not needed here,
And I myself, perhaps, unwanted too.

But never mind!
Forgive me, my native place!
I am content with what I did for you.

---

[1] Scene of Bolshevik victory against White armies during the Civil War.
[2] Propaganda poetry by the ultra-"proletarian" versifier of the twenties.

This day they need not sing my verse—
I did my singing when my native land was sick.

I'll take what comes.
Accept things as they are.
I'm ready to follow in their steps.
To October and May I'll offer up my soul,
But never surrender my beloved lyre.

I will not pass it on to alien hands—
Not even to my mother, friend, or wife.
The lyre to me alone its sounds entrusted,
And sang its gentle songs to me alone.

Flourish, young people! Strong in your bodies grow!
Your life is different, and so is your refrain.
But I, to a bourne unknown, shall go alone,
And for a rebel soul find lasting peace.
But even when,
Upon this whole wide planet,
An end is put to all the enmity of peoples,
And sorrow and falsehood thrive no more,
I still shall praise in song,
With all my poet's being,
This sixth part of the earth,
Which bears the name of Russia.

In *Paustovsky's reminiscences (entitled* A Time of Great Expec-
tations), *published in 1960 in Moscow, the novelist tells of his
early life in Kiev, where he was born in 1892, and of the small
but vivid literary world of Odessa in the first years after the Revolution. This excerpt (the original text has been cut here and there
by the editors) about his friend, Isaac Babel, is noteworthy
for its warm sympathy for Jews. Although Paustovsky himself
is of mixed Polish and Cossack origin, he is one of those Soviet
intellectuals who have recently gone out of their way to try and
counter anti-Semitic trends in the Soviet Union. In 1956, Paustovsky courageously defended Dudintsev's* Not by Bread Alone
*at a stormy meeting of the Moscow Union of Writers. In this
connection, he spoke out against the philistinism and anti-Semitism of the kind of bureaucrat depicted in Dudintsev's novel. In
recent years, Paustovsky has been one of the most forthright
champions of a more reasonable and liberal approach to literature.* Translation by Andrew R. MacAndrew.

KONSTANTIN PAUSTOVSKY

Reminiscences of Babel

I Can Guarantee You Maupassants

An issue of *The Seaman* carried a short story entitled "The
King." It was signed: I. Babel.

The story was about the chieftain of the Odessa bandits,
Benzion Krik (better known as Benya Krik), forcibly marrying off his faded sister Dvoirah to a puny, whimpering thief.
The thief was only marrying Dvoirah out of intolerable fear
of Benya.

This was one of Babel's first Moldavanka[1] stories. . . .
The piece was written tersely and precisely. It hit you in
the face like seltzer. Ever since I was a boy, I have felt
that certain literary works were a form of witchcraft.
After I had read "The King," I knew that a new sorcerer had
entered Russian literature and that whatever this man was
to write it would never be feeble or colorless. . . .

Babel was brought into the editorial offices of *The Seaman* by Izya Lifshits and I don't believe I had ever met a
man who looked less like a writer than Babel. His shoulders
were hunched, he had no neck to speak of as a result of
the hereditary Odessa asthma; his nose looked like a duck's
bill; his brow was deeply furrowed and there was an oily
gleam in his eyes. Not interesting at all, he could easily
have been taken for a traveling salesman or a dealer. But,
of course, only until he opened his mouth. The very first
words changed everything. A persistent irony was heard in
the fine ring of his voice.

Many people were unable to look at his burning eyes.
By nature Babel was a debunker. He loved to catch people
off balance and this gave him a reputation all over Odessa
for being a difficult and dangerous man.

Babel arrived in our office carrying a volume of Kipling
under his arm. When he talked to our chief editor, Ivanov,
he put the book down on the table. But he kept looking
at it impatiently, even carnivorously, as he shifted rest-
lessly in his chair, getting up and sitting down again. He
was visibly on edge. He was longing to read instead of con-
ducting a polite conversation.

At the first opportunity, Babel switched the conversation
to Kipling. Writers, he said, should write in Kipling's ironclad prose; authors should have the clearest possible notion
of what was to come out of their pens. A short story must
have the precision of a military communique or a bank
check. It must be written in the same firm, straightforward

---

[1] The Moldavanka was the bandits' and thieves' district of Odessa.

hand one uses for commands and checks. Kipling's hand
was just like that.

Babel concluded his remarks on Kipling with a quite unexpected statement. As he made it, he removed his glasses,
which immediately made his face look kind and helpless.

"Here in Odessa," he said, with a mocking glint in his
eyes, "we won't produce any Kiplings. We like a peaceful,
easy life. But to make up for it, we'll have our home-grown
Maupassants. That's because we have plenty of sea, sun,
beautiful women, food for thought. Yes, we'll have our Maupassants, that I can guarantee."

I looked out of the window to watch Babel leave our
building, his shoulders hunched, and walk off along the
shady side of the street. He walked very slowly and, the
moment he was out in the street, opened his Kipling and
started reading as he went. Now and then he stopped to
give passers-by a chance to go around him, but he never
once raised his head to look at them.

And the people in the street did avoid bumping into him.
Some stared, rather bewildered, but they didn't say a word.
Soon he disappeared in the shade of the plane trees whose
velvety foliage quivered in the liquid Black Sea air.

Later, I often met Babel in town. He was never alone.
What we called the "Odessa literary boys" hung around him
like flies. They caught up his witticisms and immediately
spread them all over Odessa. He sent them off on all sorts of
errands, which they carried out without a murmur. If one
of them was not zealous enough, Babel would tell him off
sharply, and when he got tired of them, he chased them
away mercilessly. But the harsher Babel was with them, the
more the literary boys liked it; the objects of Babel's ire
seemed to thrive on it. But it was not only the literary boys
for whom Babel was a god. Older writers too—there were
several in Odessa at that time—as well as young Odessan
writers and poets had great respect for him. At that time
he was, for us, the first really Soviet writer. . . .

I came into close contact with him toward the end of the

summer. He was living at Fontan. Izya Lifshits and I had
rented a dilapidated little summer cabin there, not far from
Babel's. . . .

I saw a lot of him. Sometimes we spent the whole day together on the beach, fishing with homemade nets and listening to Babel's leisurely stories. There was real genius in the
way he told things. When he told a story, it sounded even
stronger, even more flawless than when it was written. He
was very fond of talking about Gorky, about the Revolution,
and about how he had lived in the Anichkov Palace in Petersburg where he slept on a couch in Alexander III's study.
One day he had looked into a drawer of the Czar's desk and
found a box of magnificent cigarettes, a gift to the Czar
from the Turkish Sultan, Abdul-Hamid.

These fat cigarettes were rolled in pink paper with a
gilded arabesque design. With an air of mystery Babel gave
one cigarette each to Izya and to me. Their delicate odor
was wafted over Fontan. Immediately we both got terrible
headaches and for a whole hour staggered around like
drunks, groping our way along the stone walls as we
went.

It was at this time that Babel told me the strange story
of Cires, a meek old Jew.

Babel had moved to the center of the Moldavanka district, renting a room in the apartment where Cires lived with
his gloomy, slow-moving wife, Hava. He had decided to
write a few stories which would be situated in this Odessa
suburb, notorious for its racy way of life. Babel was attracted by the peculiar and unquestionably talented bandits,
like Mishka Yaponchik (Mike The Jap, or the Benya Krik of
his stories) who was already a living legend. The dreary
Cires apartment was as good a place as any from which
Babel could study life in the Moldavanka.

Steadfast as a rock, it was an island among the stormy,
raucous dives and the deceptively respectable apartments
with their crocheted doilies and seven-branched silver can-

delabra on the chests of drawers—places where, under their parents' roofs, the robbers could find refuge.

All around Cires' apartment one felt the presence of daring, armed young men.

Babel explained to Cires that his purpose was to study the Moldavanka district. The old man did not like it at all. In fact, he grew quite worried.

"Oi, Mister Babel!" he said, shaking his head. "Think of it: you're the son of such a well-known papa. And your mamma, she was a real beauty too. I even heard that none other than the nephew of Brodsky himself asked for her hand. So you can see that the Moldavanka is no place for you, whatever kind of a writer you may be. You'd better forget the Moldavanka for, I promise you, no good'll come of it, and if you earn anything at all, it will be a pocketful of trouble."

"What trouble?" Babel asked.

"Do I know what trouble?" Cires said, dodging the point. "Who knows what nightmares a man like, say, Five-Rubles can dream up? And I'm not talking about bullies like Luska Kur and the rest of them. No, Mister Babel, the best thing you can do is go back to your papa's house on Ekaterinskaya Street. And I tell you frankly, I'm sorry already that I rented you that room. But then, how could I possibly say no to such a nice young man?"

Sometimes, from his room, Babel heard Hava nagging at her husband in an angry whisper for renting the room to him and letting a stranger into the house.

"What will you get out of it, you skinflint? Perhaps another hundred thousand?[2] But then he'll make you lose your best customers. . . ."

The nights in the Moldavanka seemed long. The bleary light of a distant street-lamp fell on the shabby wallpaper that had a vinegary smell. Often from the street came the

---

[2] There was galloping inflation at that time.

sound of businesslike steps, a shrill whistle, and once even
an actual gunshot followed by hysterical female laughter.
The sound came through the brick wall and seemed to be
sealed into it at once.

He longed to go back to Ekaterinskaya Street. There, behind the thick walls of his apartment of the fourth floor, it
was quiet, dark, and safe, and the manuscript of his latest
story, corrected and rewritten dozens of times, lay on the
desk.

Babel would go up to his desk and stroke his manuscript
cautiously as though it were a wild creature which had still
not been properly domesticated. Often he would get up during the night and reread three or four pages by the light of
an oil lamp against which he propped an enormous encyclopedia as a shade. He would always find a few unnecessary words and throw them out with malicious glee. He
used to say, "Your language becomes clear and strong, not
when you can no longer add a sentence, but when you can
no longer take away from it."

Everybody who saw Babel at work, particularly at night
(and this was difficult because he always hid himself away
to write), was struck by his sad face and his peculiar expression of kindness and sorrow.

Babel would have given a great deal during those barren
nights in the Moldavanka to be able to return to his manuscripts. But as a writer he felt like a soldier on reconnais-
sance patrol and thought that in the name of literature he
had to endure everything: the loneliness, the stench of the
extinguished kerosene lamp that caused bad fits of asthma,
the sobs and cries of women behind the walls of the houses.
No, he couldn't give up.

One night it suddenly occurred to Babel that Cires must
be a finger man. That was how he made his living. He received a cut for his services and that was why Babel was
such an inconvenient lodger for the old man. He was liable
to scare off the old man's daring but cautious clients. . . .

Now Babel finally understood Cires' hints about his

pocketful of troubles and made up his mind to leave in a
few days. He needed a little time to worm out of the old
finger man everything of interest he could tell him; Babel
knew he had a genius for finding everything out about
people, for "gutting" them mercilessly and persistently, or,
as they used to say in Odessa, for "knocking their souls right
out of them."

But on this occasion Babel was too late. One day, while
Babel was out, Cires was stabbed to death in his apartment.

When Babel returned to the Moldavanka he found the
militia all over the place and, in his room, the inspector in
person, sitting at his desk writing a report. He was a polite
young man in blue twill riding breeches. His ambition was
to become a writer too. His attitude to Babel was therefore
respectful.

"I must request," he told Babel, "that you remove your
things immediately and leave this house. Otherwise I will be
unable to guarantee your personal safety even during the
next twenty-four hours. You must understand that this is
the Moldavanka!"

And Babel fled, shuddering at the hoarse howls of Hava,
who called down all sorts of curses on Senka's head, and
on everyone who had, in her opinion, been involved in Cires'
murder. . . .

"May Semyon," she shouted, swaying and sobbing and
calling Senka by his full name on this occasion, "may he
drink vodka mixed with rat poison and croak on his vomit!
And may feet trample to death his mother, the old viper
Miriam who gave birth to this hellhound and satan! May all
the Moldavanka boys sharpen their knives and cut him to
shreds for twelve days and twelve nights! I wish, Senka, you
may burn in a slow flame and burst in your own boiling fat!"

Soon after, Babel learned all the details of Cires' death. It
appeared that Cires himself was to blame and therefore not
a soul in all the Moldavanka, except Hava, was sorry for
him. Not a soul! The fact was that Cires had proved to be

a dishonest old man and, hence, no power on earth could
have saved him. This is what had happened: the day before his death, Cires went to see Senka Flop-Ears.

Senka was shaving before a magnificent mirror in an or-
nate frame. He squinted at Cires and said:

"So you've got yourself mixed up with a stranger, haven't
you, Mister Cires? Congratulations! And now, you know
the new Soviet law: if you come to see a man while he's
shaving, state your business quickly and beat it. I give you
ten words to explain what brings you here, like in the tele-
graph office. For every extra word, I'll reduce your commission by two hundred thousand rubles."

"You were born, maybe, making such bad jokes, Senka?"
Cires said with a sugary smile. "Or maybe it came with practice? What do you think . . . ?"

"Come on, tell me what you've come for, you old clown,"
Senka said, drawing his straight razor like a bow on an invisible violin. . . .

"Tomorrow, one P.M., at the Concordia Workshop. They'll
bring four billion."

"All right," Senka answered quietly, "you'll get your commission. Without deductions."

Cires ambled home. He didn't like the way Senka had behaved. Normally Senka never joked when it came to serious
business. At home, he shared his apprehensions with Hava.
As usual she shouted at him:

"How long do you have to live, how long before you learn
any sense? Obviously Senka won't take that job: why should
he get his nose dirty for a measly four billion? And you'll
make a bagel hole with butter on it, at the most."

"What am I to do then?" Cires groaned wretchedly. "These
bandits will drive me crazy!"

"You just go and see Five-Rubles. That one may be interested in your phony billions. At least that way maybe you
won't be left with nothing, like a fool."

Old Cires put on his cap and dragged himself off to Five-

Rubles' place. The man was asleep in his little garden under
a white acacia tree.

Five-Rubles listened to what Cires had to say and answered sleepily:

"All right, you can go. You'll get your cut."

Old Cires left quite happy, feeling like a man who had
taken out a life insurance policy that would be paid in
gold. . . .

The next day, Senka and Five-Rubles met in front of the
cashier's window of the Concordia Workshop. They looked
straight into each other's eyes and Senka asked:

"Would you mind telling me who fingered this job for
you?"

"Old Cires. And what about you, Senka?"

"Old Cires too."

"And so?" Five-Rubles said.

"And so he won't go on living."

"Amen," Five-Rubles agreed.

Each bandit went peacefully on his way. According to
the regulations, when two bandits meet on a job, the job is
canceled.

Forty minutes later, Cires was killed in his home while
his wife Hava was out in the courtyard hanging her washing. She didn't see the murderer, but she knew that no one
but Senka, or one of his crowd, could have done it. Senka
never forgave a double cross.

That Kid!

Babel's father, a fussy old man, was a dealer in a small
depot of agricultural machinery in Odessa. From time to
time, he sent his son Isaac to Kiev to buy machines from the
manufacturer Gronfein.

In Gronfein's house, Babel met his daughter, then a high-
school senior. Soon they were in love.

Marriage was ruled out. Babel, a threadbare student, the

son of a small Odessa merchant, was obviously no match for
the heiress to Gronfein's fortune. When the matter was first
mentioned to him, Gronfein unbuttoned his coat, stuck his
fingers into the armholes of his vest, and swaying back and
forth on his heels, let out a scornful hissing sound, "F-ss-sss!"
thus leaving no one in doubt as to how he felt. He didn't
even bother to put his contempt into words. This would
have been to honor the puny student too much.

The only thing left for the lovers to do was to elope, and
they did just that. Afterward everything developed on Old
Testament lines: Gronfein laid his curse on Babel's de-
scendants unto the tenth generation and disinherited his
daughter. . . .

But time went by. Came the Revolution. The Bolsheviks
confiscated Gronfein's plant. The old industrialist fell so
low that he would go out into the street unshaven, without
his collar, and with just one gold stud holding his shirt
closed.

And then, one day, an extraordinary piece of news
reached the Gronfeins: that whippersnapper Babel had
turned out to be a famous writer and, just imagine, was on
familiar terms with none other than Maxim Gorky himself. . . . It seems that the Gronfeins had made a mistake
and it was time to make peace. . . .

Their change of heart was followed by the sudden arrival
of Babel's mother-in-law at his Fontan summer house. . . .
Apparently unsure that she could clinch the reconciliation
by herself, she brought along with her from Kiev her eight-
year-old grandson, a boy called Lusya. . . .

The mother-in-law tried hard to live down her past attitude toward Babel. . . . We often had breakfast at Babel's
house, and the same scene would occur again and again.

When the boiled eggs were brought in, the old woman
would watch Babel very closely and if he didn't help himself to an egg, she would ask in a pained voice:

"Babel," she would say—she always addressed him thus
—"why don't you eat your eggs? You don't like them?"

"Thanks, I just don't feel like it now."

"So you don't like your mother-in-law?" she would go on, playfully rolling her eyes. "I cooked them specially for you."

Babel, choking, would bolt down the rest of his breakfast and rush out. . . .

The boy Lusya's ears burned unbearably with curiosity from morning till night, as though somebody were constantly tweaking them. That kid wanted to know everything. He would spy on Babel and on all of us; he was diabolically watchful and there was no escaping his scrutiny. Wherever we might go we would very soon catch sight of Lusya's ears, translucent in the sun, sticking up from behind a tamarisk shrub, or a rock on the seashore. Apparently because of the curiosity which consumed him, Lusya was incredibly thin and bony. His olive-black eyes darted about with uncanny speed. At the same time, he would ask up to thirty questions a minute without ever waiting for an answer.

Lusya was a monstrously tiresome child with a grasshopper mind. He was at rest only when asleep. During the day he was continually on the move, prancing around, turning cartwheels, making faces, smashing things on the floor, racing around the garden with bloodcurdling shrieks, tumbling on the ground, swinging on doors, emitting theatrical guffaws, tormenting the dog, meowing, tearing out his hair in temper tantrums, wailing hideously without tears, pocketing dying lizards with their tails cut off, and crabs (which he released onto the breakfast table), begging things, insulting people, stealing fishing tackle—and to crown it all, he spoke in a raucous, hoarse voice.

"And what's that?" he'd ask. "And what's it for? And is it possible to make dynamite out of a blanket? And what would happen if a man drank a glass of tea with sand in it? And who invented your funny name Paustovsky which my grandma can only pronounce after dinner? And could you catch a streetcar from behind with your fishing hook and pull it back? How would it be if one made jam out of crabs?"

It is easy to imagine how we loved the company of that kid. "That spawn of hell!" was how Babel spoke of him, a blue flame shining in his eyes.

Lusya's very presence made Babel so nervous that he couldn't write. He used to come to our *dacha* to get relief from Lusya, groaning with exhaustion. He addressed Lusya as "my boy," in such a voice that the lop-eared child's hair would have bristled in terror, if only he had had enough imagination.

The sultry days dragged on but the mother-in-law showed not the slightest sign of leaving. "All is lost," Babel moaned, holding his head in his hands, "this is the end of everything. My skull is humming like a brass kettle, as though that spawn of hell were banging on it with a stick from morning to night."

We were trying to devise a way of getting rid of Lusya and his garrulous grandma. But, as often happened, Babel was saved by an unexpected little incident.

Once I went to pick up Babel in the morning to go for a swim as we had agreed the night before. He was writing at his desk, looking very harassed. As I entered the room, he jumped, and without looking around began to stuff his manuscript into a drawer, almost tearing it in the process.

"Oof!" he sighed, recognizing me. "I thought it was that kid. I can only work while the monster is asleep."

Babel was holding the indelible pencil he had been writing with. . . .

Then Lusya burst triumphantly into Babel's room. He immediately went for the drawer, assuming that the most interesting things must be hidden there. But Babel skillfully managed to lock the drawer and put the key in his pocket. Then Lusya began to snatch things off the table, demanding to know what they were. Finally he started clutching at the indelible pencil in Babel's hand, and after a struggle, managed to seize it. . . .

We went to the beach. Lusya kept diving in close to the shore and blowing bubbles. Babel was watching him very closely. At one point he seized my arm and said in a con-spiratorial tone:

"Do you know what I noticed, back in my room? He broke off the point of the indelible pencil and stuck it in his ear."

"So what?" I asked. "Nothing will come of it," Babel agreed gloomily. "The hell with him then, let him dive to his heart's content."

. . . We were all sitting around the breakfast table and Mrs. Gronfein was working up to her daily performance about the egg. . . . Suddenly Lusya slid from his chair, grabbed his ear, and started to roll around on the floor, emitting heart-rending howls and kicking everything within range. We all jumped up. A disgusting, purplish liquid was running from his ear.

He shrieked uninterruptedly, on one horrendous note, and the women dashed around him in circles. The whole house was panic-stricken. Babel sat rigid and looked at Lusya in dismay, while he writhed on the floor and shouted, "It hurts, oh it hurts!"

I was about to announce that Lusya was shamming, that he could not be in pain, that he had simply been diving with a piece of indelible pencil in his ear. But Babel caught my arm under the table and squeezed it hard.

"Not a word," he hissed. "Keep quiet about the indelible pencil or you'll spoil everything!"

The mother-in-law was sobbing. Mary, Babel's sister, was wiping off the purplish fluid with a piece of absorbent cotton. Babel's mother demanded that the child be taken immediately to Odessa to see an ear, nose, and throat specialist.

Then Babel leaped to his feet, threw his napkin on the table next to his unfinished tea and, red with indignation, shouted:

"You must be out of your mind, Mother! What are you try-ing to do? You want to kill the boy, or what? Do you call those Odessa quacks physicians? They're horse doctors, the lot of them, charlatans, ignoramuses! . . ."

"What am I to do then?" Mrs. Gronfein exclaimed, sobbing pathetically. . . .

"You ask me what to do!" Babel cried angrily. "You, a native of Kiev! Don't you know that you have a world-famous
specialist for ear, nose, and throat diseases, Professor Grinblat? My advice is to take the child to Kiev. Without a moment's delay! . . ."

And a week later a letter arrived from Kiev.

"Would you believe it?" the mother-in-law wrote, indig-
nantly. "What do you think Professor Grinblat found? He
found that brat had stuffed a piece of indelible pencil into
his ear, and that's all there was to it. Now how do you like
that?"

After the incident with Lusya, we felt that peace was restored. . . . Babel began working hard and I would see
him coming out of his room silent and rather sad.

Hard Labor

. . . "I have no imagination," Babel once told me. "I'm very
serious about this. I can't invent. I have to know everything,
down to the last vein, otherwise I can't write a thing. My
motto is *authenticity*. That's why I write so little and so
slowly. Writing is very hard for me. After each short story, I
feel several years older. Don't talk to me about creative
work à la Mozart, about the blissful time spent over a manuscript, about the free flow of imagination! Somewhere I
once wrote that I'm rapidly aging from asthma, that strange
illness which lodged itself in my puny body when I was a
child. But I was lying. When I'm writing the shortest story, I
still have to work at it as if I were required to dig up Mount
Everest all by myself with a pick and shovel. When I start
working I always feel that it's too much for me. Sometimes
I get so tired I cry. All my blood vessels ache from the
work. I have heart spasms when I can't manage a sentence.
And how often they don't work out, those wretched sentences!"

"But your prose is so smooth," I said. "How do you manage it?"

"Only because of style. It's style that does it," Babel said and let out an old man's guffaw, imitating someone, apparently Moskvin. "He-he, young man, it's style that does it, it's style that does it. I can write a short story about washing underwear and it will read like Julius Caesar's prose. It's all a matter of language and style. But then, you know as well as I do that this isn't the essence of art, but simply high-quality—perhaps even valuable—building material for it.

" 'Just give me a couple of ideas,' as one of our Odessa journalists used to say, 'and I'll try to make a masterpiece out of them.' Come along and I'll show you how I do it. I'm tightfisted and cagey, but dammit, I'll show you." It was already dark at the *dacha*. . . . He took a fat typescript from his desk which was easily two hundred pages long.

"You know what this is?"

I was puzzled. Surely Babel hadn't at last written a long work and kept it secret from everybody? I couldn't believe it. We all know the almost telegraphic conciseness of his stories; he regarded any story longer than ten pages to be overblown and padded.

Surely there couldn't be two hundred pages of concentrated Babel prose in this work. It was impossible. I looked at the first page and saw the title—"Lyubka the Cossack"—and was even more astonished.

"For heaven's sake," I said, "I've read that "Lyubka the Cossack" is a short story you haven't yet published. Have you made a novel out of it?"

Babel put his hand on the typescript and looked at me gleefully. Tiny wrinkles gathered at the corners of his eyes. "Yes," he said, and blushed in embarrassment, "this is my short story 'Lyubka the Cossack.' It's only fifteen pages long, but here I have twenty-two versions, including the last one, which makes two hundred pages in all."

"Twenty-two versions!" I muttered, quite at a loss.

"Listen!" said Babel, who was angry now. "Literature is not potboiling. What's so terrible about twenty-two versions of the same story? You think that's extravagant, do you? But I'm not even sure that the twenty-second version is publishable. I think it could still be cut down. It's this sort of pruning, my friend, which brings out the independent force of language and style. Language and style!" he repeated.

"What I do," Babel said, "is to get hold of some trifle, some little anecdote, a piece of market gossip, and turn it into something I cannot tear myself away from. It's alive, it plays. It's round like a pebble on the seashore. It's held together by the fusion of separate parts, and this fusion is so strong that even lightning can't split it. And people will read the story. They'll remember it, they'll laugh, not because it's funny but because one always feels like laughing in the presence of human good fortune. I take the risk of speaking about good fortune because we're alone. As long as I live you mustn't tell anyone about this conversation. Give me your word. It is, of course, none of my doing that, I don't know how, a demon or an angel, whatever you want to call it, has taken possession of me, the son of a petty merchant. And I obey him like a slave, like a beast of burden. I have sold my soul to him, and I must write in the best possible way. I guess it's an affliction. But if you take it away from me—either my good fortune or my affliction—the blood will gush out of my veins and my heart along with it; I will be worth no more than a chewed cigarette butt. It's this work that makes me into a man, and not an Odessa street-corner philosopher."

He remained silent for a while and added with a fresh surge of bitterness: "I have no imagination. I have only the desire to possess it. Remember Blok's 'I see an enchanted shore, an enchanted horizon'? Blok reached this shore but I shan't. I see this shore at an unendurable distance. My mind is too matter-of-fact. But I should at least be thankful that fate has put into my heart a longing for that enchanted horizon. I work to the very limit of my powers. I do my utmost

because I want to be at the feast of the gods and I'm afraid I
might be driven away."

A tear gleamed behind the convex lenses of his glasses.
He took them off and wiped his eyes with the sleeve of his
drab patched jacket.

"I did not choose my race," he said suddenly in a broken
voice. "I'm a Jew, a kike. Sometimes I think there's nothing I can't understand, but one thing I'll never understand:
the reason for this black vileness which bears such a humdrum name as anti-Semitism." He fell silent. I too was silent
and waited for him to calm down and for his hands to stop
trembling.

"I went through a pogrom when I was a child and survived. But they twisted the head off my dove. Why? . . . I
hope my wife doesn't come in," he whispered. "Lock the
door. She doesn't like this sort of talk. And she might easily
cry all night. She thinks I'm a very lonely man and perhaps
she's right."

What could I say? I was silent.

"So there!" said Babel, bending myopically over his typescript. "I work like a mule, but I'm not complaining. I chose
this forced labor myself. I'm like a galley slave, chained for
life to his oar and in love with it, with every detail of it,
with the very wood polished by his hands. After years of contact with human skin the roughest wood takes on a fine color
and becomes like ebony. It's just the same with our words,
with the Russian language. You have only to put your warm
hand to it and it becomes a living and precious thing.

"But one thing at a time. When I write down the first
version of a story, the manuscript looks disgusting, absolutely horrible! It's a conglomeration of more or less
successful bits, joined together by the dreariest connecting links, what are called 'transitions,' but which are really
like dirty ropes. Read the first version of 'Lyubka the Cossack' and you will see that it is nothing but a futile, toothless prattling, a clumsy assortment of words. It's at this
point that you have to get down to work. This is where it

begins. I check sentence after sentence, and not once but many times. First I throw out the useless words. You need a sharp eye for that, because language is very good at concealing its garbage of repetitions, synonyms, and outright absurdities; it seems to be trying to outwit you all the time.

"After this, I retype the manuscript to see the text better, and put it aside for two or three days—that is, if my impatience doesn't get the better of me—and then I check it again, sentence by sentence, word by word. And again I'm certain to find a number of weeds and nettles I've missed. And thus I go on, retyping the text each time; I work until I get to the point where, despite the most ferocious scrutiny, I can't find a speck of mud in the manuscript.

"But that's by no means the end of it. There's more to come. When the garbage has been thrown out, I check all the images, similes, and metaphors for freshness and accuracy. If there's no accurate simile, I'd rather go without one. Let a noun live by itself, in its simplicity.

"A simile must be as precise as a slide rule and as natural as the smell of dill. Oh yes, I was forgetting: before removing the verbal rubbish, I break the text up into easy sentences. Use as many periods as possible! I would like to see that rule become a state law for writers! Each sentence is one thought, one image, and no more. So don't be afraid of periods. Perhaps my sentences are too short. This may be partly due to my chronic asthma. I can't talk long-windedly; I'm short of breath. The longer the sentences, the harder it is for me to breathe. . . . I think that a noun needs only one adjective and it must be very carefully chosen. Only a genius can afford to use two adjectives.

"The paragraphs and punctuation must be used correctly, not because of some dead scholastic rules, but so as to have the maximum effect on the reader. Paragraphs are particularly magnificent. They allow us to change the rhythm with ease, and often, like flashes of lightning, they illuminate some particular sight in a quite unexpected aspect. There are good writers who are careless about their punctuation and their paragraphs. So, despite the excellence of their prose, it is obscured by haste and carelessness. . . ."

"Yes," I said, "it really is like hard labor. It makes you think twenty times before becoming a writer."

"But the main thing," Babel said, "is not to allow this hard labor to deaden the text. Otherwise it's all for nothing, and will turn into God knows what."

This story is largely autobiographical, as Paustovsky suggests in his reminiscences of Babel which appear in this book. As a child in Odessa, Babel had endured the pogroms of Czarist Russia; as a young Bolshevik during the Civil War he was witness to the White Army's acts of violence against Jews, described here. During the Civil War and the war with Poland, Babel was a political commissar in Budyonny's cavalry, and, for a brief period, a clerical worker for the Cheka. In "Red Cavalry" and other stories, like "The Journey," Babel described the savagery of war with scrupulous objectivity, making no attempt to draw the moral which socialist realism demanded. As a result he was often under attack for "naturalism." Publication of his work ceased altogether in 1937; he was arrested two years later and died in a concentration camp in 1941.

"The Journey," written in the twenties, was first published in the literary magazine 30 Days, in 1932. It reappeared in a censored version in a collection of Babel stories published in Moscow in 1957, after his posthumous rehabilitation. The censored passage, which is restored in this translation, was evidently omitted for reasons of prudery. Translation by Mirra Ginsburg.

ISAAC BABEL

The Journey

The front collapsed in 1917. I left it in November. At home mother prepared a bundle of underwear and dry bread for me. I got to Kiev the day before Muraviev began to bombard the city. I was on my way to Petersburg. For twelve days we sat it out in the cellar of Chaim the Barber's hotel in the Bessarabka. I got a permit to leave the city from the Soviet commandant of Kiev.

There is no drearier sight in the world than the Kiev railroad station. For many years its makeshift wooden barracks have blighted the approaches to the city. Lice crackled on the wet boards. Deserters, gypsies, and black marketeers were lying all over the place. Old Galician women urinated standing on the platform. The lowering sky was furrowed with clouds, suffused with rain and gloom.

Three days went by before the first train left. At first it stopped at every verst, but then it gathered speed; the wheels began to rumble with a will, singing a song of power. Everyone was happy in our freight car. In 1918, rapid travel made people happy. During the night the train shuddered and came to a stop. The doors of our car slid open and we saw the greenish gleam of snow. A railroad telegrapher entered the car, wearing a wide fur coat fastened with a leather belt, and soft Caucasian boots. He stretched out his hand and rapped his palm with one finger.

"Your papers. Put them here!"

Near the door, a quiet old woman lay huddled on some bales. She was going to her son, a railroad worker in Luban. Next to me, a teacher, Yehuda Weinberg, and his wife sat dozing. The teacher had been married a few days earlier and was taking his young wife to Petersburg. All the way they had talked in whispers about new methods of teaching, and then had fallen asleep. Even in sleep their hands were linked, clinging to each other.

The telegrapher read their travel document, signed by Lunacharsky, took a mauser with a slender, grimy muzzle from under his coat, and shot the teacher in the face.

A large, stooping peasant wearing a fur cap with the earflaps undone shuffled behind the telegrapher. The telegrapher winked at the peasant, who put his lamp on the floor, unbuttoned the trousers of the dead man, cut off his genitals with a knife, and began stuffing them into his wife's mouth.

"*Treif* wasn't good enough for you," said the telegrapher. "So here's some kosher for you." [1]

The woman's soft neck bulged. Not a sound came from her. The train had come to a halt in the steppe. The snowdrifts shimmered with an arctic glitter. Jews were being flung out of the cars onto the roadbed. Shots rang out like exclamations. A peasant in a fur hat with dangling ear-flaps led me behind a frozen woodpile and began to search me. A cloud-dimmed moon shone down on us. The violet wall of forest was smoking. Stiff icy fingers like wooden stumps crept over my body. The telegrapher shouted from the open door of the car:

"Jew or Russian?"

"Russian," the peasant muttered, feeling me over. "Some Russian! He'd make a fine rabbi . . ."

He brought his crumpled worried face closer to mine, ripped out the four ten-ruble gold coins my mother had sewn into my underpants for the journey, took off my boots and coat, then turned me around, struck the back of my neck with the edge of his hand, and said in Yiddish:

"*Ankloif,* Chaim . . . Get going, Chaim . . ."

I walked away, my bare feet sinking into the snow. My back lit up like a target, its bull's-eye centered on my ribs. The peasant did not shoot. Between the columns of pines, in the subterranean shelter of the forest, a light swayed in a crown of blood-red smoke. I ran up to the hut. Its chimney smoked from dung fire. The forester groaned when I burst in. Swathed in strips of cloth cut out from overcoats, he sat in a little bamboo, velvet-cushioned armchair, shredding tobacco in his lap. His image was drawn out in the smoky air. He moaned. Then, rising from the chair, he bowed low before me:

"Go away, my good man . . . Go away, my good citizen . . ."

He led me out to a path and gave me rags to wrap my feet.

---

[1] The two previous paragraphs were excised in the censored 1957 version.

By late morning I had dragged myself to a little town. There was no doctor at the hospital to amputate my frozen feet. A male nurse was in charge of the ward. Every day he raced up to the hospital on a short-legged black colt, tethered him to a post, and came in blazing, with glittering eyes.

"Friedrich Engels," he would say bending over my pillow, his pupils glowing like embers, "teaches the likes of you that there mustn't be any nations, but we say: a nation must exist. . . ."

Tearing the bandages from my feet, he would straighten up and, gritting his teeth, ask me in a low voice:

"Where are you headed? What devil drives you? Why is it always on the move, this tribe of yours? . . . Why are you making all this trouble, why all this turmoil? . . ."

One night the town Soviet had us taken away in a cart—patients who didn't get along with the male nurse, and old Jewish women in wigs, the mothers of local commissars.

My feet healed up. I set out further along the hunger-stricken road to Zhlobin, Orsha, and Vitebsk.

From Novo-Sokolniki to Loknya, I found shelter under the muzzle of a howitzer. We were riding on a flatcar. Fediukha, my chance companion who was on the great odyssey of a deserter, was a storyteller, punster, and wit. We slept under the mighty, short, upturned muzzle of the gun, keeping each other warm in a canvas den lined with hay like the lair of a beast. Past Loknya, Fediukha stole my traveling box and disappeared. The box had been given to me by the town Soviet and contained two sets of army underwear, some dry bread, and a little money. For two days —we were then approaching Petersburg—I had no food. At the Tsarskoye Selo station I had my last taste of shooting. A patrol fired into the air to greet the oncoming train.

The black marketeers were led out onto the platform and the soldiers began to strip off their clothes. The liquor-filled rubber bags in which they were encased flopped down on the asphalt next to the real men. At nine in the evening, the howling prison of the station disgorged me onto Zagorodny

Prospect. Across the street, on the wall of a boarded-up pharmacy, the thermometer registered twenty-four degrees below zero. The wind roared through the tunnel of Gorokhovaya Street. A gas light flickered wildly over the canal. Our chilled, granite Venice stood motionless. I entered Gorokhovaya, an icy field hemmed in by cliffs.

The Cheka was housed in Number 2, in what had been the Governor's palace. Two machine guns, two iron dogs, stood in the vestibule with raised muzzles. I showed the commandant a letter from Vanya Kalugin, the N.C.O. under whom I had served in the Shuisky Regiment. Kalugin, who was now an interrogator in the Cheka, had written me to come.

"Go to the Anichkov Palace," said the commandant. "That's where he works now. . . ."

"I'll never make it," I smiled in reply.

Nevsky Prospect flowed into the distance like the Milky Way. Dead horses punctuated it like milestones. Their raised legs propped up a low-fallen sky. Their slit bellies gleamed white and clean. An old man who looked like a guardsman went by, pulling a carved toy sled. Straining forward, he dug his leather feet into the ice. A Tyrolean hat was perched on his head, and his beard, tied up with string, was tucked into his scarf.

"I'll never make it," I said to the old man.

He stopped. His furrowed, leonine face was calm. He thought about his own troubles and went on with his sled.

"And so, there is no longer any need to conquer Petersburg," I thought, and tried to recall the name of the man who was trampled to death by Arab horses at the very end of his journey. It was Yehuda Halevi.

Two Chinese in bowler hats, with loaves of bread under their arms, stood on the corner of the Sadovaya. With frozen nails they marked off tiny portions of the bread and showed them to approaching prostitutes. The women went past them in silent parade.

At the Anichkov Bridge I sat down on a ledge below one

of Klodt's bronze horses. My arm slipped under my head, and I stretched out on the polished slab. But the granite stung me, struck me, and catapulted me toward the palace.

The door of the cranberry-colored wing was open. A blue gas light gleamed over the doorman, who was sleeping in a chair. His lower lip drooped; his wrinkled face was inky and deathlike. Under his brilliantly lit, unbelted tunic he wore court uniform trousers embroidered in gold braid. An arrow, raggedly drawn in ink, pointed the way to the commandant's office. I climbed the stairway and walked through empty low-ceilinged rooms. Women, painted in dark and gloomy colors, danced in endless rings over the walls and ceilings. Metal gratings covered the windows, forced bolts hung from the window frames. At the end of this suite of rooms, behind a table, sat Kalugin with his cap of straw-colored peasant hair, lit up as on a stage. On the table lay a pile of children's toys, bits of colored cloth, torn picture books.

"So here you are," said Kalugin, raising his head. "Hello . . . We need you. . . ."

I brushed aside the toys littering the table, lay down on the gleaming top, and woke—seconds or hours later—on a low sofa. The bright rays of a chandelier played over me in a cascade of glass. My rags had been cut from me and lay in a puddle on the floor.

"And now for a bath," said Kalugin, who stood over the sofa. He lifted me and carried me to a bathtub. The tub was the old-fashioned kind, with low sides. There was no water in the faucets; Kalugin poured water over me from a pail. Clothing was laid out for me on the pale yellow satin cushions of the backless wicker chairs: a dressing gown with clasps, a shirt and socks of heavy silk. I sank into the underpants up to my neck. The dressing gown was made for a giant; I stepped on the flapping ends of the sleeves.

"Don't joke with Alexander Alexandrovich," said Kalugin, rolling up my sleeves. "The fellow must have weighed three hundred pounds."

We managed to tuck up the dressing gown of Alexander the Third and returned to the first room. It was a library of Maria Fyodorovna—a perfumed box in which gilded bookcases with raspberry stripes were pushed against the walls.

I told Kalugin who had been killed in our Shuisky Regiment, who had been elected commissar, who had gone to join the Whites in the Kuban. We drank tea, the stars swam and dissolved in the cut-glass walls of our tumblers. With the stars, we ate horsemeat sausage, black and moist. The dense fine silk of the curtains divided us from the world; the sun suspended from the ceiling splintered and shone, waves of stifling heat came from the radiators.

"Hell, we only live once," said Kalugin when we had finished off the horsemeat. He went out and returned with two boxes—a present from Sultan Abdul-Hamid to the Russian sovereign. One was made of zinc, the other was a cigar box pasted over with ribbons and paper insignia. "*A sa majesté l'Empereur de toutes les Russies,*" was engraved on the zinc lid, "From your loving cousin . . ."

The aroma which Maria Fyodorovna had known so well a quarter of a century before drifted across the library. The cigarettes, twenty centimeters long and as thick as fingers, were wrapped in pink paper; I do not know whether anyone but the Emperor of all the Russias ever smoked such cigarettes, but I chose a cigar. Kalugin smiled, looking at me.

"We'll chance it," he said, "maybe they weren't counted. . . . The servants told me Alexander the Third was a great smoker: he loved tobacco, kvass, and champagne. . . . Yet look at those five-kopek earthenware ashtrays on his table, and the patches on his trousers. . . ."

Indeed, the dressing gown I wore was greasy, shiny, and had often been mended.

We spent the rest of the night sorting the toys of Nicholas the Second, his drums and locomotives, his christening shirts and copybooks covered with childish scrawls. There were photographs of grand dukes who had died in infancy, locks of their hair, diaries of the Danish Princess Dagmara, letters from her sister, the Queen of England, breathing perfume and decay, crumbling away in our fingers. On the flyleaves of Bibles and of a volume of Lamartine, friends and ladies in waiting—daughters of burgomasters and state councilors—bid their farewells in slanting, diligent lines to the princess who was departing for Russia. Queen Louise, her mother, who ruled over a small kingdom, had taken care to place her children well: she married off one of her daughters to Edward VII, Emperor of India and King of England; another was married to a Romanov; her son George was made King of Greece. Princess Dagmara became Maria in Russia. Far away now were the canals of Copenhagen and King Christian's chocolate-brown sideburns. Bearing the last Czars, this little woman raged like an angry vixen behind her guard of Preobrazhensky Grenadiers, but her blood flowed into an implacable vengeful granite earth. . . .

Till dawn we could not tear ourselves away from this mute, disastrous chronicle. Abdul-Hamid's cigar was smoked to the end. In the morning Kalugin took me to the Cheka at Number 2 Gorokhovaya Street. He spoke to Uritsky. I stood behind the draperies which flowed to the floor in waves of cloth. Snatches of the conversation reached me through them.

"He is one of ours," said Kalugin. "His father is a shopkeeper, but he has broken with them. . . . He knows languages. . . ."

The Commissar of Internal Affairs of the Northern Communes walked out of the office with his swaying gait. Behind his pince-nez bulged swollen flabby eyelids, scorched with sleeplessness.

I was made a translator in the Foreign Department. I received a soldier's uniform and meal coupons. In a corner assigned to me in the large hall of the former Governor's palace, I went to work translating the testimony of diplomats, incendiaries, and spies.

Before the day was over, I had everything—clothes,

food, work, and comrades, true in friendship and in death, such comrades as are found in no country in the world but ours.

Thus, thirteen years ago, began my splendid life, a life of thought and merriment.

Alexander Grin (Grinevsky) was born in Vyatka (now Kirov)
of Polish parents in 1880. As a child, living in this suffocating
Russian province, he dreamed of exotic and romantic worlds
where men were strong and free. He nourished himself largely
on American literature: Poe, Mayne Reid, and Cooper. As a
youth he longed to escape the dreary realities of life in Czarist
Russia and run away to sea. But he was not able to get farther
than Odessa, which nonetheless provided him with much of the
romantic material for his works.

A protégé of Gorky, Grin became a prolific writer of fantastic
tales (much in the spirit of Gorky's early "bosyak" ["bum"] stories), whose action usually takes place in the imaginary country
of "Grinland." Because of his exotic plots, his use of Anglo-
Saxon-sounding names, and his peculiar "translated" style, he
was often thought by his readers to be a foreign author in translation. It is interesting to note that he sometimes appears to anticipate the existentialist trend in Western literature, as in the
story translated here.

This totally anomalous Soviet writer died of natural causes in
1932. Selections of his work were often reprinted until 1950,
when he was posthumously denounced as an "arch-cosmopolitan";
it was said that the Soviet intelligentsia had been infected by him
with a disease quaintly defined as "Grinomania." Since Stalin's
death he has again been published, in large printings, and
his influence, thanks partly to the efforts of friends such as Paustovsky and other Grinomaniacs, is as strong as ever among Soviet intellectuals of all ages for whom he provides an antidote to
socialist realism. Translation by Christopher Bird.

ALEXANDER GRIN

The Making of Asper

In the gloomy valley of Engra, near the quarries, Judge Gakker confessed the most extraordinary things to me.

"My friend," began Gakker, "man's higher purpose is creative work. The kind of work to which I have dedicated my life demands ironclad secrecy during the creator's lifetime. The artist's name must remain unknown; more than that, people should not suspect that certain phenomena which astonish them are nothing but works of art.

"Painting, music, and poetry create an internal world of artistic fancy. That is estimable, though less interesting than my sort of creation. I make living people, and this is a lot more troublesome than color photography. Carefully putting the finishing touches on the tiny parts, fitting them together, tidying them up, devising intellectual faculties for the newly created subject and also making sure that it acts in accordance with its status—all this takes considerable time.

"No, no," he continued, noting the unease and distrust on my face, "I'm dead serious and you'll soon see it. Like every artist, I'm ambitious and want to have disciples; therefore, knowing that I shall end my life tomorrow, I've made up my mind to confide to you my method of attaining certain results.

"Our earth is parsimonious in originating new forms of plants, animals, and insects. I had the idea of extending nature's luxurious diversity by creating new forms of animal life. If each discovery of a new variety of luminous beetle or orchid immortalizes the name of some lucky professor, then how much prouder would I be if I were able—not through crossing, that is nature's way—to alter artificially the characteristics of the species in separate individual specimens, and transmit these mutations to their offspring. I found a sure way, so strange and so infinitely simple that if I let you in on my discovery, you'll surely be amazed. I'm not going to tell you about this, however, so as not to make certain poor animals into amusing oddities, the pariahs of the scientific world; for now they are objects of reverential study which crown their discoverers with fame.

"I have created a swimming snail with new respiratory organs; six kinds of May bettles of which one is specially noteworthy for the secretion of an aromatic fluid; a white sparrow; a duck-billed pigeon; a crested snipe; a red swan; and many others. As you see, I chose well-known and common species with a view to their earliest possible discovery by the scientists. My creations caused a furor; nature was held to be the creator, but I read about the fins on a new snail with a smile and with tender feelings toward these little creatures, whose maker was none other than I. Trying to see how far I could go, I then started to create human beings. I devised three, and released them into life: 'The Veiled Lady,' the 'Poet Teklin,' well known to you, and the robber, 'Asper,' about whom everybody agrees that he is the terror of the region.

"It seemed a pointless amusement to produce ordinary people, of whom there are quite enough. Mine should be able to hold the center of universal attention and make a strong impression, just like famous works of art; the trail conceived and blazed by me must make a deep impression on the souls of men.

"I began with 'The Veiled Lady' as an experiment. One day a shapely young lady called on the public prosecutor of the High Court in D. A black veil hid her face. She explained that she wished to see the prosecutor to make secret disclosures relative to the sensational trial of X., indicted for high treason. A servant went in to announce her and returned to find that the lady had disappeared. At the very same moment on that very day, as was later discovered, the mysterious lady came on a similar errand to Senator G., to the Minister of Justice, to the Minister of Defense, to the Police Inspector, and in each and every place she vanished without waiting to be received.

"The speculation in the newspapers and in society about this inexplicable occurrence gave me many a pleasant hour. The gutter press shrieked about a Madame K., the mistress of a staff general who was interested in getting rid of the defendant. Others, foaming at the mouth, declared that the lady was the cunning invention of the conservatives, bribed by the Ministry Police in order to smother the scandal. Still others concocted an intrigue on the part of foreign powers, accusing the government of treason and asserting that the Veiled Lady was Prince V.'s morganatic wife, a beauty dangerous to all men, however high the offices they held. Ladies in high society as well as women of the demimonde were slandered in whispered drawing-room gossip; the mysterious lady personified graft, depravity, intrigue, party conspiracy, cowardice, and treachery. At last she was universally proclaimed to be Mariana Chen—the ailing sister of Captain Chen—a lady who always fancied herself privy to the truth on any subject.

"For three years and in four cities she appeared and disappeared at self-appointed meetings which concerned all kinds of weighty matters of world import. Her face was never seen except once, in a picture she placed in the *Paris Herald* together with a letter in her own handwriting. Here is that picture."

Gakker's tale had stirred me. I began to believe him. It was like an echo in a ravine which allows us to gauge the height of the precipice. Gakker's tale resounded like an echo of human power.

He handed me the photograph; it would be difficult to take a better picture of a face that expressed secretiveness. The gaze of half-shut eyes was steady under a high, proud forehead. The face shone in its pale, hard oval. A finger had, it seemed, only lately been poised against the compressed lips.

"Mariana Chen is a symbol of all the obscurity surrounding any tangled affair that involves a large number of people.

"Making the poet Teklin, whose translator I was until his death, was a far more difficult business. As you know, this writer was a man of the people, and the artistic demands made upon persons of natural talent are no higher than the usual ones; being prolific and enjoying democratic sympathies they can generally be sure of great popularity.

"In editorial offices a shy country giant began to appear, offering verses presentable enough for an uneducated man; he attracted attention, and within a year he was already writing with marked improvement. Then, after several impressive articles and reviews, Teklin vanished, reporting from time to time that he was in India or Bukhara or Australia, moving with the speed of lightning from one end of the world to the other. Teklin continued to write verse of lofty social significance; his 'wholesome' poetry satisfied a broad sector of society, and his fame increased. I began to translate him into all possible languages and I can assure you I attained a reputation as a pretty fair translator.

"Teklin recently died of yellow fever in Palestro. Even after he got rich, the poet managed without servants, was a vegetarian, and enjoyed physical work."

"You're joking!" I shouted. "It's unthinkable!"

"And, pray, why?" Gakker was sincerely amazed. "Can't I compose bad verse?" He fell silent.

"Yes, Teklin was a fine work of art," said Gakker, rousing himself from his thoughts. "I took great pains with him. But now I come to the one who, to me, is the most interesting of all—Asper. I shall not go too closely into the question of technique. In this example you will see the artist at work on his first draft.

"Asper is the idealized robber type—the romantic, the scourge of merchants, a friend of the poor, and an object of the platonic love of women who seek heroism wherever bullets fly. Strange as it seems, society, while waging a bitter fight against crime, nevertheless crowns thieves with a peculiar kind of halo, offering with one hand what it takes away with the other. After sleep, hunger, and love, man's greatest need is perhaps for the unusual, and writers of all nations and peoples have immortalized the pursuits of robbers in their works: Cartouche,[1] Morgan,[2] Rocambole,[3] Fra Diavolo,[4] Stenka Razin.[5] However much they stink of blood, the man in the crowd is drawn relentlessly toward them as a puppy yelping in fright is drawn to the slowly swaying head of a boa constrictor. It's a tonic for the nerves, so I created the legendary Asper. Roving through the slums where men's faces are overgrown with hair and voices are cracked by drink, I hit on a runaway convict, a dangerous man indeed. I had no trouble, with the help of money, in sending him overseas; he was well known to the police and his arrest was not to my advantage. Taking someone else's mousetrap but putting my own mouse in it, I made use of his name: 'Asper.' Armed robberies are commonplace in our region and I skillfully exploited them—but only those which were committed without violence or murder. Having created Asper, I then created a gang for him; after each robbery, the victim received a short notice which read: 'Asper thanks you.' At the same time the poorest among the peasants received money from me and notes 'From Asper the generous' or 'To each his own, Asper.' Sometimes these messages were longer. Frightened farmers, for

---

[1] Cartouche, 1693-1721, otherwise known as Louis-Dominique Bourguignon, was the leader of a band of robbers. He was broken on the wheel.

[2] Sir Henry Morgan, seventeenth-century buccaneer, whose exploits included the capture of Panama in 1671.

[3] Rocambole, the adventurer who was the hero of a series of novels by Ponson du Terrail, 1829-1871, called *Les Exploits de Rocambole*.

[4] Italian bandit and soldier who resisted the French invasion of the kingdom of Naples in 1799.

[5] Celebrated Cossack chief who led a rebellion against the Czar in 1670.

instance, would get the following: 'I'll be coming soon. Signed for Asper—his helper who reveals not his name.' Sometimes these farmers were actually attacked, but whenever the robbers were captured they naturally denied any connection with Asper's gang. This offered even stronger proof of the wonderful discipline imposed by the elusive, and—a trait by now universally acknowledged—courageous bandit.

"The daring and effrontery of Asper attracted the keenest attention. It was rumored that he hardly ever showed himself and opinions as to what he looked like differed widely. His victims' imaginations were of enormous help to me. From time to time I would add a little color. For instance, if I saw a peasant traveling all by himself along a road, I'd put on a mask and pass silently by him; the age-old urge to show off would force the poor dolt to tell everything about his encounter with none other than Asper himself. Once I prepared a burnt-out campfire near a small railroad station, leaving two masks, several spent cartridges, and a knife nearby on the grass. This was then solemnly declared to have been a bivouac hastily abandoned by the robber.

"His good deeds became more and more varied and frequent. I dispatched money to poverty-stricken brides, to widows, to starving workers, and toys to sick children, etc. With each passing month Asper's popularity waxed stronger and the police exhausted themselves trying to locate the villain. Whole villages suspected one another of harboring Asper, but it was impossible to follow the comings and goings of this remarkable man. Once, when I had heard that the village of Garrakh was to be put under close surveillance and every one of its citizens searched, following a denunciation by some lying or imaginative individual, I sent a letter to the newspaper *Dawn* in Asper's name. In it Asper certified on oath that Garrakh was hostile to him.

"About that time Asper fell in love.

"A young lady, R., had taken up residence not far from Zurbagan in her sister's villa. During a stroll in the woods a stone wrapped in a piece of paper fell at her feet. Picking up the object, R., in fright and amazement, read the following lines: 'My power is great but your power is greater. I have loved you long and secretly. Do not worry—although I am hunted and an outcast, in pronouncing your name I become transformed. Asper.' The young lady hurried home. A family council decided that this was the silly prank of one of the neighbors and calmed the perturbed beauty. In the morning they discovered a garden full of roses under her window; the whole area from the flower beds to the windowsills was covered with gigantic bouquets. A dagger of blue steel with a mother-of-pearl handle impaled a note on the wooden wall of the house. On the note was inscribed: 'From Asper.'

"R. immediately departed for another part of the country, followed by the not unenvious gaze of the ladies in her circle.

"Elusiveness is more disturbing than crime. On several occasions the police laid an ambush in mountain passes, on river banks, at fords, in caves, and everywhere one might possibly assume Asper to have his secret haunts. But the bandit's supernatural elusiveness, which deprived the police of even the meager consolation of a skirmish or a chase, little by little cooled the ardor of the authorities. Half-heartedly, with no enthusiasm, they took increasingly bureaucratic measures, like a chronically ill person who has lost all hope of being cured, engaging in endless official correspondence. Then, full of concern for my brainchild, I sent a denunciation which revealed the location of his permanent residence: a small hut I had built deep in the forest. Cavalry and infantry forces were sent to follow up this clue.

"Early in the morning as the pursuers were approaching Asper's hut, shots rang out from the green undergrowth. Robbers were firing from behind the shrubbery. These were blank cartridges I had wired and hidden with fantastic skill in various parts of the forest; when the mounted policemen passed along the only trail in this area they did not suspect that their horses rode over a board concealed underground which pressed a button. I had taken enormous trouble with this. The police raced in the direction of the shots, but found nobody; the robbers had disappeared. In the hut, coals were still smoldering on the hearth. The remains of food on pewter plates, knives and forks, jugs of wine all told of a hasty getaway. In chests under the bed, on the walls, and in one small secret hiding-place several wigs, false beards, pistols, and stores of firearms were discovered. On the floor lay a tortoise-shell fan, a belt, and a woman's silk handkerchief which were thought to be the belongings of Asper's mistress.

"The game has dragged on for six years. Many songs have been composed by young people in Asper's honor. But I am now convinced that Asper must be captured; recently the police have infested the region to such an extent that robbery has ceased entirely. Nothing has been heard of Asper for a year now, and many people dispute his very existence.

"I must save him—that is, I must kill him. I shall do this tomorrow."

Gakker rolled back one of the sleeves of his shirt to show me a tattoo. The design was composed of the letter A, a skull, and a bat.

"I copied this from the arm of the real Asper," said Gakker. "The police will recognize the design."

I understood. "You're going to die?"

"Yes."

"But, look, life is worth more than Asper; think of that, my friend."

"I have a special attitude toward life: I consider it an art; art demands sacrifices; furthermore, a death of this kind attracts me. In dying, I shall merge with Asper, knowing, unlike authors who are unsure of the significance of their works, that Asper shall live on a long time and serve as material for other creators, founders of legends about magnanimous robbers. So now, farewell, and pray for me to whomever can grant absolution."

He rose and we shook hands. I knew that sleep would not find me this night and walked along slowly. Asper, as a robber, continued to exist for me, despite Gakker's tale. I looked toward the mountains and sensed quite clearly that the bandit was there; hiding, he was lying in wait along the highway and cocking his weapons; my invincible certainty in this was stronger than reason.

"About 11:00 P.M. at the Vul cliffs, in the abyss, the legendary Asper was killed. Holding up a mail stage, the robber, while cocking his carbine, slipped and fell; the postman took advantage of this and shot him in the head. The wounded Asper, rushing through the undergrowth, came to the precipice but could not remain on his feet and hurtled downward onto sharp rocks scattered at the bottom of the 400-foot void. The disfigured corpse was identified by a tattoo on the left arm and a stiletto with the robber's name on the blade. Details in a special issue."

That's what I read in yesterday's paper, bundles of which were being passed out by hoarse-voiced newsboys. "Death of Asper!" they shouted. I have put this newspaper into a special box of curiosities and sad memories. Anyone can see it if he wants to.

The "M.Ts." of the title is the poetess Marina Tsvetayeva, whose work Pasternak so greatly admired and with whom he became close friends, largely by correspondence. "M.Ts." was written in 1928 when Tsvetayeva was living as an émigrée abroad. In his autobiographical essay Pasternak wrote of his sense of kinship with her: "a similarity of points of departure, tastes, and aspirations." When he met her at an anti-Fascist congress in Paris in 1935, she asked him whether he thought she and her husband and children should return to Russia; her pro-communist family was pressing her to flee the loneliness and isolation of émigré life. Pasternak did not know what to reply. "I was afraid that these remarkable people would have a difficult and troubled time at home," he wrote. "But the tragedy which was to strike the whole family surpassed my fears beyond all measure." The family returned to Russia in 1939. Her husband was arrested and perished in prison; her daughter was also arrested, her son died at the front. Tsvetayeva herself was exiled to a small town where she could not find work, even as a cleaning woman. There, she hanged herself in 1941. Translation by George Reavey.

BORIS PASTERNAK

M.Ts.

Turning your pocket inside out,
You justly say: Search, probe, and rummage.
I'm far from caring how raw the mist is.
What's done is like a wild March morning.

The trees in fluffy peasant coats
Stand rooted in brown gamboge soil,

Though probably the branches find
This covering difficult to bear.

The dew sets all the branches trembling
As it ripples like merino fleece.
Dew scurries like a hedgehog, shaking
Dry tufts of bristle on its nose.

I'm far from caring whose the chatter,
Floating from nowhere, I catch by chance.
What's done is like a farm in spring
When wrapped up in a smoking haze.

I'm far from caring what the cut
Fashions impose on clothing now.
Like dreams, they'll sweep away what's done,
Cooping up the poet in it.

Then drifting out through many gaps,
He'll seep, as does the curling smoke,
Through all the cracks of this age of doom
Into an alley just as blind.

In wisps of smoke he'll then burst free
From rifts in shattered lives.
His grandsons will say, as of the peat:
"The age of so-and-so's aglow."

Pilnyak (*the pseudonym of Boris Vogau*), *together with Za-myatin, was the object, in 1929, of the first Soviet literary frame-up. Both writers were accused of having published anti-Soviet works in the bourgeois press abroad. Pilnyak's "Mahog-any" had indeed been published in Berlin in 1929; until this time it had been the standard practice for Soviet authors to simultane-ously publish their works abroad to establish copyright. In the case of* Mahogany, *the work had been published in Germany without the author's consent. Nevertheless, this was used as a pretext to smash the quasi-independent Russian Writers' Associ-ation of which Pilnyak was president. After making a groveling submission, Pilnyak was permitted to continue working. He re-vised* Mahogany *which later appeared in Russia in the novel* The Volga Flows into the Caspian Sea (1930). *Unlike Zamyatin, who refused to submit, Pilnyak was rewarded for his weakness by arrest in 1938. He was sent to a concentration camp during the Yezhov period. His ultimate fate is unknown, but he did not survive imprisonment and, like so many other Soviet writers arrested at that time, he no doubt died in camp.*

By a tragic irony, it appears that Pilnyak intended to give Mahogany *an anti-Trotskyist twist, in the spirit of the times. He made a political miscalculation in believing that the Bukharin "right-wing" line might be followed by Stalin; at the time of writ-ing Bukharin's fate had not yet been decided. Readers may note one curious aspect of* Mahogany, *namely, an anticipation of Burnham's* Managerial Revolution.

Mahogany, *which has never been available to Soviet readers, is a splendid example of the ornamental style derived from Leskov, Bely, and Remizov. This prose style with its thematic repetitions and its peculiar rhythms was characteristic of the So-viet twenties, and was subsequently denounced as "formalist." The greater part of* Mahogany *is translated here.* Translation by Max Hayward.

BORIS PILNYAK

Mahogany

The year is 1928.

The town is a Russian Bruges and a Russian Kamakura.[1] Three hundred years ago the last Czarevich of the Ryurik dynasty was murdered in this town; on the day of the murder the boyars Tuchkov played with the Czarevich;[2] and the Tuchkov family has persisted in the town to this very day, as have the monasteries and many other families of less distinguished origin. . . . This is the Russia of olden days, the provincial Russia of the upper reaches of the Volga with its forests, marshes, monasteries, manorial estates, and a chain of towns—Tver, Uglich, Yaroslavl, Rostov the Great. The town is a monastic Bruges of the Russian principalities, of streets sprouting medicinal camomile, of stone monuments to murders and bygone ages. It is two hundred miles from Moscow, but fifty miles from the nearest railroad station.

The ruins of manor houses and the wreck of mahogany furniture are still to be found here. The curator of the museum walks the town in a top hat, morning coat, and checked trousers, and he has grown side whiskers like Pushkin's. He keeps the keys of the museums and the monasteries in the pockets of his morning coat; he drinks tea in the tavern and vodka in the solitude of his woodshed. In his house there are piles of Bibles, icons, archimandrites' hoods, miters, cassocks, chasubles, psalters, breviaries, altar cloths,

---

[1] An ancient Japanese provincial town which Pilnyak visited on his travels.
[2] This reference to the murder of the Czarevich Dmitri, on the orders of Boris Godunov, identifies the "Russian Bruges" as Uglich.

and vestments of the thirteenth, fifteenth, and seventeenth centuries. In his study he has some mahogany which once belonged to the Karazin family and on his writing table there is an ash tray in the form of a nobleman's cap with a red band and a white crown.

Vyacheslav Pavlovich Karazin is a nobleman who once served in the Horse Guards. He resigned his commission about twenty-five years before the Revolution because he was too honest. A colleague of his had got involved in a theft and Karazin had been sent to investigate; he reported the truth of the matter to the authorities, but the authorities had covered up for the thief. Karazin, unable to tolerate this, sent in his letter of resignation and retired to his country estate. He used to travel to the town once a week in his carriage, with two footmen, to do his shopping; with a wave of his white glove he would command the salesmen to wrap up half a pound of caviar, three quarters of a pound of *balyk*, and a whole sturgeon; one of the footmen would then settle the bill while the other collected the purchases. A shopkeeper once tried to shake hands with Karazin, but Karazin repulsed him, saying, "That is unnecessary."

Karazin wore a greatcoat of the period of Nicholas I and a nobleman's cap. The Revolution had ejected him from his country estate and exiled him to the town, but it had left him his greatcoat and cap; he wore this cap when he stood in queues, now preceded not by his footmen but by his wife.

Karazin lived off the sale of his antiques; in connection with this business he would call on the museum curator. At the curator's he recognized certain articles which had been confiscated from his country house by the will of the Revolution; he would glance with contemptuous unconcern at these articles, but one day he noticed the ash tray shaped like a nobleman's cap.

"Remove it," he said curtly.

"Why?" the curator asked.

"A Russian nobleman's cap cannot serve as a spittoon,"

Karazin replied. The two antiquarians quarreled. Karazin departed in a rage. He never crossed the curator's threshold again.

There was a saddler in the town who remembered with gratitude how Karazin, for whom he had worked as a groom in his youth, had knocked out seven of his teeth with a blow of his left hand because he had been too slow about something.

A deep silence hung over the town; the tedium was relieved once every twenty-four hours by the wail of the riverboat's siren and by the pealing of the town's ancient bells—that is, until 1928, when the bells were removed from many of the churches for the use of the Metallurgical Trust. With pulleys, beams, and jute ropes the bells were pulled down from their high perches on the belfries and then, poised high above the ground, they hurtled down. As they were moved slowly by the ropes, the bells still chanted their ancient lament. They fell with a roar and a thud, digging holes some five feet into the ground. At the time of this tale the whole town was full of the moaning of these ancient bells.

The most important thing in the town was to have a Trade Union card; there were two queues in the shops—one for those with cards and another for those without them. Rowboats on the Volga were rented to people with cards for ten kopecks, and to the others for forty kopecks an hour. Movie tickets cost some people twenty-five, forty, and sixty kopecks, but they were sold to card-holders at only five, ten, and fifteen kopecks. A Trade Union card, wherever it was shown, had priority together with the bread card; the bread card, and accordingly bread itself, were issued only to people who had the vote—they got four hundred grams a day; the disenfranchised and their children had no allocation of bread at all. The movie house was situated in the Trade Union park, in a heated shed; the beginning of the performances was announced, not by the customary ringing of a bell, but by

signals from the power station which reached everybody in
the town at once. The first signal meant that it was time to
drink up one's tea and the second that it was time to put on
one's coat and leave the house. The power station worked
till one o'clock in the morning, but on the occasion of birth-
days, "October days," [3] and other such unpredictable festiv-
ities at the house of the chairman of the Soviet executive
committee, the chairman of the industrial combine, and
other such high officials, the electric power would sometimes be kept on throughout the night and the rest of the
populace arranged for their own celebrations to coincide
with these occasions. In the movie house one evening a
representative of the ministry of Internal Trade, a certain
Satz (or it may have been Katz), though he was quite sober, accidentally happened to shove, as the result of an awkward movement, the wife of the chairman of the executive committee and she, with utmost scorn, said to him: "I
am Kuvarzina." Satz, not having been informed of the power
of this family, excused himself with an air of surprise and
was, as a consequence of his surprise, booted out of the district. The leading officials of the town kept very much to
themselves and, with their inborn suspiciousness, were wary
of the rest of the population; they conducted public life by
means of cabals and year after year they re-elected each
other to the leading posts in the district in accordance with
arrangements between the different feuding cliques. . . . In
view of the shut-in nature of their life, which proceeded
in secret from the rest of the populace, the leading officials
are of no interest for the purposes of this tale.

The Skudrin house stood by the Skudrin bridge, and the
house was inhabited by Yakov Karpovich Skudrin, a go-
between in peasant lawsuits, who was eighty-five years old.
Apart from Yakov Karpovich Skudrin, there dwelt separately from him in the town his two much younger sisters,

---

[3] In early Soviet times, a substitute for christening in orthodox communist
circles.

Kapitolina and Rimma, and Ivan the outcast, who had changed his name to Ozhogov. More will be said of these later.

For the last forty years Yakov Karpovich had suffered from hernia, and when he walked about, he supported his hernia with his right hand through a slit in his trousers. His hands were puffy and greenish in color and he would take great pinches of salt for his bread from the common salt-cellar and, gritting the salt on his teeth, he would carefully pour back into the saltcellar any that had been spilled. During the last thirty years Yakov Karpovich had lost the habit of normal sleep; he used to wake at night and pore over the Bible till dawn, and then fall asleep till noon. But in the middle of the day he would always go to the public reading room to peruse the newspapers—no newspapers were sold in the town, for subscription money was short—so the papers were read in reading rooms. Yakov Karpovich was fat, bald, and quite gray; his eyes were always running, and whenever he was about to speak, he always wheezed and puffed for a while. The Skudrin house had once belonged to the landowner Vereisky, who had gone bankrupt after the emancipation of the serfs while performing his duties as an elected justice of the peace.[4] Yakov Karpovich, having served his term in the pre-reform army,[5] worked for Vereisky as a scribe and learned all there was to be learned about legal juggling, and finally he bought Vereisky's house, together with the office of justice of the peace, when the landowner went bankrupt. The house had not changed since the days of Catherine the Great and in the hundred and fifty years of its existence it had grown as dark as its mahogany furniture and the windowpanes had turned bottle-green. Yakov Karpovich remembered well the days of serfdom. The old man remembered everything—the master

---

[4] After the abolition of serfdom in 1861 there was a legal reform providing for the election of law-enforcement officers.
[5] Serfs were often required to serve as long as twenty-five years in the army before the Emancipation.

of the village in which he had been a serf and the recruit-
ment of conscripts for Sebastopol; for the past fifty years he
had memorized the Christian names, patronymics, and surnames of every Russian minister and people's commissar, of
every ambassador to the Imperial Russian Court and to the
Soviet Central Executive Committee; he remembered all
the Ministers of Foreign Affairs of the Great Powers and all
the Prime Ministers, Kings, Emperors, and Popes. The old
man had lost count of the years and he would say: "I have
outlived Nicholas the First, Alexander the Second, Alexander the Third, Nicholas the Second, and Vladimir Ilyich
Lenin. And I shall outlive Alexei Ivanovich Rykov!" [6]

The old man had a very nasty smile which was both ob-
sequious and malicious, and his whitish eyes watered when
he smiled. The old man was quick-tempered, as were his
sons as well. The eldest son, Alexander, had once—it was
long before 1905—been sent to the steamship office with an
urgent letter, but he had been late for the steamer and his
father had slapped his face with the words: "Get out of here,
you scoundrel!" This was the last straw. The boy was only
fourteen, but he turned on his heel and left the house, returning six years later as a student of the Academy of Arts.
In the meantime his father had sent him a letter command-
ing him to come home and promising, otherwise, to deprive
him of his parental blessing and bestow his eternal curse
upon him. The son scribbled "To hell with your blessing!"
on this letter, just below his father's signature, and sent the
epistle straight back to him. When Alexander entered the
sitting room one sunny morning six years after his departure,
his father got up to meet him with a gleeful smile and
with his hand raised to strike him; but, grinning cheerfully,
the son seized his father by the wrists; he smiled again—
his smile glowed happily with strength—and he held his
father's hands in a vise. Pressing slightly on his wrists, he

---

[6] Rykov, as chairman of the Council of People's Commissars, was the nominal
successor to Lenin as head of the Soviet State. He was shot in 1938.

forced him down into an armchair by the table, and then he said:

"How are you, papa? Why put yourself out, papa? Sit down, papa!" The old man wheezed, giggled, and breathed hard; a wicked look of benevolence came over his face and he shouted to his wife:

"Mariushka, yes . . . he-he-he, a little vodka, bring us a little vodka, my dove, a little chilled vodka from the cellar with some nice cold *zakuski*. He's grown, our little boy, he's grown. He's come back our little boy, to our sorrow, the son of a bitch!"

The eldest son, Alexander, was an artist, and then came the other sons: one was a priest, another a doctor, and the youngest was an engineer. The two younger brothers took after the eldest, Alexander, and their father. Like Alexander they had left home, and the engineer, Akim, had become a communist. He never went near his father, and whenever he came on a visit to the town he always stayed with his aunts, Kapitolina and Rimma. By 1928 Yakov Karpovich's oldest grandsons were already married, yet his daughter, the youngest of his children, was still only twenty. She was the only daughter and, in the tumult of the Revolution, she had received no education.

This daughter, Katerina, lived in the house with the old man and her mother, Maria Klimovna. In wintertime half the house, and the second floor, were not heated. The household lived as people lived long before the time of Catherine, or even before the time of Peter—though the mahogany, which brooded in the house, was only of Catherine's day. The old couple lived off their garden. Matches, kerosene, and salt were the only products of industry in the house and the old man controlled the use of all three. From spring to the fall Maria Klimovna, Katerina, and he tended their cabbages, beets, turnips, cucumbers, carrots, and licorice, which they used instead of sugar. In the summer one could meet the old man at dawn in his nightclothes, barefoot, his right hand thrust into the slit in his trousers and his left hand holding a long switch, pasturing his cows in the dew and the mist on the outskirts of the town. In wintertime he lit the lamp only in his waking hours and at certain times his wife and daughter were obliged to sit in the dark. At midday the old man went out to read the newspapers in the public reading room and there absorbed the names and the news of the Communist Revolution. Katerina would then sit down at the spinet and practice the hymns of Kastalsky— she sang in the church choir. The old man came home at dusk, ate his meal, and went to bed.

The father would wake toward midnight, have something to eat, and apply himself to the Bible, reciting aloud from memory. At about six in the morning he fell asleep again. No longer afraid of either death or life, the old man had lost all sense of time. His wife and daughter were silent in his presence. The mother cooked gruel and cabbage soup, baked pies, made scalded and sour cream, and prepared jellied meats from pigs' trotters, putting aside the knuckles for her grandchildren[7]—in other words, she lived as Russians lived in the fifteenth and seventeenth centuries, and even the food she cooked went back to those days. Maria Klimovna, very old and shriveled, was a wonderful woman, the sort of woman who is still found in the heart of provincial Russia, together with ancient icons of the Mother of God. Fifty years ago, on the day after her wedding, when she had donned her rich red velvet jacket, her husband had said: "What's that for?" She did not immediately understand and he repeated his question: "What's that for? Take it off! I know you well enough without these fiddle-faddles and the others had better keep their eyes off you!" Then he moistened his finger and gave her a painful lesson in how she should brush her hair back from her temples. The cruel will of her husband forced her to put away forever her rich red velvet jacket and sent her to work in the kitchen. Whether her will was broken by his, or whether she was

---

[7] These bones—*babki*—are used by Russian children for various games.

tempered by her subjection to it, she was at all times meek
and dignified, silent and sad, but never devious or dishonest.
Her world went no farther than the gate and her only path
beyond it led to the church and the grave. She sang Kastalsky's hymns together with her daughter. She was sixty-
nine years old. At night the old man, who was no longer
afraid of life, declaimed aloud from the Bible. Very rarely
—every few months or so—the old man would walk to his
wife's bed, in the silent hours of the night, and whisper:

"Mariushka, yes . . . ha, h'm . . . yes, h'm, Mariushka,
this is life, Mariushka!" He held a candle in his hand, his
eyes watered and twinkled, his hands trembled.

"Mariushka, he-he . . . here I am, yes . . . That's life,
Mariushka, he-he!"

Maria Klimovna made the sign of the cross.

"Have shame, Yakov Karpovich! . . ."

Yakov Karpovich put out the light.

Their daughter Katerina had small yellow eyes, which
seemed to have been immobilized from endless sleep. All
year round freckles sprouted around her puffy eyes. Her
arms and legs were like logs and her bosom was as large as
the udder of a Swiss cow.

The town is a Russian Bruges and a Russian Kamakura.

. . . Moscow rumbled with trucks and deeds, with proj-
ects and achievements. Automobiles and buildings together
hurtled into space. Posters blared in the language of Gorky's
GIZ,[8] of the movies, and of congresses. The din of street cars,
buses, and taxis proclaimed the capital from end to end.

A train was departing from Moscow into a night as black
as soot. The hectic glow and roar of Moscow were dying
away, and they died very quickly. The fields lay wrapped
in black silence and this silence came to dwell in the carriage. In a double compartment of a "soft" first-class carriage
sat two men, the brothers Pavel Feodorovich and Stepan

---

[8] The State publishing house.

MAHOGANY   **[83**

Feodorovich Bezdetov, connoisseurs and restorers of mahogany furniture. It was impossible to weigh them up from their
appearance. Like merchants in the days of Ostrovsky,[9] both
wore frock coats over their Russian tunics, and their faces,
though clean-shaven, had the slavonic cast of Yaroslavl.
Their eyes were vacant, yet shrewd.

The train went on dragging time across the black expanse
of the fields. In the carriage there was a smell of tanned
leather and hemp. Pavel Feodorovich extracted a bottle of
cognac and a silver liqueur glass from his valise; he poured
out a glassful and drank it down; he poured out another and
handed it silently to his brother. His brother emptied the
glass and passed it back. Pavel Feodorovich put the bottle
and glass into the valise.

"Are we buying beadwork?" asked Stepan.

"Absolutely," replied Pavel.

Half an hour elapsed in silence. The train dragged time
with it, halting it only at the stations. Pavel extracted the
bottle and the glass again, drank, poured out some for his
brother, and then put them away.

"Shall we give the girls a treat? And are we buying china?"
asked Stepan.

"Absolutely," Pavel replied.

After another half hour in silence, the brothers drank
again.

"Are we buying so-called Russian tapestries?" asked Stepan.

"Absolutely," replied Pavel.

By midnight the train arrived at a village on the Volga
which is famed throughout Russia for its craft in the making
of boots. The smell of leather grew stronger and stronger.
Pavel poured out a last nip for each of them.

"We're not buying anything later than Alexander the
First?" asked Stepan.

"Absolutely not," replied Pavel.

_____

[9] Alexander Ostrovsky (1823-1886), Moscow dramatist, who in many of his
plays described the life and manners of the merchant class.

· · ·

Without speaking a word Pavel Feodorovich hired a cart
for forty kopecks to take them to the steamship office.

By midday the steamer arrived in the seventeenth- and
eighteenth-century Russian Bruges. The town sloped down
to the Volga with its churches, its citadel, and the ruins left
over from the fire in 1920, when a good portion of the central
part of the town had been gutted. The fire had started in the
Commissariat of Food Supplies. Instead of trying to extin-
guish the fire, they started tracking down members of the
local bourgeoisie and put them in prison as hostages. They
hunted them for three days—for as many days as the town
burned, and stopped hunting them when the fire had
burned itself out without any intervention on the part of
the fire brigade or the population. At the hour when the
antique dealers disembarked, flocks of frantic jackdaws
were wheeling over the town, which was filled with the
weird groan of bells being cast down from their belfries. It
looked as though there was going to be a bit of rain.

Without speaking a word Pavel Feodorovich hired a carriage to take them to Yakov Karpovich Skudrin's at Skudrin
bridge. The carriage rattled over the medicinal camomile of
the ancient cobbled streets and the coachman told them the
latest town gossip about the bells, explaining that many
people's nerves had been shattered by the tension of waiting
for bells to fall and the thunder of the impact when they
hit the ground—the same as happens to inexperienced rifle-
men who shut their eyes to brace themselves for the report.
When the Bezdetovs arrived, old Yakov Karpovich was in
the yard, chopping logs for firewood. Maria Klimovna was
shoveling dung out of the cowshed. Yakov Karpovich did not
at first recognize them, but when he did, he looked pleased
and began to smile. Groaning and wheezing, he said:

"Ah, the dealers! . . . I've got a new theory about the
proletariat for you!" Maria Klimovna, her hands under her
apron, gave a low bow and sang out her greeting:

"Dear guests, a good welcome to you, long-awaited guests!"

Katerina, in a skirt tucked up to her thighs and covered with dirt, rushed headlong into the house to change. From over the housetops, startling the rooks, came the whine of a falling bell. Maria Klimovna crossed herself. The bell thudded louder than a cannon and the windowpanes tinkled. It certainly was enough to set your nerves on edge.

They all went into the house. Maria Klimovna went to her pots and pans and soon the samovar sang out at her feet. Katerina came in in her Sunday best and curtsied to the visitors. The old man threw off his felt boots and, cooing like a dove, walked barefooted around his guests, who went to wash up and then sat down side by side at the table, in silence. Their eyes were vacant like those of dead men. Maria Klimovna inquired after their health and laid out an assortment of seventeenth-century food on the table. The visitors put a bottle of cognac on the table. Yakov Karpovich was the only one to talk. He hummed and hawed and giggled as he told the Bezdetov brothers of the places to which they should go in search of antiques and which he had noted for their benefit.

"But you yourself won't give in? You're not selling?" inquired Pavel Feodorovich.

The old man, fidgeting and giggling, replied in a whimpering voice:

"Yes, yes, seems so. I can't, no, I can't. I'll not part with my own. I may need it myself. We shall see what we shall see . . . yes, h'm . . . I'd better tell you about my theory. . . . I'll outlast you all yet!"

After lunch the guests retired to bed. They closed the creaking door, stretched out on the feather beds, and silently drank cognac out of old silver cups. By evening they were quite drunk. Katerina sang her hymns all afternoon and Yakov Karpovich lurked near the visitors' door, hoping they might come out or start talking, so that he could drop in and have a chat with them. The rooks departed with the day which they had been busily pilfering all through sundown, and the water carriers came on their evening round, distributing the darkness. When the guests came down for tea their eyes were quite dead and fixed in a stupefied glaze. They sat down at the table, side by side and in silence. To be within easy reach of their ears, Yakov Karpovich settled himself right behind them. The guests sipped tea from their saucers, lacing it with cognac, and unbuttoned their jackets. A charcoal brazier of Catherine's day gave off its fumes near the dining table, which was round and made of mahogany.

Yakov Karpovich talked, spluttering in his haste to have his say: "I have a new thought for you, h'm, a new thought. . . . Marx's theory about the proletariat will soon be forgotten, because the proletariat itself must disappear: there you have it, my thought! . . . It follows that the whole Revolution was for nothing, a mistake, h'm, of history, because, yes, in two or three generations the proletariat will have disappeared—first of all in the United States, in England, and in Germany. Marx wrote down his theory in the age of manual labor. Now machines are taking the place of brawn. That's what I think. Before long the machines will be tended only by engineers and the proletariat will disappear. The proletarians will turn into engineers. That's, h'm, what I think. And an engineer is not a proletarian, because the more cultured a man is, the less fussy he is about his needs, and he finds it easier to live with everyone on a footing of material equality, to distribute the goods of this world equally in order to set the mind free. Yes, just look at the English: rich and poor alike sleep in pajamas and they live in the same houses, all of three stories. Just compare how the merchants and the peasants used to live in this country, with the merchants all dressed up like priests and living in palaces. But a man like me can go barefoot and be none the worse for it. You may argue, yes, h'm, that there will still be exploitation, but how can there be exploitation? The peasants who can be exploited because they are like wild beasts, will not be allowed near the machines—they might break them and they cost millions, these machines. Machines are too expensive to make petty economies in wages. You've got to have a man who knows the machine, and one man will do where they used to need a hundred. They'll take good care of a man like that. The proletariat will disappear! . . ."

The visitors drank their tea and listened, their eyes glazed and unblinking. Yakov Karpovich snorted and hawked and babbled on, but he didn't manage to develop his thought to its final conclusion because of the arrival of his brother, Ivan the outcast, who had changed his name from Skudrin to Ozhogov. He was tidily dressed in a fantastic array of cast-off clothing and his hair was neatly clipped. He wore no socks under his galoshes. He bowed politely to the company and sat down silently a little to one side. Nobody acknowledged his bow. His face was that of a madman. Yakov Karpovich fidgeted uneasily.

"And what was it that brought you here, my dear?" Maria Klimovna asked in dismay.

"I've come to see some aspects of the counterrevolution, my dear," replied the outcast Ivan.

"What kind of counterrevolution is there here, my dear?"

"As far as you are concerned, my dear, it is only your way of life which is counterrevolutionary. But you have wept for me, which means that you have within yourself the rudiments of communism. Brother Yakov has never wept and I am very sorry that I did not put him up against the wall, when I had the chance, and shoot him."

Maria Klimovna sighed and shook her head.

"And how's your dear son?" she asked.

"My dear son," Ivan the outcast answered with pride, "is finishing his studies in the university and he has not forgotten me. When he comes on vacation he visits me in my domain and warms himself by the furnace while I compose revolutionary verse for him."

"And his wife?"

"I don't meet her. She manages a Party bureau for women's

affairs. Do you know how many managers we have for every two workers engaged in production?"

"No."

"Seven. With seven nurses, the child runs wild, as the proverb says. Your guests, by the way, represent the counterrevolution in its historical aspect."

Glassy-eyed, the visitors drank their tea. Yakov Karpovich, swelling with purple rage, began to look like a beet. He went toward his brother, and giving a polite giggle, vigorously rubbed his hands together as though they were very cold.

"Listen, brother dear," said Yakov Karpovich politely in a hoarse voice, "get out of here and go to the devil. I implore you from the bottom of my heart! . . ."

"I beg your pardon, brother Yakov," replied Ivan, "but I didn't come to see you. I came to look at the counterrevolution in its historical aspect and to engage it in conversation."

"And I'm asking you to clear off and go to the devil."

"I shall not go to the devil."

Pavel Feodorovich Bezdetov slowly turned one glassy eye to his brother and said:

"We cannot talk with cranks. If you don't get out, I shall instruct Stepan to remove you by the scruff of your neck."

Stepan returned his brother's glance and shifted slightly in his chair. Maria Klimovna put her face in her hands and sighed. Ivan the outcast sat on in silence. Stepan rose reluctantly from the table and went toward him. The outcast got up in fright and retreated backward to the door. Maria Klimovna sighed again and Yakov Karpovich giggled. Stepan stopped halfway across the room and the outcast halted, grimacing, by the door. Stepan took another step toward him and he went outside. Then from behind the door, he said in a begging voice:

"Well, in that case give me a ruble and twenty-five kopecks for vodka." Stepan glanced at Pavel and Pavel said:

"Give him enough for a half-bottle."

The outcast departed. Maria Klimovna went out of the

gate to see him off and thrust a piece of pie into his hand. Beyond the gate the night was black and still. Ozhogov the outcast walked to the Volga down dark side streets, past the monasteries and over vacant lots, along paths which he alone knew. The night was very black. Ivan talked to himself, muttering indistinctly. He went down to the brickworks belonging to the Industrial Combine; here he crawled through a gap in the fence and made his way through the clay pits. Amid the clay pits was a kiln and it was working. Ivan crawled underground into the hollow of the kiln; it was hot and stifling here and a red light glowed from cracks in the doors of the furnace. Here, on the bare earth, sprawled a band of ragged men with matted hair as thick as felt: these were Ivan Ozhogov's communists who had a tacit agreement with the Industrial Combine whereby they fired, without wages, the kiln of the brickworks—the kiln in which the bricks were baked—and in return lived here, near the furnace, free of charge; these were men for whom time had stopped in the period of War Communism[10] and they had elected Ivan Ozhogov as their chairman. On the straw beside the board which served them as a table three of the ragged crew lay resting.

Ozhogov squatted down beside them, shivered a little as one does when warming up after being in the cold, and placed the money and the piece of pie on the table.

"They didn't weep?" asked one of the ragged men.

"No, they didn't weep," replied Ozhogov.

They were all silent for a while.

"Your turn to go, Comrade Ognev," Ozhogov said.

Two more men with matted beards and mustaches crawled into the clay interior of the underground and, in all their ragged poverty, slumped on the bare earth, placing some money and bread on the boards. Ognev, about forty years of age and an old man already, who was lying stretched out where it was darkest and warmest, crawled up

---

[10] The short period (1917-1921) preceding N.E.P., during which there was an attempt at the vigorous application of communist principles.

to the board, counted the money, and climbed out of the underground. The rest remained lying or sitting in silence, except one of the new arrivals who remarked that they would have to load the barge with logs first thing in the morning. Before long Ognev returned with bottles of vodka. Then the ragged crew moved to the board, pulled out their mugs, and sat down in a circle. Comrade Ognev poured a round of vodka; they clinked their mugs and drained them in silence.

"Now I shall speak," Ozhogov declared. "There were the brothers Wright, and they decided to fly into the sky, and they perished, crashing to earth after falling from the sky. They perished, but their cause was not abandoned; men reached for the sky and grasped it, and men are flying now, comrades, they are flying above the earth like birds, like eagles! Comrade Lenin perished like the Wright brothers. In our town I was the first chairman of the Soviet executive committee. In twenty-one everything came to an end. The only real communists left in the whole town are we and the only place left to us is this underground. I was the first communist in the town and a communist I shall remain until my dying day. Our ideas shall not perish. And what ideas they were! Now no one remembers them, comrades, except us. We are like the Wright brothers! . . ."

Comrade Ognev poured out another round of vodka and, interrupting Ozhogov, said:

"I'll tell you, chairman! The great things we did! the way we fought! I was in command of a partisan unit. We marched through a forest for a day and a night, and then another day and another night. And at dawn what do we hear? Machine guns!"

Ognev was interrupted by Pozharov, who asked:

"And when you use your saber how do you hold your thumb, straight or bent?"

"Against the blade. Straight," Ognev replied.

"That's what they all do. Here, show me on this knife, show me how you do it!"

Ognev took the cobbler's knife which they used to cut bread and demonstrated how he placed his thumb on the blade.

"That's the wrong way!" Pozharov cried out. "That's not how I hold it—it cuts like a razor when I use it. Here, I'll show you, you've got it all wrong!"

"Comrades!" said Ozhogov softly, his face wincing with pain and madness. "We must talk of ideas today, of great ideas, and not about saber-slashing!"

A fourth man interrupted Ozhogov, shouting:

"Comrade Ognev! You were in the Third Division and I was in the Second. Do you remember how you missed the crossing near the village of Shinky? . . ."

"We missed it? No, it was you who missed it, not we! . . ."

"Comrades!" Ozhogov again interjected in a voice at once calm and insane. "We must speak about ideas! . . ."

By midnight these ragged men who had asserted their right to live underground in the kiln of the brickworks were already asleep in their subterranean shelter next to the furnace. They slept all in a heap, the head of one resting in the lap of another, and rags were their only covering. The last to fall asleep was their chairman, Ivan Ozhogov. He had lain for a long time with a sheet of paper near the mouth of the furnace. He lay on his stomach, with the sheet spread on the ground. Licking the point of his pencil, he tried to write verse. "We raised a world . . ." he wrote and crossed it out. "We lighted a world . . ." he wrote and crossed it out. "You who warm your thievish hands," he wrote and crossed it out. "You, be ye lackeys or lunatics," he wrote and crossed it out. The right words did not come. He fell asleep, dropping his head on the scribbled sheet of paper. Here slept the communists who answered the call of War Communism and who had been disbanded in nineteen hundred and twenty-one, men of arrested ideas, madmen and drunkards who in their underground refuge and in their labor of unloading barges and sawing timber had created for themselves a strict brotherhood, a strict communism, men who possessed noth-

ing for themselves, neither money nor belongings nor wives
—their wives had left them to their dreams, their madness,
and their alcohol. It was very stifling in the underground,
very hot and very bare.

Midnight descended on the town, as turgid and as black
as the history of these parts.

At midnight, Stepan, the younger of the two antique-
dealers, stopped Katerina on the staircase leading to the
second floor, touched her shoulders, which were as strong as
a horse's, felt them with his drunken hand, and said in a
low voice:

"Go and tell your sisters . . . you know . . . we'll do it
again. They should find a place, tell them . . ."

Katerina stood there meekly and meekly whispered back:
"Very good. I'll tell them."

Downstairs at that minute Yakov Karpovich was unfolding his theory of civilization to Pavel Feodorovich. On the
round table in the sitting room stood a glass and bronze
frigate which had been specially adapted as a receptacle for
liquor; dispensed through a tap into glasses and thence to
human throats, the liquor enabled one to journey on the
frigate through the world of fantasy. The frigate was an
eighteenth-century object. It was filled with cognac. Pavel
Feodorovich sat in silence. Yakov Karpovich fussed around
him, strutting like a pigeon and holding his hernia through
the slit in his trousers.

"Yes, h'm," he was saying, "what is it then in your opinion
that makes the world go round, and civilization and science
and steamships? Well, what?"

"Well, what?" Pavel Feodorovich repeated the question.

"Well, what do you think? Labor? Knowledge? Hunger?
Love? No! The prime mover of civilization is memory! Just
think what it would be like if tomorrow morning men were
to lose their memory. They still have their instincts and their
reason, but no memory. I wake up in bed and fall out of it,
because I know of space only from memory and without
memory I am ignorant of it. My trousers are lying on a chair

and I feel cold, but I don't know what to do with my trousers.
I don't know how to walk—on my hands or on all fours. I
do not remember the previous day and since I am ignorant
of it, I have no fear of death. The engineers have forgotten
the whole of their higher mathematics, and all the streetcars
and locomotives are at a standstill. Priests don't know the
way to their churches and they remember nothing of Jesus
Christ. Yes, h'm! . . . I have my instincts left, and it's true
that they're a sort of memory, but suppose I don't know
whether to eat the chair or the bread left on it overnight
and suppose, when I see a woman, I take my daughter for
my wife?"

With northeast winds the alcohol-laden frigate on the table was blowing the cobwebs from Yakov Karpovich's mind.
Amidst the mahogany of the sitting room, this Russian Voltaire and his frigate were relics of the eighteenth century. A
provincial Soviet night held sway outside these eighteenth-
century windows.

An hour later the Skudrin house was asleep. And then,
in the musty silence of his bedroom, Yakov Karpovich
shuffled in his slippers over to Maria Klimovna's bed. The
old woman was sleeping. The candle trembled in Yakov
Karpovich's hand. He giggled and touched Maria Klimovna's shoulder, which was as dry and shriveled as parch-
ment, and his eyes grew moist with pleasure.

"Mariushka," he whispered, "this is life, Mariushka, this is
life." The eighteenth century vanished in Voltairean darkness.

In the morning church bells again went to their doom and
howled and were smashed to smithereens. The Bezdetov
brothers woke early, but Maria Klimovna had got up even
earlier and hot pies with onion and mushrooms were served
with the morning tea. Yakov Karpovich was still in bed.
Katerina looked sleepy. Tea was drunk in silence. The day
rose up gray and sluggish. After breakfast the Bezdetov
brothers went off to their work. Pavel Feodorovich drew up
on a piece of paper a list of all the houses and families they

had to visit. The streets lay mute amidst the provincial pave-
ments, the brick walls, the weeds growing under them, the
elder bushes in the ruins left from the great fire, the
churches and the bell towers. The silence of the streets was
deafened by the whining of the bells and it shrieked when
they smashed to the ground.

The Bezdetovs walked silently, side by side, into the
houses they visited and their eyes were blank as they looked
around.

Vyacheslav Pavlovich Karazin was lying on a sofa in the
dining room; he was covered by an impossibly worn jacket
made of squirrel fur. The dining room and the combined
study and bedroom which he shared with his wife presented the spectacle of an antique shop housed in the
cramped quarters of a post office clerk. The Bezdetov brothers paused in the doorway and bowed. Karazin studied them
for some time and then he roared:

"Get out! Swindlers! Get out of here!"

The brothers did not budge.

"Out of my sight, scoundrels!" barked Karazin once more,
the blood rushing to his face.

His wife appeared at the shout. The Bezdetov brothers
bowed to Madame Karazin and left the room.

"Nadine, I cannot bear to see these rogues," Karazin said
to his wife.

"Very well, Vyacheslav. Go into the study and I'll talk with
them. You know the situation," Madame Karazin replied.

"They've disturbed my rest. Very well, I'll go to the study.
Only mind you, no familiarity with these menials."

Karazin left the room, trailing his squirrel jacket after
him. The Bezdetov brothers returned on his heels and once
more they bowed politely.

"Show us your Russian tapestries and tell us what you
want for the secretaire," said Pavel Feodorovich.

"Take a seat, gentlemen," said Madame Karazin.

The door of the study flew open and Karazin thrust his

head out. Averting his eyes to the windows—so that they should not by accident fall upon the Bezdetovs—he shouted:

"Nadine, don't let them sit down! How can they possibly understand the beauty of art! Don't offer them a choice! Sell them only what we see fit to sell! Let them have the porcelain clock, and the bronze stuff! . . ."

"We can leave, if you like," said Pavel Feodorovich.

"Oh, just a minute, gentlemen. Allow Vyacheslav Pavlovich to calm down, he's very ill," said Madame Karazin, sitting down helplessly at the table. "Oh dear, gentlemen, we simply have to sell off a few things! . . . Vyacheslav Pavlovich, I beg you, shut the door, don't listen to us, go for a walk. . . ."

In the evening, when the jackdaws had torn the day to shreds and the falling bells had ceased their whine, the Bezdetov brothers returned home and dined. After dinner Yakov Karpovich went out on an expedition. In his pocket he had money and a list given to him by the Bezdetovs. The old man donned his broad felt hat, his sheepskin jacket, and his leggings. He was going to see the carpenter and the carter, obtain ropes and matting, and make all the necessary arrangements for the packing of the purchases and their transport to the wharf for dispatch to Moscow. The old man knew his business and on leaving he said:

"We should give the job to the down-and-outs in the brickworks: they're as honest as the day is long, crackpots though they may be. But we can't. Their revolutionary-in-chief, brother Ivan, would never hear of them doing a job for the counterrevolution, he-he-he! . . ."

The Bezdetov brothers settled down to rest in the sitting room and night was settling on the earth. Throughout the evening people came and knocked furtively on Maria Klimovna's window. Katerina would go out to see them, and fawning like beggars, the people would say: "Your visitors buy all kinds of antiques, don't they?" and they offered old ruble and kopeck coins, broken lamps, ancient samovars,

books, and candlesticks. These people, who were poverty-
stricken in all respects, knew nothing of antiques. Katerina
did not allow them to come into the house with their brass
candlesticks and proposed that they leave their stuff until
the morning when the visitors, having rested, would look at
it.

At about eight o'clock Katerina asked her mother's permission to go out for the evening—first to choir practice
and then to visit a friend. She put on her best clothes and
left the house. Half an hour later Pavel Feodorovich and his
brother Stepan followed her out into the rain. Katerina was
waiting for them on the other side of the bridge. Stepan
Feodorovich took Katerina's arm, and they walked in the
pitch dark along a path which ran by the side of a ravine
to the outskirts of the town, where Yakov Karpovich's old
sisters, Kapitolina and Rimma, had their house. Katerina
and the Bezdetovs crept into the yard like thieves and, like
thieves, slipped through the garden. In the depths of the
garden stood a solitary bathhouse.

Katerina knocked and the door was half opened. A light
was burning in the bathhouse and three girls were waiting
for the guests. They had covered up all the chinks in the
windows with curtains and moved the table to the brick
steps in the middle of the bathhouse. The girls were in their
Sunday best and they greeted their visitors with great cere-
mony.

The Bezdetov brothers drew bottles of cognac and port
wine, brought with them from Moscow, out of their pockets.

On the table, which was covered with paper, the girls laid
out salami, sprats, candy, tomatoes, and apples. Klavdia, the
eldest of them, produced a bottle of vodka from behind the
stove. They all spoke in whispers. The Bezdetov brothers sat
down side by side on the brick steps, where an iron lantern
was burning. Within an hour the girls were drunk, yet even
so they continued to speak in whispers. When people are
drunk—and this is particularly true of women—the expres-

sion induced by alcohol tends, the drunker they get, to become fixed on their faces. Klavdia was sitting at the table,
propping her head on her hands like a man; her teeth were
bared in a fixed grin of contempt. Sometimes her head
slipped from her hands and then she would tear her bobbed
hair, without feeling pain. She smoked one cigarette after
another and drank cognac. She was crimson-cheeked and
beautiful in a monstrous way. Disgustedly she said:

"I'm drunk? All right, I'm drunk. What of it? Tomorrow I'll
be teaching in school again. But what do I know? What the
hell am I teaching? And at six o'clock I go to a parents'
meeting that I called myself. Look at my notebook here, I've
got it all down. . . . So I'm drinking . . . well, what the
hell . . . and now I'm drunk. And who the hell are you?
Relatives of mine or something? You buy mahogany? Antiques? And you want to buy us as well, with wine? You
think I don't know the facts of life, but I know 'em all right!
Going to have a kid before long . . . don't know who the
father is . . . but what the hell!"

The lips were drawn back from her teeth and her eyes
had a fixed stare. Pavel was pestering Zina, the youngest of
the girls. She was a short-legged giggly girl with very flaxen
hair. Her legs apart and her arms akimbo, she sat on a
wooden block at some distance from the others. Pavel Feodorovich was saying:

"I bet you daren't take off your blouse, Zina, I bet you
daren't undo your brassiere!"

Zina held her hand pressed to her mouth so as not to burst
into loud laughter and she replied with a giggle:

"Yes, I dare!"

"No, you daren't."

Klavdia said with contempt:

"She'll do it all right. Show 'em your tits, Zinka! Let 'em
have a good look. Want to see mine as well? You think I'm
drunk, don't you? Well, I'm not. I've not been drunk since
the last time you came. Today I just wanted to get boiled.

Boiled, you understand? Boiled, boiled, boiled! So what the hell? Show 'em your tits, Zina! You show 'em to your Kolya, don't you? . . . Want to see mine as well?"

Klavdia ripped at the collar of her blouse. The other girls rushed over to her and Katerina said soberly:

"Klavdia, don't tear your clothes, or they'll find out at home."

Zina had difficulty in standing up. Klavdia caught hold of Zina and put her arms round her. Klavdia kissed her.

"I mustn't tear my clothes? All right, I won't. . . . You show them yours, then. Let them have a good look. We've got no prejudices here! . . . So you buy mahogany?"

"All right, I'll show them," said Zina obediently, and she began to unbutton her blouse in a businesslike way.

The fourth girl went outside to be sick.

The Bezdetovs, of course, felt that this was just another deal. Buying and selling was all they knew about.

It was raining outside and the trees rustled in the wind. At this same hour Karazin was having one of his fits of senile hysteria and the down-and-outs in the brickworks, sitting by the furnace in their underground, were praising, with the eyes and voices of the madmen, the year nineteen hundred and nineteen, when everything—both bread and labor— was shared in common, when there was neither past nor future, when people lived for ideas and when there was no money, because money was not needed.

An hour later the bathhouse was empty. The Bezdetov brothers went home and so did the drunken women, creeping silently into their beds. A notebook remained lying on the bathhouse floor. In it was written: "Call parents' meeting for 6 P.M. on the 7th." "At the trade-union meeting suggest subscription of month's salary to the industrialization loan." "Ask Alexander Alexeyevich to go through the A.B.C. of communism again."

In the early morning the bells set up their whine again and carts laden with mahogany of the time of Catherine, Paul, and Alexander lumbered down to the wharf under the

supervision of Yakov Karpovich. The Bezdetov brothers
slept till noon. By this time a crowd had gathered in the
kitchen, eager to learn the fate of their old rubles, lamps,
and candlesticks.

The town is a Russian Bruges.

About the time of which we are speaking, a couple of days
after the arrival of the Bezdetov brothers, the engineer
Akim Skudrin, the youngest son of Yakov Karpovich, also
visited the town. He did not go to his father's, but stayed
with his aunts, Kapitolina and Rimma. Akim did not come
on business, it was just that he happened to have a free
week.

Kapitolina Karpovna went up to her window. What a
backwater it was! The wall of crumbling red brick ran to an
ocher-colored house with a belvedere at one corner, and to
a church at the other; and further on were a square, a weigh-
bridge, and another church. It was raining. A pig was sniff-
ing at a puddle. A water carrier came around the corner.
Klavdia went out of the gate in chamois leather boots, and a
black overcoat that reached down to her ankles; a blue kerchief was tied around her head. With her head bent down,
she crossed the street, walked along the crumbling wall, and
turned the corner on the square. Kapitolina's eyes, shining brightly, followed Klavdia for some time. In the next
room Rimma Karpovna was feeding her granddaughter, the
daughter of her eldest child, Varvara. The room was very
bare and spotlessly clean; it was very tidy and had that air
of having been lived in for many years—it was all that one
could expect of an old maid's room. It was furnished with
an old maid's narrow bed, a worktable, and a tailor's dummy,
and there were curtains on the windows. Kapitolina Karpovna went into the dining room.

"Rimma dear, let me feed the little one. I saw Klavdia go
out. Has Varvara gone too?"

The two old ladies, Kapitolina and Rimma, came of a long

line of much respected townsfolk and they were seam-
stresses and dressmakers of good standing. Their life was as
simple as the life lines on the palms of their left hands. There
was only a year between them, and Kapitolina was the elder.
Kapitolina had lived a life of righteousness in the best tradi-
tions of her class. She had lived it in full view of her fellow
citizens and in full accord with the standards which ruled
them. She was a highly respectable member of her class.
And not only she herself knew, but the whole town knew,
that all her Saturday evenings had been spent at vespers,
that she had passed every weekday of her life stooped over
the hems and stitches of shirts and blouses—countless thousands of them—and that never, never had she been kissed
by a stranger. But only she knew those thoughts and that
pain of the soured wine of life by which the heart is withered. She had lived through all the seasons of her life—childhood and youth and the later years—but never once had she
been loved and never once had she sinned in secret. By
the standards of the town she was a paragon—a virgin and
an old maid whose life had gone rancid in service to chastity,
God, and the ways of her fathers. The life of her sister
Rimma, who was also a seamstress, had taken a different
turn. It had happened twenty-eight years before and lasted
three years—three years of shame that had clung to her for
the rest of her life. It had happened in the days when
Rimma, already turned thirty, was losing her freshness and
sowing the seeds of despair. At that time there was a Treasury official in the town, a good-looking fellow who took part
in local dramatics, and a prize swine. He had a wife and
children and drank like a fish. Rimma fell in love with him
and was unable to resist the consequences of her love.
Everything about it was shameful. This love affair was a
total disgrace from the standpoint of the local conventions; it
was disastrous from beginning to end. All around there were
woods where it could have been carried on in secret, but
she chose to yield herself to this man one night in one of
the main streets, and not once during the three years of her

shame did she meet the man in privacy, preferring assignations in a neighboring wood, in the street, in an empty tumbledown house, or in a derelict barge. Yakov Karpovich disowned his sister and threw her out of the house, and even Kapitolina turned against her. She was pointed out in the street and ostracized. The lawful wife of the Treasury official used to come and slap her face and egged on the local boys to do likewise. The town, by virtue of all its laws and conventions, sided with the legal wife. Rimma gave birth to a daughter, Varvara, who was the very incarnation of her shame and the witness thereof. Klavdia, her second daughter, was a further witness to her disgrace. The Treasury official left the town and Rimma, now well over thirty, was left with the two small children to live a life of abject poverty and shame. Varvara, the elder daughter, was now married— very happily married—and had two children of her own, the granddaughters of Rimma Karpovna. Varvara's husband worked in an office and so did Varvara herself. Rimma Karpovna, as the founder of the family, now had quite a large household on her hands. The good woman was now well pleased with life. Old age had shrunk her, but happiness had rounded her out. Small and plump, she had kind, lively eyes. As for her sister Kapitolina, she was completely preoccupied by the life of Rimma, Varvara, Klavdia, and the granddaughters. All her chastity and all her decency in the eyes of the town had proved to be pointless and she had no life of her own.

"Let me feed the little one," she said. "I saw Klavdia go out. Has Varvara gone too?"

In the provincial backwater outside autumn rain was falling. The door creaked in the hall and a man's boots stamped on the floor to shake off the dirt and the mud. He came into the room and stared round helplessly as do all shortsighted people without their spectacles. It was the engineer Akim Yakovlevich Skudrin and he looked exactly like his father thirty years back. He had come for no particular purpose that anybody knew of.

"Greetings to you, my dear aunts!" he cried, kissing Aunt Rimma first of all.

Here was the Russia of the provinces with its autumn rain and its samovars.

. . . Akim had come for no particular purpose. His aunts greeted him with a samovar, some pancakes made in the twinkling of an eye, and all the hospitality of rural Russia. Akim did not call on his father, nor did he visit the local officials. Dying bells whined over the rooftops and the streets bloomed with medicinal camomile. Akim left after twenty-four hours, having established that he had no need of his birthplace and that the town had no use for him. He spent the day with his aunts, roaming in memory with all its vanities, partaking of the dire poverty of his aunts, sharing their thoughts, their cares, and their dreams. The arrangement of the furniture was much the same as it had been twenty or twenty-five years ago, and the tailor's dummy, which had frightened him in childhood, frightened him no longer. At dusk Klavdia came home from the school. The two cousins—the difference in age was ten years or so—sat down side by side on the sofa.

"How's life?" asked Akim.

After some small talk Klavdia told Akim of her main preoccupation. She spoke very simply. She was very beautiful and quite calm. The twilight dragged on slowly into the darkness.

"I should like your advice," Klavdia ventured. "I'm having a child. I don't know what to do. I don't know who the father is."

"How do you mean, you don't know who the father is?"

"I'm twenty-four," Klavdia replied. "In the spring I decided to become a woman and now I am one."

Akim was at a loss for further questions.

"I was absorbed not by love, but by myself and my own feelings," Klavdia continued. "I picked different men in order to get to know everything. I didn't want to get pregnant. Sex is a joy in itself and I didn't think of a child. But

I am pregnant and I've decided not to have an abortion."

"And you don't know who the man is?"

"I'm not certain who it is. But that isn't important. I'm a mother now. I'll manage somehow and the state will help me. And as for morality, I just don't know what it is. It doesn't make sense to me any more. Or rather, I've got my own morality. I can only answer for myself and through myself. What's immoral about giving yourself to a man? I know exactly what I want and I don't have to answer to anybody. Do I know the man, you ask. I don't want to involve him. A husband's all right when you really need him and when he's not tied in any way. I don't want a fellow who just walks round the house in his slippers and gives me kids. People will help me out—I believe in people. People like you when you've got a sense of your own dignity and when you don't want to impose on them in any way. And the state will help me too. I went with the men I liked simply because I wanted to. I'll soon have a son or a daughter. At the moment I don't give myself to anybody, because I don't need it. Yesterday I got drunk for the last time. I'm just telling you what I think as it comes into my head. I hate myself for getting drunk yesterday, but I may need a father for the child. You ran away from your father and I never had one, or rather I heard nothing but bad of him, and this made me very mad when I was a child and I was angry with my mother. Yet all the same I've decided not to have an abortion. My womb is full of the child. It's an even greater joy than . . . I am young and strong!"

Akim found it hard to collect his thoughts. Before him on the floor lay patchwork rugs, proclaiming the poverty of life in a small provincial town. Klavdia was strong and beautiful and very self-possessed. It was drizzling outside. As a communist Akim liked to think that a new way of life was in the making, but the old way was so hallowed by time. Klavdia's view of morality was both new and extraordinary for him, but if that was how she saw things, perhaps she was right. Who knows?

"Have your child then," he said.

Klavdia nestled against him, put her head on his shoulder, tucked up her feet, becoming limp and cozy.

"The body is everything for me," she said. "I love eating, I love bathing, I love physical exercise. I love it when our dog Sharik licks my hands and feet. I get pleasure from scratching my knees till the blood comes. . . . And the life all around us is so vast. I can't make head or tail of it, and I can't make any sense of the Revolution either, but I don't mind. I *believe* in life and in the Revolution and that's all that matters. I only understand the things that concern me personally and I couldn't care less about anything else."

A cat walked over the carpet and, in a familiar movement, jumped onto Klavdia's lap. It had grown dark outside. In the room next door a lamp was lit and a sewing machine began to rattle. Darkness descended on the world.

That evening Akim went to see his uncle Ivan, the uncle who had changed his name from Skudrin to Ozhogov. The outcast came out of the kiln to meet his nephew. The earth is constantly being churned up in the neighborhood of a brickworks, the roofs of brick sheds are long and low and a brickworks always has an air of ruin and mystery. Ivan the outcast was drunk. It was impossible to talk with him, but he was very, very glad that his nephew had come to see him. Shaking like a dog, he kept his feet with difficulty.

He took his nephew into one of the brick sheds.

"You've come, you've come," he whispered, pressing his trembling hands to his trembling breast.

He gave his nephew a seat on an upturned wheelbarrow.

"They've kicked you out?" he said jubilantly.

"Kicked me out of where?" asked Akim.

"Out of the Party," said Ivan.

"No."

"No? They haven't?" Ivan asked again and a note of sadness crept into his voice, but he added cheerfully:

"Well, they haven't done it yet, but they will sooner or

later. All the Leninists and all the Trotskyists will go. They'll all be kicked out!"

Ivan Karpovich now went into a delirium and in his delirium he spoke about his commune, about his having been the first chairman of the executive committee of the local Soviet, about those awesome years that had gone never to return, about how he had been cast off by the Revolution and was now a pilgrim among men, enjoining them to weep, remember, and love; he spoke again of his commune with its brotherhood and equality. Communism, he affirmed, was above all a matter of love, of solicitude for others, of friendship, fellowship, and labor done in common. Communism meant the renunciation of material things, and true communism was love and, above all, respect for one's fellow men. The neat little man shivered in the wind and fingered the collar of his jacket with his thin, trembling hands. The yard of the brickworks proclaimed havoc and destruction. The engineer Akim Skudrin was flesh of the flesh of Ivan Ozhogov . . . beggars and tramps, wandering cripples, and vagabond monks, the feeble-minded and the halt and the lame, prophets and seers and holy madmen—these were the leaven of life in the Holy Russia which has gone forever, a brotherhood in Christ which prayed for the world. The man who stood before the engineer Akim was a beggar and an outcast, a holy fool of Soviet Russia who prayed for the world, for justice, and for communism. Uncle Ivan was probably deranged. His particular point of lunacy was to walk the town calling on people he knew and on strangers, urging them to weep. He delivered wild and fiery speeches on communism as a result of which many people in the marketplaces did indeed weep. He visited the local officials in their offices, and it was rumored in the town that on these occasions the officials smeared their eyes with onion in order to win, through this outcast from the brickworks, the popularity which they so sorely needed. Ivan was frightened of churches but not of priests and he cursed them to their faces. His slogans were the most left-wing in the town. He was respected, as it has always been the custom in Russia throughout the centuries to respect those holy fools out of whose mouths speak truth and justice and who, for the sake of truth and justice, are prepared to lay down their lives. Ivan drank, destroying himself with alcohol. He had gathered around him men of his own kind: men who had been created by the Revolution only to be rejected by it. They had taken refuge underground and they practiced true communism, brotherhood, equality, and fellowship. Each of them had his own particular madness: one wanted to enter into correspondence with the proletarians of Mars, another proposed that all the full-grown fish in the Volga should be caught and steel bridges built over the river out of the proceeds of their sale, while a third man had a bee in his bonnet about constructing a streetcar system.

"Weep!" said Ivan.

Akim, lost in his thoughts, did not at first understand.

"What do you say?" he asked.

"Weep, Akim, weep this very minute for the communism that is lost!" Ivan shouted, pressing his hands to his breast and lowering his head as though in prayer.

"Yes, yes, I am weeping, Uncle Ivan," said Akim.

Akim was a tall, strong, and hulking man. He came up close to his uncle and kissed him.

The rain lashed down. The murky brickworks proclaimed havoc and destruction.

In 1946, Zoshchenko, Anna Akhmatova, and Boris Pasternak
were denounced for infringing the canons of socialist realism
laid down by A. A. Zhdanov at the first Congress of Soviet
Writers in 1934. They were accused of writing works devoid of
political and ideological content, and of demoralizing Soviet
youth by their pessimism. The journals in which they had published their works during the war (Zvezda and Leningrad) were
the subject of a special decree of the Central Committee of the
Communist Party. The head of the Soviet Union of Writers at
that time, N. Tikhonov, together with the editors of these journals, lost their jobs. One of the works mentioned in the decree
was Zoshchenko's "Before Sunrise," which had been published
in two installments in Oktyabr, in 1943.

"Before Sunrise" is an exercise in self-analysis—unique in Russian literature—that Zoshchenko attempted by writing down the
most vivid and compelling episodes in his life until 1926. Explic-
itly under the influence of Freud, the humorist hoped in this way
to find some clue to his own relentless unhappiness. He regarded
the episodes he describes as "snapshots," which explains their
partial incoherence.

In the first installment, of which this excerpt covers the years
1920-1926, Zoshchenko describes his checkered career in the
immediate postrevolutionary years. Besides a brief spell as a de-
tective, mentioned here, he was successively a carpenter, a telephone operator, a shoemaker's assistant, a militiaman, a gambler,
and an actor.

Zoshchenko died in 1958, apparently unforgiven, unrepentant,
and unhonored. An edition of his collected works, however, was
published in Leningrad in 1960, in an edition of 150,000 copies.
Translation by John Richardson.

MIKHAIL ZOSHCHENKO

Before Sunrise

"If I'd been a friend of luck, I vow
I certainly wouldn't be doing this now."

House of the Arts

This house is on the corner of the Moika Canal and the Nevsky Prospect.

I walk up and down a corridor waiting for the literary
evening to start.

The fact that I'm an inspector in the criminal investigation department means nothing. I already have two critical
articles and four stories to my credit. And they have all
been very well received.

I walk along the corridor and look at the writers.

Here comes A. M. Remizov. He's small and ugly like a
monkey. His secretary is with him. A cloth tail sticks out
from under the secretary's jacket. It's a symbol. Remizov is
the Dean of the "Free Monkey Parliament." E. I. Zamyatin's
standing over there. His face is rather shiny. He's smiling.
He's holding a long cigarette in a long elegant holder.

He's talking to someone in English.

Here's Shklovsky. He's wearing a Central Asian skullcap.
He has an intelligent and impudent face. He's arguing vehemently with someone. He can't see anyone but himself and
his adversary.

I say hello to Zamyatin.

Turning toward me, he says:

"Blok's here. You wanted to see him. . . ."

Zamyatin and I go into a dingy room.

A man is standing by the window. He has a deeply tanned face, a high forehead, and light, wavy, almost curly hair.

He's standing surprisingly still. He's looking at the lights of the Nevsky Prospect. He doesn't turn around when we go in.

"Alexander Alexandrovich," says Zamyatin.

I have never seen such empty, lifeless eyes. I never thought that a face could express such sadness and apathy.

Turning slowly around, Blok looks at us.

Blok holds out his hand—it is limp and lifeless.

I feel awkward at having disturbed a man lost in his oblivion. . . . I mumble an apology.

Blok asks me in a rather dull voice:

"Will you be speaking at the evening?"

"No," I say. "I've come to listen to the others."

Apologizing once again, I leave hurriedly.

Zamyatin is left with Blok.

Again I walk along the corridor. An emotion is stifling me. I almost know my fate now. I see the finale of my life. I see the misery which will inevitably stifle me.

I ask someone: "How old is Blok?" I receive the answer: "About forty."

Fancy, not yet forty! But Byron was thirty when he said:

> It is that weariness which springs
> From all I meet, or hear or see?
> To me no pleasure Beauty brings
> Thine eyes have scarce a charm for me . . .

Byron did not put a question mark at the end of the second line. It is I who am mentally asking the question. I wonder whether this is really "that weariness." The literary evening begins.

The Cafe "Twelve"

This cafe is at 12 Sadovaya Street. I sit there at a table with my friends.

Drunken shouting, noise, and tobacco smoke all around me.

A violin is playing.

I mutter Blok's verse:

> I will again befriend the tavern fiddle . . .
> I will again drink wine . . .
> I still won't have the strength to reach the end
> With a sober, sad smile, beyond which
> Is the terror of the grave, the anxiety of a corpse . . .

A man comes to our table, walking uncertainly. He's wearing a black velvet blouse. There is a large white muslin bow on his chest.

His face is smeared with powder.

His lips are made up and his eyebrows penciled.

On his face is a smile—a drunken and rather embarrassed smile. Someone says:

"Seryozha, come and sit with us."

Now I see it is Esenin.

He sits down heavily at our table. He looks angrily at one of the drunks. He mutters:

"I'll push your face in . . . get out . . ."

I pat Esenin's hand. He calms down. He smiles again sadly, and with embarrassment.

Behind the made-up mouth I see pale lips.

Someone else comes over to our table.

Someone shouts: "We must put the tables together."

They start moving the tables.

I go outside.

At Gorky's

We go into the kitchen. On the stove are large copper saucepans.

We go through the kitchen into the dining room.

Gorky comes toward us.

There is something elegant in his noiseless walk and in his movements and gestures.

He doesn't smile as a host ought to, but his face is friendly.

He sits down at the table in the dining room. We settle down on chairs and on a low brightly colored divan. I see Fedin, Vsevolod Ivanov in a soldier's greatcoat, Slonimsky, and Gruzdev. . . .

Coughing from time to time, Gorky talks about literature, the people, and the tasks of a writer.

He speaks in an interesting and even absorbing way. But I hardly listen to him. I watch him drumming his fingers nervously on the table, and almost imperceptibly smiling to himself. I watch his amazing face—a clever, rather coarse, and far from simple face.

I look at this great man who has become a legendary figure. It's probably bad, disconcerting, and tiring to be one. I wouldn't like it.

As though answering my thought, Gorky says that by no means everyone knows him; a few days before he was traveling by car when some guards stopped him. He told them he was Gorky, but one of them said: "We don't care whether you're Gorky [1] or sweet. Show your pass."

Gorky smiles faintly. Then he starts talking again about literature, the people, and culture.

Someone behind is writing down everything he says.

We get up. We say good-by.

With his hand barely touching my shoulder, Gorky asks: "Why do you look so glum and grim? Why?"

In reply I mumble something about my heart.

"That's bad," says Gorky. "You must get better . . . come and see me in a few days—we'll talk about your affairs."

We go through the kitchen again. We go out onto the stairs.

We go out into the Kronversky Prospect—the Gorky Prospect.

---

[1] Gorky means "bitter" in Russian.

An Encounter

I go up and down endless stairways. I am holding a file containing papers and forms. I write down information about the tenants on these forms. It's a national census.

I undertook this work to find out how people live.

I only believe what I see. Like Harun-al-Rashid I go to other people's houses. I go along corridors, through kitchens, into rooms. I see dull electric lights, tattered wallpaper, washing on the line, ghastly crowding, garbage, and rags. Yes, of course, it is only recently that the difficult years, famine, and devastation passed . . . but I didn't expect to see what I've seen.

I enter a dingy room. A man is lying on a bunk on a dirty mattress. He is not friendly. He does not even turn toward me. He stares at the ceiling.

"Where do you work?" I ask.

"Only asses and horses work," he says. "I don't work myself and don't intend to. So write that down on your lousy papers . . . you can add that I go to the club and play cards. . . ."

He's annoyed. Perhaps he's sick. I want to go on to the neighbors. As I leave, I look at him. I've seen him somewhere before.

"Alyosha!" I say.

He sits up on the bunk. He has an unshaven, gloomy face.

I see before me Alyosha N., a school friend. He was one grade ahead of me. He was a sissy, a teacher's pet, first in the class, and a mommy's darling. . . .

"What happened, Alyosha?" I mutter.

"Absolutely nothing happened," he says. And I see annoyance on his face.

"Maybe I can help you?"

"I need absolutely nothing," he says. "Incidentally, if you have any money, give me five rubles. I'll run down to the club."

I offer much more, but he takes only five.

A few minutes later I'm sitting on his bunk and we're talking as we used to ten years before.

"Really a very commonplace business," he says. "My wife went off with some heel. I began drinking. I drank everything I had. I lost my job. I began playing cards at the club, and now, you understand, I don't want to go back to the past. I could, but I don't want to. Everything is rubbish, rot, comedy, nonsense, smoke. . . ."

I make him promise to visit me.

At Night

There are letters to the *Red Gazette* on my pillow. They are complaints about inefficiency in the public baths. I am supposed to write a *feuilleton* about it.

I scan through the letters. They are inept and comic. But at the same time serious. They certainly are! The issue concerns an important aspect of everyday life—baths.

I draft an outline and start writing.

Even the first few lines amuse me. I laugh. I laugh louder and louder. I finally roar with laughter to such an extent that the pencil and pad drop from my hands.

I start writing again. And again I'm convulsed with laughter.

No, later on, when I'm rewriting the story, I shan't laugh so loudly. But the first draft always amuses me to an incredible degree.

I feel sick with laughter.

A neighbor knocks on the wall. He's an accountant. He has to get up early tomorrow. I'm preventing him from sleeping. Tonight he's pounding with his fist. I must have wakened him. Annoying.

I call out:

"Sorry, Pyotr Alexeyevich . . ."

I take up the pad again. Again I laugh, this time with my face in a pillow.

Twenty minutes later the story is complete. A pity I wrote it so quickly.

I go across to the desk and copy out the story in nice, neat handwriting. While copying it out, I continue to laugh quietly. But tomorrow, when I'm reading the story to the editors, I shan't be laughing. I shall read it glumly and even grimly.

Two A.M. I go to bed. But for a long time I can't sleep. I think up subjects for new stories.

Dawn. I take bromide in order to sleep.

More Rubbish Again

The editorial office of the literary journal *Contemporary*.

I gave five of my best little stories to this magazine, and now I've come for the answer.

Sitting in front of me is one of the editors—the poet M. Kuzmin. He is affectedly polite. Much too much so. But I see from his face he's about to tell me something unpleasant.

He hesitates. I come to his rescue.

"My stories probably aren't what you need for the magazine," I say.

He says: "Ours is a big magazine, you see . . . and your stories . . . no . . . they're very funny and amusing . . . but they're written . . . well, it's . . ."

"Rubbish, do you mean?" I ask him. And the comment written on a school essay—"rubbish"—lights up in my mind.

Kuzmin spreads his hands.

"For heaven's sake. I don't mean that at all. On the contrary. Your stories show great talent . . . but you must agree they're rather exaggerated."

"They're not exaggerated," I say.

"Well, just take the language. . . ."

"The language isn't overdone. It's the syntax of the street . . . of the people. . . . I may have exaggerated a little to make it more satirical, to make it critical. . . ."

"Don't let's argue," he says softly. "Give us an ordinary novel or story of yours . . . and believe me, we rate your work very highly."

I leave the editorial office. I no longer have the same feelings I had at school. I'm not even annoyed.

"To hell with them," I think. "I'll do without big magazines. They want something 'ordinary.' They want something like a classic. That impresses them. That's very easy to do. But I don't intend writing for readers who don't exist. The people have a different idea of literature."

I'm not bitter. I know I'm right.

In a Beerhall

Daytime. Sunshine. I go along the Nevsky Prospect. Esenin's coming toward me.

He's wearing a smart navy blue coat with a belt. No hat.

His face is pale. His eyes dull. He walks slowly. He mutters something. I go up to him.

He is sullen and not inclined to talk. Despondency is written all over him.

I try to go, but he won't let me.

"Do you feel bad? Do you feel ill?" I ask him.

"Why?" he asks in alarm. "Do I look bad?"

Suddenly he laughs and says:

"I'm getting old, dear friend. . . . I'll soon hit thirty. . . ."

We arrive at the Hotel Europe.

Esenin stands for a moment at the entrance, then says:

"Let's go across the street. To the beerhall. For a moment."

We go into the beerhall.

The poet V. Voinov is sitting at a table with his friends. He comes toward us looking delighted. We sit down at his table. Someone pours out mugs of beer.

Esenin says something to the waiter. He brings him a glass of rowanberry liqueur.

Closing his eyes, Esenin drinks. And I see life returning to him with every swallow. His cheeks become brighter. The gestures more certain. The eyes light up.

He's about to call the waiter again. To distract him I ask him to recite some poetry. . . .

He readily agrees for some reason and is even delighted.

Standing up, he recites the poem "The Black Man."

People gather around the table. Somebody says: "It's Esenin."

Practically the whole beerhall crowds round us.

A moment later Esenin is standing on the chair and, gesticulating, recites a short poem.

He recites wonderfully and with such feeling and such pain that everyone is shaken.

I have seen many poets on the stage. I have seen them received with tremendous success, and I've heard the delighted ovations and the delight of entire audiences, but I have never known such feeling and warmth as for Esenin.

Dozens of hands raise him from the chair onto the table. Everyone wants to clink glasses with him. Everyone wants to touch him, clasp him, and kiss him.

The crowd is tightly ringed around the table where he's sitting.

I leave the beerhall.[2]

It's My Fault

Evening. I go along the Nevsky with K.

I met her in Kislovodsk.

She is pretty, witty, and amusing. She has the *joie de vivre* which I lack. Perhaps that attracts me most in her.

We go along, tenderly holding hands. We come out by the Neva. We go along the dark embankment.

K. talks endlessly about different things. But I don't listen very carefully to what she's saying. I listen to her words like music.

---

[2] Esenin committed suicide in Leningrad in 1925.

Then suddenly I hear displeasure in the music. I listen carefully.

"This is the second week we've been walking about the streets," she says. "We've covered all these silly embankments and parks. I just want to sit with you in a hotel, and talk a bit, and drink tea."

"No, we might be seen there."

"Ah, yes. I had forgotten." She has quite a complicated life. A jealous husband and a very jealous lover. Many enemies who would report that they had seen us together.

We stop on the embankment. We hold each other. We kiss. She murmurs:

"Oh, how stupid. We are in the street!"

We walk again and kiss again. She covers her eyes with her hand. She is dizzy from the endless kisses.

We reach the gates of a house. K. murmurs:

"I must go in here and see the dressmaker. Wait for me here. I'll just try on a dress and be right back."

I walk up and down by the house. I walk up and down for ten minutes, fifteen. Finally she arrives. Happy. Laughing.

"Everything's all right," she says. "It's a very pretty dress. It's very modest and unpretentious."

She takes me by the hand and I see her home. I meet her five days later. She says:

"If you like, we can meet today at the house of a friend of mine."

We arrive at the house. I recognize it. It was where I waited twenty minutes for her. It's the house where the dressmaker lives.

We go up to the fourth floor. She opens the door with her key. We go into the room. It is a well-furnished room. Not like a dressmaker's room.

From professional habit I leaf through a book I find on a small table. On the front page I see a familiar name. It is the name of K.'s lover.

She laughs.

"Yes, we're in his room. But don't worry. He's gone away to Kronstadt for two days."

"K.! It's not that I'm worried about. So you were here with him then?"

"When?" she asks.

"When I waited twenty minutes for you by the door."

She laughs. She closes my mouth with a kiss. And says: "It was your fault."

September Twenty-third

The window of my room looks out onto the corner of the Moika and the Nevsky Prospect.

I go over to the window. A very strange sight—the river has swollen and turned black. Another half meter and it will overflow its banks.

I run out into the street.

Wind. An unheard-of-wind blows from the sea.

I go along the Nevsky Prospect. I am excited and aroused. I reach the Fontanka Canal. It is practically level with the roadway. Here and there water is splashing on the sidewalk.

I jump into a streetcar and go over to the Petrograd side of Leningrad. That's where my family lives—my wife and tiny son. They live with relatives. I moved to the House of the Arts so that the infant's crying wouldn't disturb me.

Now I hurry to them. They live on the first floor in Push-karskaya Street. Perhaps they'll have to move up to the second floor.

The streetcar turns into the Alexander Prospect. We ride through water. We stop. We can't go any further. Wooden blocks from the roadway are floating about and prevent the streetcar from moving.

The passengers jump out into the water. It's not deep here—knee-high.

I walk through the water and reach the Bolshoi Prospect. There is no water yet on the Prospect.

I almost run all the way to Pushkarskaya Street. The water has not reached it yet. My dear ones are upset and alarmed. They are very glad I've come and am now with them.

I put on my coat again and go out into the street. I want to see whether the water is still rising.

I come into the Bolshoi Prospect. I buy bread at the baker's. I go on to Vvedenskaya Street. It's dry.

Suddenly I see a strange light—there is water pouring from every manhole and flooding the roadway at a great rate. I wade home through the water.

The water has already reached the stairway.

We moved up to the second floor with our belongings.

I make chalk marks on the stairway to see whether the flood is rising.

At five P.M. the water is splashing at the door.

It grows dark. I sit at the window and listen to the wind howling.

Practically the entire city is under water now. The water has risen four meters.

The dark sky is lit by the glare of some kind of conflagration.

Dawn. From my window I see the water gradually receding. I go out into the street. A ghastly sight. A barge piled with wood in the street. Beams. Boats. A small sailing ship with a mast is lying on its side. Devastation, chaos, and destruction everywhere.

The Train Was Late

Alya came in breathlessly and said:

"Didn't want to let me go . . . you've got to realize, Nikolai, I said, I must see my best friend off—she's leaving for Moscow and doesn't know when she'll be back. . . ."

I asked Alya:

"When does the train leave with your friend?"

She laughed and clapped her hands.

"You see," she said, "and you believed it . . . no one's

leaving. I just made it up to be able to come and see you."

"The train for Moscow leaves at 10:30," I said. "That means you have to be home about 11:00."

It was already midnight when she looked at her watch. She gave a shriek and ran over to the telephone without even putting on her slippers.

She sat down in a chair and picked up the receiver, trembling with cold and emotion.

I threw her a shawl. She covered her legs with it.

She was strikingly pretty—almost like a painting by Renoir.

"Why are you telephoning?" I asked her. "You had better get dressed and leave."

She waved her hand at me in annoyance.

"Nicky," she said into the mouthpiece. "Just imagine, the train was late and has only just left. I'll be home in ten minutes."

I don't know what her husband said, but she replied:

"I'm telling you, the train was late. I'll be home presently."

Her husband probably said it was midnight. "Really?" she said. "Well, I don't know what your watch says, but here, by the station clock . . ."

She threw back her head and looked at my ceiling.

"The station clock here," she repeated, "says exactly eleven." She narrowed her eyes as though looking at a distant station clock. "Yes," she said, "exactly eleven, actually two minutes past eleven. You must have a funny sort of watch. . . . Your watch must be wrong."

She hung up and began to laugh. Today this little sawdust-filled doll would be a most welcome guest. But then I was angry with her. I said:

"Why do you tell lies so brazenly? He will check his watch and see you've told a lie."

"But he believed I was at the station," she said, putting on lipstick.

Having finished painting her lips, she added:

"Why tell me off anyway? I don't want to listen. I know

what I'm doing. He runs around with a revolver threatening to kill my friends and me too in the bargain. . . . Incidentally, he won't care whether you're a writer or not . . . I'm sure he'll shoot you just as splendidly."

I mumbled something in reply.

Putting on her coat, she said:

"So you were angry? Perhaps you don't want me to come any more?"

"Just as you please," I answered.

"No, I won't come to see you any more," she said. "I see you don't love me at all."

She left with an imperious nod of her head.

She did it beautifully for her nineteen years.

Heavens, how I could cry now! But at the time I was glad. Anyway, she came back in a month.

At Table

Moscow. I'm sitting at a table in a theater club. The table is set for two. Mayakovsky is going to have supper. He ordered his meal and went off to play billiards. He'll be back in a moment.

I hardly know Mayakovsky. We've met only at the theater and at parties.

Here he comes toward the table. He's breathing heavily. His face is grim. He's morose. He wipes his forehead with a handkerchief.

He won the game, but this hasn't cheered him up. He sits down heavily at the table.

We scarcely exchange a word. I pour him some wine. He takes only one sip, then leaves the glass.

I'm also morose. And I don't want to make artificial conversation. But Mayakovsky is a *maître* for me. I am almost a novice in literature; I have only been working five years. I feel guilty that I'm silent. I begin to mumble something about billiards and literature.

For some reason it's extraordinarily heavy going for me.

I speak incoherently and uninterestingly and stop after every word. Suddenly Mayakovsky laughs.

"No, really," he says, "I find it very pleasant. I thought you would make jokes, be witty, and clown, but you . . . no, it's just wonderful! Absolutely wonderful . . ."

"Why should I make jokes?"

"Well, you're a humorist! You're supposed to. You . . ."

He gives me a rather pained look. He has surprisingly unhappy eyes. There's a dim light in them.

"Why are you . . . like that?" he asks.

"I don't know. I'm trying to find out."

"Yes?" he asks cautiously. "Do you suppose there's a reason? Are you sick?"

We begin to talk about illness. Mayakovsky enumerates several ailments from which he is suffering—something wrong with his lungs, stomach, and kidneys. He can't drink and even wants to give up smoking.

I notice one more ailment in Mayakovsky—he is even more concerned about his own health than I am about mine. He wipes his fork twice on his napkin. Then he wipes it with a piece of bread. Finally, he wipes it with his handkerchief. He also wipes the edge of the glass.

An actor I know comes up to our table. Our conversation is interrupted. Mayakovsky says to me:

"I'll call you in Leningrad."

I give him my number.

Public Appearance

I had agreed to speak in several cities. It was an unfortunate day in my life. My first appearance was in Kharkov, then in Rostov.

I was taken aback. I was greeted with stormy applause, but at the end they hardly clapped at all. So in some way I displeased the public, deceived them in some way. How?

It's true I don't read like an actor; I read monotonously, sometimes boringly. But surely they don't come to my eve-

ning to hear me as a "humorist"? Really! Maybe they think
that if actors can recite a work humorously, what will the
author himself be like?

Each evening is torture for me.

I mount the stage with difficulty. The knowledge that I
am about to deceive the audience spoils my mood even
more. I open the book and mumble a story.

Someone cries from the back:

"Give us 'The Bathouse' . . . 'The Aristocrat' . . . why
are you reading that rubbish?"

"Heavens!" I think. "Why did I agree to these evenings?"

I look wretchedly at my watch. Pieces of paper fly onto
the stage. A chance for a rest. I close the book.

I unfold the first note. I read it out.

"If you're the author of these stories, why do you read
them?"

I am annoyed. I shout in reply:

"And if you're a reader of these stories, why in hell do you
listen to them?"

The audience laughs and applauds.

I open the second note:

"Rather than read what we all know, tell us in a funny
way how you came here."

In a furious voice I shout:

"I got on the train. My relatives wept and implored me not
to leave. They warned me I'd be pestered with stupid questions."

A burst of applause. Laughter.

Ah, if only I could walk around the stage on my hands or
ride around on one wheel, the evening would be a success.

The man who organized my appearances whispers to me
from the wings:

"Tell them something about yourself. They like that."

Submissively I begin to tell them my biography.

Pieces of paper come flying onto the stage again.

"Are you married? . . . How many children do you have?
. . . Do you know Esenin?"

It's a quarter to eleven. I can finish.

Sighing sadly, I leave the stage amid sparse applause. I am consoled by the fact that they are not my readers. I am consoled by the fact that this is an audience which would attend a performance given by any comedian or conjurer with just as much zeal.

I leave for Leningrad without fulfilling my contract.

Beasts

I wander around the Leningrad zoo.

There is a huge and superb tiger in a cage. Alongside him is a small white dog—a fox terrier. It was she who suckled the tiger. And now, as the tiger's mother, she is in the same cage.

The tiger looks at her lovingly.

An amazing sight.

Suddenly, I hear a horrifying cry behind me.

Everyone rushes to a cage in which are some brown bears.

We see a ghastly scene. Next to the brown bears is another cage containing bear cubs. The two cages are separated by a wooden partition, as well as by iron bars.

A little cub has climbed up this partition, but his paw has got stuck in a crack. And now a brown bear is viciously worrying the little paw.

While trying to free himself, the squealing bear cub gets his other paw wedged in the crack. Now a second bear seizes this paw.

They both tear at the cub so much that one of the onlookers faints.

We try to drive the bears away with sand and stones. But they only get more vicious. There's a paw with black claws lying on the floor of the cage. I grab hold of a long pole and hit the bear with it.

Keepers and officials come running up at the sound of the terrible squealing and roaring of the bears. They pull the cub away from the partition.

The brown bears pace furiously up and down the cage. Their eyes are bloodshot. Their muzzles are covered with blood. Growling, the male mounts the female.

The unfortunate bear cub is taken to the office. Its front paws have been torn off.

It's not squealing any more. It will probably be shot. I begin to understand what beasts are. And the way they differ from humans.

Enemies

Sunday. I go down the street. Someone calls out "Misha!" I see a woman. She is dressed simply; she is carrying a bag of groceries.

"Misha!" she repeats, and the tears run down her cheeks.

Before me is Nadya V.'s sister—Katya.

"Good heavens!" she mutters. "It's you . . . it's you. . . ."

My heart is thumping terribly.

"I thought you'd left!" I say. "And where's Nadya? Your family?"

"Nadya and Marusya are in Paris . . . let's go to my place and I'll tell you everything . . . but don't be surprised—I live very simply . . . my husband is a very good man . . . he respects and pities me . . . he's an ordinary laborer. . . ."

We go into a little room.

A man gets up from the table. He is about forty. After greeting me he immediately puts on his coat and goes out.

"You see how good and tactful he is," says Katya. "He realized at once I wanted to talk to you."

We sit down on the couch. Emotion is choking us. Katya begins crying. She cries so loudly that someone opens the door and asks what happened.

"Nothing," shouts Katya.

She is again shaken with sobs. She's probably crying for what is past. She probably sees the past in me. Her youth, her childhood. I calm her down.

Going across to the washbasin, she wipes her tearful face and blows her nose loudly.

Then she begins to talk. In 1917 she went to the south intending to reach the Caucasus and then escape abroad. But in Rostov she caught typhus. It was not possible to wait. Only a few days were left. Her sisters drew lots to see who would stay with their father. Katya stayed. She was in dire straits when her father died. She worked as a cleaning woman, then as a housemaid. Later she managed to get to Leningrad. But it was no better there—she had no apartment and no friends.

"Why didn't you come to me?" I ask. "You must have heard about me. . . ."

"Yes. But I didn't think it was you."

Katya begins speaking of her sisters. The elder one writes to her, but Nadya doesn't. She hates everything she left in Russia.

"And what if I write to her?" I ask.

Katya says: "You know Kolya M. You remember how much he loved her. He wrote to her. She sent him a postcard on which there were four words: 'Now we are enemies.' "

Katya and I part. I promise to visit her.

It's Disgusting

Alya arrived. Her face was pale and there was misery in her eyes. Silently she untied the brightly colored scarf around her neck. She threw back her head slightly.

On her neck I saw five blue fingermarks. Someone had probably tried to strangle her.

"Alya, what happened?" I exclaimed.

She answered dully:

"Nikolai found out everything. He tried to strangle me, but I made such a noise that people came running."

She began crying. Through her tears she said:

"Ah, why did I come to see you? Now my peaceful life has

ended. I shall never go back to it. I'll move to my mother's and come to see you from time to time."

I put a hot compress on her neck, and taking a taxi, drove with her to her mother's.

I was extremely upset. I don't remember what my idea was, but the same evening I went to see her husband. To my surprise, he greeted me calmly.

I said to him:

"I didn't expect such a filthy trick from you. You could have left her and gone away . . . but to try to strangle this little girl . . . it's disgusting. . . ."

I thought he would shout at me or even throw me out. But without moving he sat down and, lowering his head, he said quietly:

"She drove me to distraction. I suspected she wasn't faithful. Then yesterday I found this note in her bag. Just look . . ."

He threw the note on the table. It was addressed to the actor N., with whom I had seen Alya a few times in the street.

The note left no doubt; she had been intimate with him to the highest degree.

I was amazed, even staggered. I was so staggered that at first I didn't realize that her husband knew nothing about me and that his only concern was with the actor.

I looked at him in confusion. He looked at me just as confused.

"And what has this to do with you anyway?" he asked. "Why, did you see her today? Was she at your place? Did she use to visit you?"

I suddenly saw in his eyes that he had guessed.

I covered my eyes with my hand.

"Good God," he cried. "So she . . . and you . . ." He was suddenly struck by the irony of it and burst out laughing. Almost calmly he said: "So she deceived you as well . . . that's a good one. . . ."

We parted coldly. Practically without saying good-by.

I went home in a daze. My mind was full of chaos. I wanted to solve the problem of why she had come to me with her bruises. Then I calmed down at the thought that before coming to me she had been with her bruises to the actor.

Madness

A man comes into my room. He sits down in an armchair.

For a moment he sits silently, listening. Then he gets up and closes the door tightly.

He goes over to the wall and, putting his ear to it, listens.

I begin to realize he is mad.

Having listened at the wall, he sits down in the chair again and covers his face with both hands. I see he is in despair.

"What's the matter?" I ask.

"They're after me," he says. "I was in a streetcar a moment ago and I heard their voices clearly: 'There he goes . . . catch him . . . seize him . . .'"

He covers his face again with his hands. Then he says quietly:

"You alone can save me. . . ."

"How?"

"We will swap surnames. You will be Gorshkov and I'll be the poet Zoshchenko." (That's what he said—"poet.")

"Good. I agree," I say.

He jumps toward me and shakes my hand.

"And who is after you?" I ask.

"I can't say."

"But I have to know since I'm taking your name."

Wringing his hands, he says:

"That's the point; I don't know myself. I can only hear their voices and at night I see their hands. They reach out toward me from all sides. I know they'll seize me and strangle me."

His nervousness is transferred to me. I feel unwell. My

head spins. There are spots before my eyes. If he doesn't go
away immediately, I shall probably faint. He has a devastat-
ing effect on me.

Gathering my strength, I mumble:

"Go away. You now have my name. You can relax." He
leaves with a joyful expression.

I lie down on the bed and feel a terrible misery overpower-
ing me.

In the Hotel

Tuapse. A small hotel room. For some reason I'm lying on
the floor. My arms are widespread and my fingers are in
water.

It is rainwater. The storm has just passed. I don't want to
get up to shut the window. Torrents of rain have come
through the window.

I shut my eyes again and lie in a kind of stupor until evening.

I probably ought to move over to the bed. It would be
more comfortable there. There's a pillow. But I don't want
to get up from the floor.

Without getting up, I reach out for the suitcase and get
out an apple. I haven't had anything to eat today either.

I bite off a piece of apple. I chew it like a straw. I spit it
out. It's nasty. I lie there till morning.

In the morning someone knocks on the door. The door is
locked. I don't open it. It's the maid. She wants to clean the
room. Only once every three days. I say:

"I don't want anything. Go away."

During the day I get up with difficulty. I sit on the chair.
Alarm seizes me. I realize that I cannot go on like this. I will
die in this wretched room if I don't go away immediately.

I open my bag, and feverishly gather up my things. Then
I ring for the maid.

"I'm sick," I tell her. "I must be taken to the station and
bought a ticket . . . immediately. . . ."

The maid brings the manager and a doctor. Patting my hand, the doctor says:

"Nerves . . . it's only nerves . . . I will prescribe bromide for you. . . ."

"I need to leave immediately," I mumble.

"You will leave today," says the manager.

Conclusions

And so my reminiscing was over.

I had reached 1926. Right up to the day when I stopped eating and almost died.

In front of me I had thirty-three stories. Thirty-three happenings which at some time or another affected me.

I began looking through each story. In one of them I had hoped to find the reason for my misery, my bitterness, my sickness.

But I did not find anything in these stories.

Yes, of course, some of them are depressing. But no more depressing than most people's experiences. Everyone's mother dies. Everybody has to leave home at some time. Or part with his beloved. Fight at the front.

No, I did not find what I was looking for in any of the stories.

Then I put all the stories together. I wanted to see the over-all picture, the over-all chord which perhaps stunned me like a fish which is taken from the water and thrown into a boat.

Yes, of course, I've had many shocks in my life. A change of fate. The collapse of the old world. The birth of a new life, new people, a new country.

I didn't see any disaster in that! After all, I was also striving to see the sunlight. And I was dogged by misery even before these events. So they were not the cause of the problem. So that's not the reason. On the contrary, they helped me to rediscover the world, my country, and the people for whom I began working. . . . There should be no misery in my heart! But there is.

I was disheartened. It seems I set myself an impossible task in seeking the reason for my misery, seeking the unhappy event which turned me into a miserable speck of dust blown about by the winds of life.

*Published in Moscow in 1953, this little frolic, unusually bold
for the time in which it was written, gives a vivid idea of the
tribulations which Soviet writers may suffer at the hands of
editors.* Translation by Andrew R. MacAndrew.

VLADIMIR POLYAKOV

Fireman Prokhorchuk or
The Story of a Story

(*The action takes place in the editorial offices of a magazine. A woman writer—a beginner—shyly enters the
editor's office.*)

SHE: Pardon me. . . . Please excuse me. . . . You're
the editor, aren't you?

HE: That's right.

SHE: My name is Krapivina. I've written a little short
story for your magazine.

HE: All right, leave it here.

SHE: I was wondering whether I couldn't get your
opinion of it right away. If you'll permit me, I'll read it to
you. It won't take more than three or four minutes. May I?

HE: All right, read it.

SHE: It is entitled "A Noble Deed." (*She begins to
read.*)

It was the dead of night—three o'clock. Everybody in the
town was asleep. Not a single electric light was burning. It
was dark and quiet. But suddenly a gory tongue of flame

shot out of the fourth-floor window of a large gray house. "Help!" someone shouted. "We're on fire!" This was the voice of a careless tenant who, when he went to bed, had forgotten to switch off the electric hot-plate, the cause of the fire. Both the fire and the tenant were darting around the room. The siren of a fire engine wailed. Firemen jumped down from the engine and dashed into the house. The room where the tenant was darting around was a sea of flames. Fireman Prokhorchuk, a middle-aged Ukrainian with large black mustachios, stopped in front of the door. The fireman stood and thought. Suddenly he rushed into the room, pulled the smoldering tenant out, and aimed his hose at the flames. The fire was put out, thanks to the daring of Prokhorchuk. Fire Chief Gorbushin approached him. "Good boy, Prokhorchuk," he said, "you've acted according to the regulations!" Whereupon the fire chief smiled and added: "You haven't noticed it, but your right mustachio is aflame." Prokhorchuk smiled and aimed a jet at his mustachio. It was dawning.

HE: The story isn't bad. The title's suitable too: "A Noble Deed." But there are some passages in it that must be revised. You see, it's a shame when a story is good and you come across things that are different from what you'd wish. Let's see, how does it start, your story?

SHE: It was the dead of night—three o'clock. Everybody in the town was asleep. . . .

HE: No good at all. It implies that the police are asleep and those on watch are asleep, and . . . No, won't do at all. It indicates a lack of vigilance. That passage must be changed. Better write it like this: It was the dead of night —three o'clock. No one in the town was asleep.

SHE: But that's impossible. It's nighttime and people do sleep.

HE: Yes, I suppose you're right. Then let's have it this way: Everybody in the town was asleep but was at his post.

SHE: Asleep at their posts?

HE: No, that's complete nonsense. Better write: Some

people slept while others kept a sharp lookout. What comes next?

SHE: Not a single electric light was burning.

HE: What's this? Sounds as if, in our country, we make bulbs that don't work!

SHE: But it's night. They were turned off.

HE: It could reflect on our bulbs. Delete it! If they aren't lit, what need is there to mention them?

SHE (*reading on*): But suddenly a gory tongue of flame shot out of the fourth-floor window of a large gray house. "Help!" someone shouted. "We're on fire!"

HE: What's that, panic?

SHE: Yes.

HE: And it is your opinion that panic ought to be publicized in the columns of our periodicals?

SHE: No, of course not. But this is fiction . . . a creative work. I'm describing a fire.

HE: And you portray a man who spreads panic instead of a civic-minded citizen? If I were you I'd replace that cry of "help" by some more rallying cry.

SHE: For instance?

HE: For instance, say . . . "We don't give a damn! We shall put it out!" someone shouted. "Nothing to worry about, there's no fire."

SHE: What do you mean, "there's no fire," when there *is* a fire?

HE: No, "there's no fire" in the sense of "we shall put it out, nothing to worry about."

SHE: It's impossible.

HE: It's possible. And then, you could do away with the cry.

SHE (*reads on*): This was the voice of the careless tenant who, when he went to bed, had forgotten to switch off the electric hot-plate.

HE: The what tenant?

SHE: Careless.

HE: Do you think that carelessness should be popularized in the columns of our periodicals? I shouldn't think so. And then why did you write that he forgot to switch off the electric hot-plate? Is that an appropriate example to set for the education of the readers?

SHE: I didn't intend to use it educationally, but without the hot-plate there'd have been no fire.

HE: And would we be much worse off?

SHE: No, better, of course.

HE: Well then, that's how you should have written it. Away with the hot-plate and then you won't have to mention the fire. Go on, read, how does it go after that? Come straight to the portrayal of the fireman.

SHE: Fireman Prokhorchuk, a middle-aged Ukrainian . . .

HE: That's nicely caught.

SHE: . . . with large black mustachios, stopped in front of the door. The fireman stood there and thought.

HE: Bad. A fireman mustn't think. He must put the fire out without thinking.

SHE: But it is a fine point in the story.

HE: In a story it may be a fine point but not in a fireman. Then also, since we have no fire, there's no need to drag the fireman into the house.

SHE: But then, what about his dialogue with the fire chief?

HE: Let them talk in the fire house. How does the dialogue go?

SHE (reads): Fire Chief Gorbushin approached him. "Good boy, Prokhorchuk," he said, "you've acted according to regulations!" Whereupon the fire chief smiled and added: "You haven't noticed it, but your right mustachio is aflame." Prokhorchuk smiled and aimed a jet at his mustachio. It was dawning.

HE: Why must you have that?

SHE: What?

HE: The burning mustachio.

SHE: I put it in for the humor of the thing. The man

was so absorbed in his work that he didn't notice that his mustache was ablaze.

HE: Believe me, you should delete it. Since there's no fire, the house isn't burning and there's no need to burn any mustachios.

SHE: And what about the element of laughter?

HE: There'll be laughter all right. When do people laugh? When things are good for them. And isn't it good that there's no fire? It's very good. And so everybody will laugh. Read what you have now.

SHE (*reading*): "A Noble Deed." It was the dead of night —three o'clock. Some people slept while others kept a sharp lookout. From the fourth-floor window of a large gray house somebody shouted: "We are not on fire!" "Good boy, Prokhorchuk!" said Fire Chief Gorbushin to Fireman Prokhorchuk, a middle-aged Ukrainian with large black mustachios, "you're following the regulations." Prokhorchuk smiled and aimed a jet of water at his mustachio. It was dawning.

HE: There we have a good piece of writing! Now it can be published!

L ev Kassil *was born in Pokrovsk (now Engels) on the Volga
in 1905. Mainly a writer for children, he is an accomplished
stylist who has perhaps put his subtle mind at the service of
children because, like a number of other Soviet writers, he has
found it easier to express himself in fairy-tale form rather than
in the cramped, plain language required for adult reading.*

This is an independent story within a children's novel called
My Dear Boys, *published in 1948. Only in this form was it
possible to put across the astonishing anti-Stalinist satire which
it patently represents. In 1949, at the height of the campaign
against "homeless cosmopolitans," Kassil, who is a Jew, was
severely criticized for having given the name "Commandos"
(from the British irregular forces) to the secret society of Young
Pioneers to whom this story is told in the book. Translation by
John Richardson.*

LEV KASSIL

The Tale of the Three
Master Craftsmen

Once upon a time there was a country called Sinegoriya.
There, amid the blue mountains, for that is what the name
means, lived hard-working and happy people. Nature was
kind to them and the climate was very mild so that the inhabitants neither froze in winter nor suffered in summer from
excessive heat, since they could always find a cool spot
under the palms and monkeybread trees. And the once
terrible volcano Quiproquo had long been asleep and now

only snored from time to time, which no longer frightened anyone. Children tobogganed down from its snow-capped top and people roasted chestnuts in the very crater.

Travelers came from far-off countries to gaze with awe upon the blue mountains, to taste the delicious fruit which grew there in abundance, and to purchase mirrors of peerless clarity and the famous swords which were strong and sharp and yet so slender that you only had to turn them edgeways to make them invisible.

The fruit, mirrors, and swords of Sinegoriya were famed throughout the world, and who did not know that at the foot of the volcano Quiproquo lived three great Master Craftsmen: Amalgam, the glorious Maker of Mirrors and Crystal; Isobar, the highly skilled armorer; and wise John Greenfingers, the renowned gardener and fruit-grower.

Isobar's mighty hands could easily bend the thickest iron bar, yet they could also weave the thinnest chain mail. He forged both swords and plows, while the children of Sinegoriya played with intricately designed rattles which the kind craftsman made for them. John Greenfingers grew grapes which were as large as apples, and apples which were as huge and heavy as watermelons. In his garden were roses and lilies of unmatched beauty. Their aroma made people gay like a very strong wine. But the Master Craftsman whom the people of the blue mountains loved most was Amalgam. He could make glass, the facets of which caught the seven colors of the rainbow, and his mirrors possessed the mysterious power of retaining sunbeams in their depths and radiating them in the dark. And when the finest of these sunbeams were plucked, they sang like the strings of a lute. Everyone loved the Master Craftsman, for the people of Sinegoriya were fair of face and there were few who were distressed by the mirrors. The children were delighted at the seven-colored tinker-bells which danced from the mirrors.

Then it happened that for many years no travelers were able to reach Sinegoriya. Raging storms barred the way to

all ships that tried to approach the island. Nevertheless, one
daring seafarer and his valiant comrades finally managed
to sail to the shores of Sinegoriya. But when the ship had
dropped anchor and the weary travelers had gone ashore,
they hardly recognized the once happy and prosperous country where they had so often tasted the fruit and breathed
the intoxicating scent of the flowers, fenced with lightweight
invisible swords, and gazed at themselves in crystal-clear
mirrors.

The streets were deserted. Shutters and wide-open doors
banged constantly. Unabating, the wind whistled in chimneys, howled in the streets like a dog, and tore at people's
clothing. The citizens walked about with their heads down
as though bowing to the wind, and the trees bent down to
the ground. The wind blew dried leaves along the dust-
laden road and there was no sound of children's laughter
or the song of birds, nor was there any scent of flowers. The
only noise was a squeaking and rattling from all around as
the weathervanes twirled on the rooftops.

"What has happened?" asked the voyagers in dismay.

"Can't you see?" came the reply. "The winds have ruined
us. Everything has gone with the wind."

The travelers then learned that the country had been
seized by the evil and stupid king who lived on a neighboring island. He was called Vainglorious the Eleventh-and-
Three-Quarters, because Vainglorious the Eleventh had long
since ended his reign and died, and the whole numbers
were awarded only after a certain number of years service.
Hence the first Vainglorious had been called Zero, and then
had come Vainglorious the First-and-a-Half, Vainglorious
the Second-and-a-Half, and so on. Before the Vainglori-
ouses the dynasty of Braggarts had been on the throne.
They had ruled for so long that the people lost count, and
the last of them had simply been called Braggart and Five-
Figures-Point-Something. King Vainglorious the Eleventh-
and-Three-Quarters was an extremely frivolous person. He
spent so much money dandifying himself that he finally

squandered his entire wealth. His people began saying that
he had thrown prudence to the wind, and he was full of hot
air, and just a windbag. And they were right. It was because
of this that the winds of the whole world decided that
King Vainglorious was just the right person for them—the
most scatterbrained king in the world. They gathered on the
island and sought to persuade the king. "Would you like us
to broadcast your fame to all corners of the earth? Would
you like us to waft away your sad thoughts, O King?" "Go
on, then," said the stupid king.

And the winds became the masters of the country. Power
was seized by the Secret Council of Winds. All inhabitants
were ordered to fit weathervanes to their roofs so that all
and sundry could see which way the wind was blowing.
Under penalty of death the inhabitants had to keep their
doors open wide. All the children caught chills. Drafts penetrated into houses through every door, window, and crack,
caught up every word, and reported back to the king. The
Chiefs of the Chimney Draft, specially appointed by the king,
saw to it that people disposed of all their possessions up the
chimney. Only wind instruments were allowed. The king
surrounded himself with weathercocks and windbags. The
Court Windgauge, who was a sly rogue called Once-Upon-
a-Time, became the Prime Minister, and, in effect, the ruler
of the land. The king awarded him the Order of the Fan,
the Chain of the Great Ventilator, and the highest distinction of all, the "Wind Rose."

The three splendid Master Craftsmen were seized by the
king's weathercocks and taken to the island. John Greenfingers was only allowed to grow dandelions. The armorer
was ordered to make weathervanes—weathervanes and
nothing else. And the splendid Amalgam was told to break
all his mirrors and never make any more, for the king was
extremely ugly and it had often happened that having
seen himself in the mirror, he had smashed it in fury. The
winds hated all forms of glass because it prevented them
from blowing through windows, and the evil and greedy

Once-Upon-a-Time forbade mirrors so that people could not see for themselves how the winds had dried them up. And the great Master Craftsman, whose mirrors had been an abode of light and beauty, was now forced to become a purveyor of soap bubbles. King Vainglorious was very fond of blowing bubbles, and Master Craftsman Amalgam knew some secret mixtures. He mixed them into soap, and the king blew silvery, mirrorlike bubbles of an enormous size. They rose high into the air and took a long time to burst. But Amalgam knew that the phase would not last, for art is eternal only when man can freely put the whole of his heart into it.

Hard times came upon Sinegoriya. The evil winds dried up the fields and gardens; where there had once been forest land was now a mass of wind-fallen trees, where there had once been sweet-scented roses was now overgrown with weeds. All that was heard was the howl of the winds in the chimneys and the rattle of the iron weathervanes, while the king kept blowing soap bubbles, listening to the spinning of the weathervanes and the blaring of brass bands, and gazing with pleasure at the thistledown floating through the air.

In the meantime John Greenfingers' daughter Melchiora had grown up a thousand times more beautiful than the finest lily that had ever adorned his flowerbeds. And the clear-eyed Amalgam, languishing in his dingy dungeon, fell in love with her. Melchiora's eyes reminded him of the rainbow and her laughter was like the crystal tinkle of rays reflected in a mirror.

The girl also fell in love with the Master Craftsman for his eyes, light-colored hair, and sunny nature. John Greenfingers tried to hide his daughter from the king, but the drafts got to know this and reported to Vainglorious.

"Whew!" whistled Vainglorious, seeing how beautiful Melchiora was. "I didn't know that the old gardener had been hiding his finest flower from us . . . why shouldn't I make his daughter a member of my court?"

The beauty started back in horror from the greedy monster.

The king realized that Melchiora would never love him, so, on Once-Upon-a-Time's advice, he resorted to cunning. He knew there was not one mirror in the palace and that Melchiora had never seen her face and had no idea she was beautiful. So Vainglorious ordered all those who surrounded John Greenfingers' beautiful daughter to tell her she was monstrously ugly. From then on, whenever they met Melchiora, the courtiers would turn away in disgust and horror, and the king took advantage of every occasion to say to her: "You see how kind I am! I, the king and mighty conqueror of the winds, offer you my love and invite you to become a courtier. See, they all turn away from you, you are so ugly. But I have a kind heart, I remember your father's services to me, and I'm not squeamish. Consent and perhaps I may make you my queen."

But Melchiora stubbornly continued to reject the king.

"Am I really so ugly?" she used to ask Amalgam in dismay. "How is it you love me?" "Believe me, you are the most beautiful girl in the world," Amalgam would answer. "And I am ready to say it anywhere, even if the winds tear me to pieces for those words. Alas, if I had but one mirror, I could let you look at yourself and you would never be able to take the mirror away."

But Melchiora was never able to see her face. Whenever she went into the streets, the king ordered her face to be covered so that the people should not be frightened at her ugliness.

"Look into my eyes," Amalgam said to her. "Can you not see how beautiful you are?" "No," answered Melchiora, "in your eyes I can only see the love which overpowers everything and dazzles me, and probably you too, and I see nothing else."

"Then go to the lake and look at yourself—the water will tell you the truth!" exclaimed Amalgam.

So the beautiful Melchiora ran to the lake. She leaned over

its mirrorlike surface and began to gaze at her reflection. But one of the winds hastened after her and began blowing on the water. The mirror rippled and Melchiora's beautiful features were hideously distorted. She shrank back in horror, covering her eyes with her hands. "The king is right," she said. "I am really extremely ugly. Amalgam must surely have loved me out of pity."

Yet, she still wanted to find out once and for all whether or not she was ugly. "If I am so ugly, Your Majesty," she said to the king, "why do you not help me to be certain? Allow Master Craftsman Amalgam to make one mirror, no matter how small."

The king did not know what to say. He was not very clever or quick-witted, that conqueror of the winds. But the cunning Once-Upon-a-Time helped him out once more. "Let him make an untrue mirror," he advised. "Let her admire herself in a curved mirror."

The king sent for Amalgam and said: "They say you are very bored without your mirrors, Master Craftsman. I will allow you to make one mirror, but it must be curved so that whoever looks in it will see himself ridiculous and unattractive. And the better looking the person, the more hideous he will be in the mirror. Let the nose be twisted across the face, let the eyes pop out onto the cheeks, let the mouth stretch from ear to ear and the ears hang like a dog's!" "No! Never," answered Amalgam. "My mirrors shall never distort the true face of beauty."

The king was enraged: "Do you dare disobey my commands? Do you want to be thrown down the ventilator? Seize him!" "Wait . . . let me think first," said Amalgam.

He was silent for a moment, and then, as though making up his mind, he said, looking into the king's face with his clear eyes: "All right, let it be as you say; I will make a mirror of that kind." "But don't try any tricks," the king warned him. "I shall look into the mirror myself to test it."

Amalgam went off to his workshop, fanned the fire until it blazed, and set the crucible to heat. He spent three days and three nights making the mirror and another three days and three nights polishing it. And the mirror he made was finer than anything he had ever made before. Then he told the king the work was completed.

The king looked at the mirror from the side and said: "The surface doen't look curved to me." "That is the whole secret, Your Majesty," answered Amalgam. "It looks like an ordinary mirror, but won't you take a look in it?"

The king looked at himself in the mirror. He was hideously ugly, but had not seen himself for so many years that he roared with delight.

"Well done, Master Craftsman; I shall award you the Order of the Fan. Your mirror really does distort the human face! Look! My nose goes across my face, my eyes are popping out, my mouth reaches from ear to ear, and my ears hang like a dog's. Thank heaven it is a curved mirror."

And no longer worried, Vainglorious sent for Melchiora.

"I have carried out your request, Melchiora," said the king. "Here is the truest mirror; it was made by your friend Amalgam. Look into it and admit that I told you the truth." The king snickered as he spoke those words.

Hardly had Melchiora looked into the mirror when she stepped back and covered her face with her hand in incredulity.

"Now I hope you know what you're like," said the contented king. "Yes, now I know what I'm like," said Melchiora quietly and again looked in the mirror, unable to tear herself away. "There you are," said the king. "Now you won't be so stubborn."

In a happy mood, the king sent for his courtiers and told them all to look in the mirror. The Ministers and Lords, the weathercocks and Chiefs of the Chimney Draft gazed at themselves in the mirror and then spat with disgust: "We certainly have ugly mugs in this mirror!"

They had not the slightest idea that Amalgam had made a perfectly plain and true mirror. It was only the sly Once-Upon-a-Time who suspected something was wrong. He seized the mirror, suddenly held it up before Amalgam's face and saw that the Craftsman was reflected in it just as clear-eyed as he was in actual fact.

"Look, Your Majesty," howled Once-Upon-a-Time, "the rascal has cheated us! He made a magic mirror which distorts our own faces and the beautiful countenance of the king but reflects his own face and that of this stubborn girl in undistorted fashion."

"All right, this time it's the ventilator for you!" shouted the furious king.

He smashed the mirror against the stone floor with such spite that the glass broke into a thousand pieces.

The king's weathercocks seized Amalgam and threw him into a dark dungeon without a single ray of light.

The next day the rebel was tried by the Council of Winds.

The Council of the Winds met in an enormous courtroom in which the ceiling was marked with the four points of the compass and instead of a chandelier there quivered a gigantic compass needle.

The first to enter were numerous Trade Winds and Monsoons who took up their stand on the left and right of the throne.

The Chief Windmaster of the Royal Court announced the arrival of the winds. In swept the Cyclone, gusty, twisted, tightly wrapped in his cloak. His eyes flashed lightning. He was whipping along in front of him a gigantic humming top made of water and sand . . . From the opposite door came tottering his adversary—the flabby and listless Anticyclone. He was bent low under the weight of a cylinder of compressed air. His loose, colorless clothing flapped as he went.

"Mister Northeaster, the northeast wind!" announced the windmaster.

The Northeaster blew in, red-nosed with a long white flowing beard and wrapped in furs. It became very cold in the courtroom. The wind breathed with a whistle and his breath settled on the floor as a hoarfrost. He was leading his son, Pine Forest, with his long bony hand which had icicles instead of fingers.

"Mister Southwester, the southwest wind!" called out the windmaster.

"Atchoo!" Snuffling and sneezing, the Southwester came in. He was wearing a plastic raincoat and carrying an open umbrella, dragging his rubber-shod, rheumatic feet, and leaving wet marks on the parquet flooring. Coughing and sneezing could be heard throughout the courtroom.

Then there was a piercing whistle and in came another wind, this time wearing a flapping scarf the color of meerschaum and a wreath of withered vine leaves.

"Signor Sirocco, the terror of the vineyards!" proclaimed the Windmaster.

With a pirate's ring in one ear and his swarthy cheeks puffed out, wheezing through his few teeth and slashing the air with a Samurai sword, came the slant-eyed Typhoon.

"Khan Sandstorm!"

And everyone felt a blast of hot air. The wind entered panting heavily, and licking his cracked lips with a dry, pallid tongue. His piercing eyes were inflamed and on his shaven head was a wreath of feather-grass and wormwood. He was followed by the Tornado, the wind from the West Indies and prairies, in a cowboy hat, clinking the spurs on his moccasins and twirling a swishing lasso above his head. Then came the half-naked Fang, a handsome brown-haired man with fiery eyes and a thin, dry mouth—the destroyer of the Colchis mandarins. The curly golden fleece was slung across his bronzed shoulders.

"Khamsin, Master of the desert!"

Into the courtroom staggered a scarecrow, as high as the ceiling, roaring like a bull in fury, rolling his crazy eyes and gnashing his sandy teeth; he was shaggy, red-haired, and dressed in tatters.

Finally, taking a deep breath as though about to chill the whole world, the Windmaster announced: "His Royal Majesty, King Vainglorious, Great Commander of the Winds!"

The organ bellows began to pump; puffing out their cheeks, the musicians played a fanfare. Everything squeaked and howled. The drafts flitted from corner to corner and a small eddy raced across the courtroom shouting: "Make way for the king!"

Vainglorious entered, accompanied by the Chief Windgauge, Once-Upon-a-Time, and a retinue of henchmen; he was wearing a crown with a huge weathervane on top.

"Gentlemen of the Wind," began the king, "be seated!" The winds reclined on wide divans. The Royal Court was in session.

Weathercocks led Master Craftsman Amalgam into the courtroom. As soon as they saw him, the winds began howling and roaring. A storm rose in the room. The Windmaster had great difficulty in coping with this hurricane and restoring calm in the court.

Fearless and clear-eyed, the Maker of Mirrors looked at the king and those around him.

Once-Upon-a-Time roared out the charge.

"Do you plead guilty?" asked the king.

"I am only guilty," began the Master Craftsman proudly, "in that I have never distorted the beautiful, hid the ugly, flattered the unsightly, nor avoided telling people the truth."

"Burn out his eyes!" howled the Khamsin.

"Fill his mouth with sand!" roared the Simoom.

"Lash him with rain!" proposed the Southwester.

"Twist him into a whirlwind!" shrieked the Cyclone.

"Freeze him!" said the Northeaster through gritted teeth.

"Strangle him and stamp on him!" bellowed the Tornado.

"Let him commit hari-kari!" cried the Typhoon.

"Into the ventilator with him!" shouted the king.

"Into the ventilator with him!" repeated the winds.

That was the worst kind of execution.

Amalgam was shut up in a high tower in one of the walls of the castle. The execution was fixed for the next morning. The beautiful Melchiora ran to Isobar the armorer and threw herself on her knees before him, imploring him to save Amalgam. But how could they find out which tower he was in, and how could they save him when all the towers were as straight and smooth as candles!

When Amalgam came to his senses after the tortures to which the weathercocks subjected him, he felt himself and found a piece of glass in his pocket. It was a fragment of the mirror which Vainglorious had smashed in his fury. Amalgam had managed to hide it.

He climbed up onto the ledge of the narrow window in the tower and caught a ray of sunlight in the glass. A spot of rainbow-colored light danced over the roofs, towers, and walls of the palace. Then suddenly the spot of light, the envoy of the Master Craftsman, danced into the hovel where Melchiora wept, wringing her tender hands, and Isobar clenched his mighty fists in helplessness. Melchiora immediately guessed that this was a messenger from Amalgam.

She ran to the window and saw a rainbow-colored ray coming from a window in one of the towers.

Immediately her father, the wise John Greenfingers, clapped his hand to his forehead and said: "Oh, what a greenfingers I am! I have some bindweed seed. I have grown it for fifty-five years in succession! I tended it day and night until it could look after itself. This weed grows so fast that if you stretch a thread from the top to the foot of Quiproquo and plant the seeds below, shoots will instantly weave around the thread and before you can say one-two-three, bindweed will be blossoming at the very top of the mountain. But listen. I once tried sowing it during a shower. You can imagine what happened. Like lightning it wound around a stream of rain and before the rain could reach the ground, it had already climbed up to the sky. I put these seeds aside for a rainy day, daughter, to be able to weave a wreath around the house which you would live in with your lover, but it seems the time has now come to use it. Don't cry, we will save Amalgam. I will sow the bindweed below the window of the tower in which he is imprisoned." "But the tower is high and the window is at the very top. How can we stretch the thread so high or make rain?" wondered Isobar. "My bindweed is so strong and fast-growing that it only needs a straight sunbeam and it will climb up it. But we cannot do this in the daytime," he said, "the guards will see, and at night there's no sun."

"Yes, but the moon is full just now." "The king has posted his most loyal weathercocks at the tower," warned Melchiora. "They are on guard all night." "I will undertake the task," Isobar reassured her. "I will wreck all the weathervanes on the palace. The winds will quarrel and confusion will follow!"

And that is what happened. Toward nightfall the winds saw that the arrows on the palace weathervanes were pointing in different directions and they immediately became excited.

"It's my turn to blow," howled the Northeaster, "but the weathervane shows southwest! Call the guard and have the vanes mended!"

Disorder reigned in the palace. The weathercocks rushed off to look for Isobar, but there was no trace of him.

In the meantime the moon had risen. Catching her pearly light in his piece of mirror, Amalgam sent down a slender, quivering, transparent ray. Wherever it touched the earth, John Greenfingers sowed a handful of his magic seeds. In an instant powerful shoots twined themselves around the rays and climbed to the top of the tower.

There were many of these green shoots. They bound themselves into a thick, strong rope, and Amalgam was easily able to climb down to the ground. And when one of the sentries threw himself at Amalgam, having heard the noise, the Craftsman blinded him with a ray from his mirror. And so the Master Craftsmen Amalgam and John Greenfingers escaped from the palace. It was agreed that Melchiora would wait for them on the shore where Isobar had already fitted out a small ship with a loyal crew. But when the fugitives reached the shore, John Greenfingers was unable to find his daughter and Amalgam could not find his beloved. They did not know that the sly Once-Upon-a-Time had locked up the beauty in a dungeon during the night.

Amalgam wanted to go back at once to the palace to free Melchiora, but John Greenfingers and Isobar the Armorer would not let him go, thinking that to do so would be unwise and that Amalgam would only destroy both himself and Melchiora, for she could only be saved if the three Master Craftsmen set about it while at large.

They found shelter with kind and brave people called Commandos. These were reliable fellows, hard-working and fearless, skilled craftsmen and brave soldiers. "Valiance, loyalty, labor, and victory!" was their slogan. There was no work they could not do. There was no danger which could daunt them. They had long intended to rid the country of Vainglorious and the evil winds. "He who sows the wind shall reap the storm," the Commandos used to say. They greeted the three glorious Master Craftsmen joyfully and respectfully, and invited them to join the family of Commandos.

"Valiance!" said Isobar. "Loyalty!" added Amalgam. "Labor!" said John Greenfingers. "Victory!" cried all three, repeating the Commandos' oath.

Then Isobar the Armorer said: "I know what I must do. So far I have made weathervanes which show the direction of the wind. But now it is up to us to turn the wind in the direction we want. John Greenfingers put all his heart into his bindweed seeds, and the plant acquired the magic power of growth. I will work with the weathervanes and we will subdue the winds."

And without delay he seized a hammer in his powerful hands and set to work.

"You're right!" responded Amalgam. "And I will set to work too. What have my mirrors done so far? They have obediently reflected beauty and shown people their defects. But beauty and ugliness exist apart from my mirrors. I will put my mind to it and work day and night until I make mirrors which will themselves make the world more beautiful. I want people to reflect everything with which I imbue the mirror by my toil and love, for it is said that there is no force in this world superior to creative work, provided man has chosen it of his own will."

And the Master Craftsmen set to work. They toiled day and night without fatigue, without taking sleep or rest. A great fury inspired the armorer and fanned the fire under his furnace. A great love gave the Maker of Mirrors strength and shone in his crystal.

Time passed, for toil and perfection need time. . . .

. . . Time passed while the beautiful Melchiora languished in captivity. The cruel Once-Upon-a-Time had thrown her into a filthy dungeon. Cold slimy toads kept jumping on her, smooth-tailed rats nipped her beautiful face, and wood lice crawled all over her arms. Very soon there was not a trace of her former beauty left. Once-Upon-a-Time brought her a piece of mirror which had accidentally been overlooked in the palace. How bitterly the poor Melchiora wept when the dull glass reflected a yellow, ugly, wrinkled face covered with weals, scars, welts, bruises, and sores.

"What have you done to me?" cried the poor girl.

At this point Once-Upon-a-Time thought of another crafty plan.

"Don't fret," he said, "you're as beautiful as ever. It's just a crooked mirror. We have captured your Master Craftsman and he has renounced both you and his stupid truth. As you see, he has made a crooked mirror for you. Now you must give in."

But at that moment Melchiora caught sight of Once-Upon-a-Time's face in the mirror before he had time to move aside. The face in the mirror was as spiteful and hideous, and just as horrible, as it was in reality. Melchiora realized that the evil Windgauge was trying to fool her again, though she also saw that the mirror was telling her the bitter truth.

Yet she was glad at this, for to lose faith in love seemed much more terrible to her than to lose her own beauty.

By that time the Master Craftsmen had finished their work and the Commandos were making ready for their campaign against Vainglorious. But the drafts sent by the king had already penetrated through cracks into the Commandos' camp. It was soon known at the palace where Amalgam, Isobar, and John Greenfingers were hidden, and Vainglorious sent military windcraft to the blue mountains where the Commandos were in hiding.

It was a rainy day and the showers kept falling and falling. The Winds blew heavy thunderclouds toward the mountains with windcraft hidden inside them. But John Greenfingers dropped a handful of seeds at the foot of the mountain and the bindweed instantly climbed up the streams of rain to the clouds, some of the shoots even managing to encircle the lightning which streaked from the clouds. A thick wall of greenery stretched to the very sky all around the Commandos' quarters, entangling Vainglorious's windcraft like flies in a spider's web and making them crash to the ground.

Then the Commandos made preparations to storm the palace. On the eve of their attack they replaced all the weathervanes in the country with new ones. The hardworking Isobar had made thousands of vanes imbued with a magic power. Before setting out to do battle, Master Craftsman Amalgam made each Commando look in his new mirror and as soon as he saw himself, each one became braver, abler, and more loyal to the cause.

At last the day of reckoning arrived. The arrows on all the weathervanes turned their tips in the direction of the palace. The Commandos sallied forth. Isobar armed them with newly made magic arrows. The Commando warriors carried spears with crystal points, and behind each spear there arched a tiny rainbow. In addition to this, every Commando was armed with a small mirror attached to a bracelet and a basket with bindweed seeds. At dawn the

Commando ships stealthily approached the shores of the island.

With their rainbow-colored flag flying, the Commandos launched their attack. Storm-guns rattled from the walls of the castle. The Winds were just about to throw themselves upon the Commandos when they saw that not a single weathervane had moved. Then a miracle occurred. The splendid Isobar had put so much fury into his work that the Winds were unable to do a thing with the weathervanes. The weathervanes were out of control. No matter how the winds blew, no matter how they puffed out their cheeks, all the vanes pointed in one direction—toward the palace. Since the thousands of arrows fired by the Commandos were made of the same magic metal as the vanes, they went right through the approaching hurricane and, carrying the air with them, made a powerful new hurricane of their own. The old winds were forced to surrender. The hurricane shook the palace, sweeping the guards from the walls. Then beams of yellow light from thousands of little pocket mirrors surrounded the castle and in an instant bindweed and ivy wove round and round these rays all the way up to the battlements. Commandos scrambled up the green strings as though they were rope ladders. They stormed into the castle and killed all the weathercocks. Soon, above the biggest tower, there fluttered the Commandos' rainbow-colored flag, the flag of the Great Rainbow, the herald of good weather and bright happiness.

Once-Upon-a-Time tried to escape from the palace in a windcraft, but the infuriated winds seized him, and since each one was blowing in his own direction, the Chief Windgauge was blown to pieces. The frightened king was found hiding under the stairs.

"All right," said the Armorer. "Now you are Vainglorious-Exactly-the-Twelfth, and there will be no more to come after you."

In the meantime Master Craftsman Amalgam was speeding through the passages and corridors of the castle in search

of Melchiora. He went through all the towers and case-
mates, and finally, in one of the dungeons, he found a wrinkled, starved, hideous-looking creature. When she saw him,
the unfortunate girl gave a cry and hid her face in her
hands. But her cracked voice was deliciously familiar to
Amalgam.

"Who are you?" he asked, afraid he might be wrong.

"Don't you recognize me? I was once your beloved. Now
I can die in peace, for I know that you remained loyal to
your truth. I cannot live any more as hideous as I am."

"Wait," exclaimed Amalgam, "if you believe in my love,
look into this mirror." "No, I don't want to. I haven't the
strength to see my ugliness again, not even once."

And she dropped lifeless to the ground.

Amalgam threw himself down on his knees, held a mirror
to her lips, and saw it misted for a second. She was alive.
He warmed her deathly pale face with kisses and forced her
to look in the mirror.

Overcoming her repulsion, Melchiora looked at herself in
the glass. Suddenly something wonderfully soft passed
across the mirror. And as she watched, Melchiora felt her
features obeying the spell of the mirror, her face becoming
clearer, the wrinkles smoothing out, her sores healing, and,
in effect, she felt herself growing more beautiful every
moment.

"Keep looking, keep looking," said Amalgam.

She gazed intently into the glass and suddenly she was
again as beautiful as ever—even more enchanting than before.

And when she and Amalgam went out onto the balcony
together, the Commandos met them with whoops of joy.
They shook their spears and the crystal tips sent up myriads
of colored lights which merged into one triumphant rainbow
and arched across the sky. Then John Greenfingers sowed
seed round about and roses and lilies blossomed on the spot.

That is how the three Master Craftsmen helped the free
Commandos to rid themselves of the Winds. The Winds

were all incarcerated beneath the castle and only allowed out when needed for work, that is to say to clear the sky of clouds, turn the windmills, or fill the sails of ships. The gardens bloomed again in Sinegoriya, the mirrors glittered once more, and dampers were put back on the stoves, while on the walls of the castle appeared a new coat of arms—a rainbow with an arrow entwined in bindweed.

This poem is a dramatic statement in verse of the feeling most Russians had at the beginning of World War II that, in Pasternak's words, "when the war broke out, its real horrors . . . were a blessing compared with the inhuman power of the lie, a relief because it broke the spell of the dead letter." It appeared in the almanac Literary Moscow, *#2, November 1956, whose publication represented an attempt on the part of Moscow writers to achieve some independence from bureaucratic control. It contained many outspoken poems and stories which were later, during the panic caused by the Hungarian revolution, fiercely attacked.* Translation by Walter N. Vickery.

JULIA NEIMAN

1941

Those Moscow days . . . The avalanche of war . . .
Uncounted losses! Setbacks and defeats!
Yet, comrades of that year, tell the whole truth:
Bright as a torch it flamed, that shining year!
Like crumbling plaster, subterfuge flaked off,
And causes were laid bare, effects revealed;
And through the blackout and the camouflage
We saw our comrades' faces—undisguised.
The dubious yardsticks that we measured by—
Forms, questionnaires, long service, rank, and age—
Were cast aside and now we measured true:
Our yardsticks in that year were valor, faith.

And we who lived and saw these things still hold

Fresh in the memory, and sacred still,
The watches, rooftops, and barrage balloons,
The explosive chaos that was Moscow then,
The buildings in their camouflage attire,
The symphony of air raids and all-clears—
For then at last seemed real
Our pride as citizens, pure-shining pride.

The author of this story is the son of the Russian writer, Kornei Chukovsky. It appeared in the almanac Literary Moscow, #2, 1956, at the height of the "thaw." Of the several controversial works in this almanac, this story is particularly interesting for its scrupulous objectivity in describing a character and situations which are scarcely in accord with the canons of socialist realism. Here, there is none of that tedious moralizing which has brought the doctrine into such disrepute, both in Russia and in the West. Translation by Walter N. Vickery.

NIKOLAI CHUKOVSKY

The Tramp

1

In 1916 Misha was twenty years old. He was curly-headed, broad-shouldered, strong in the legs; his appearance was spoiled only by his teeth, which were stained and rotten. He lived with his mother and father in a southern town. His father owned six fishmonger stores situated in various parts of the town.

Every evening Misha would go down to the main street and meet his friends there. The noisy gang would start off strolling along the main street. If they spotted a passer-by who looked to be of no great account, they would begin a heated argument among themselves. When the passer-by was quite close, Misha would suddenly turn toward him and say: "Listen to this!" When the passer-by stopped, Misha would turn his back on him and go on with the argument. The passer-by, thinking he had been forgotten, would start to move on. But Misha would stop him again: "Wait!" The passer-by would stand there waiting, while Misha argued about how many watermelons you could get into the *Andromeda*'s hold or how many paces it would take to walk from one street in the town to another. Then, as if he had suddenly remembered about the other's existence, Misha would say: "Go away. You're not needed here." And the passer-by would go on his way, hearing behind his back the gang's loud laughter rising through the branches into the warm, darkening sky.

Another Misha stunt was to start a fight with one of his friends. If some misguided peacemaker started to separate them and stop the fight, Misha and his friend would stop fighting each other and together would slap the peacemaker's face.

He was quite a joker, was Misha.

He was costing his father a great deal of money. The war was on with Germany and Austria-Hungary. His father was paying money to keep him out of military service. But in spite of all the money invested in this way, Misha's position was daily becoming less and less secure. He was too conspicuous in the small town. The governor himself, people said, was displeased by the fact that Misha was not yet at the front. And Misha's father felt that he would have to fix things for his son in some other way.

It took a bit of fixing, but he at length succeeded in having Misha accepted as a clerk in Supplies Administration at a prisoner-of-war camp.

The camp was in Central Asia. Misha, wearing a military greatcoat and fur cap, left for the camp in the fall.

The prisoners of war were building a railroad. In the snowless winter the frozen steppe echoed underfoot. The prisoners were divided into groups of six. Their job was to carry the rails. Each group had a sentry to watch it. The six men would pick up the rail and carry it up onto the embankment. The sentry marched alongside, rifle in hand. The black-mustached Croats and Bosnians would then walk back in single file, in the same order. Mittens had still not been issued; the skin on the men's hands tore off—their fingers froze to the iron of the rails. The small chains of men in the frozen steppe looked from a distance like notes on a gray sheet of music. They worked till dark and then lay down on the hard earth, stretching out their feet to the smoky dung fires.

Soon Misha had made himself at home in his new surroundings. He did not remain a clerk for long. He was put onto delivery work and would be sent to Ashkhabad for supplies. In Administration he made a name for himself as a wag and a good storyteller. He would tell the story of the passenger who kept on asking what the next station was called.

"Papaluki," he was told.

"And the one after?"

"Mamaluki."

"And the one after that?"

"All the little Lukis!"

Misha was much in demand socially. He was always being invited out. His superiors had complete confidence in him. They started to entrust him with more difficult missions: he would take food supplies to Ashkhabad and there sell them to the dealers. The food supplies were supposed to be for the prisoners. Misha was a bit shaken by this operation at first, but he got used to it. He had to share the profits with an enormous number of people, but in spite of this Misha was getting more money than his father was getting from all six fishmonger stores. And every month Misha was becoming noisier and more cheerful.

In the spring of 1917, when the steppe turned green and hot, when meetings started to be held and the news of the overthrow of the Czar reached Central Asia, Misha started to buy up pounds sterling. In the camp they received Kerensky's speeches. They also received a report that an inspection team was coming from Tashkent. They decided to offer up a sacrifice: all their sins would be laid at the door of one victim so that the rest could go free. Their choice was Misha.

He was young, inexperienced, and a stranger to all of them.

People became even friendlier toward Misha. Eventually he was allowed to steal as much as he wished. And he carted off whole wagon trains of food supplies to Ashkhabad. Meanwhile the camp accountants transferred to his name all the previous thefts and forgeries.

But Misha was no fool. And when the steppe turned from green to a scorched yellow, he stuffed all his pounds sterling into his boots and, providing himself with travel orders, set off in a small cart for a village close to the border.

From there it was twelve versts across the steppe to Persia. At sunset Misha left his horse in the village and started south on foot. The steppe here is rolling and he tried to keep in the depressions between the rises. The sky flamed crimson and the hot dry evening lay suspended above the earth like a purple mist.

It was almost completely dark and the sunset had shrunk to a thin strip when Misha suddenly noticed someone sitting on a nearby slope.

The man got up. He was standing on the slope immediately above Misha, and to Misha he seemed enormous. He asked something in a low voice in an unintelligible language. Two or three words sounded like Russian, and Misha suddenly guessed that the man was a Croat who had escaped from the camp. Of late everything in the camp had gone to pieces and escapes were not infrequent.

Misha did not answer and the Croat bent right down close to his face, peering at him. Misha stood motionless. He could feel the Croat's breath on his cheeks. Suddenly the Croat uttered a cry and Misha realized that he had been recognized.

The Croat started to speak rapidly, and the fact that in his unintelligible speech there were words that were intelligible made it all the more terrifying. Then he struck Misha in the face with his fist.

Misha spat out all his stained teeth, lost consciousness, and fell down in the hard grass.

When he came to his senses, the sunset was completely
over. Large stars hung low over the steppe. Weak and afraid
of moving, Misha lay on his back and looked at the stars.

The hours passed, the constellations moved across slowly
over Misha's head. Around everything was quiet. And suddenly in the distance, in the silence, three rifle shots rang
out, one after the other.

Misha listened eagerly, but again there was silence, motionless, immovable.

When the night turned to gray, Misha got up and started
slowly forward. A thin streak of dawn appeared in the east,
the tops of the rises grew pink. Bending low, Misha was
making his way across a flat, open stretch, when he stumbled over something in the grass. Looking down, Misha saw
that his toe cap had caught on someone's leg. He recognized
the man; it was the Croat.

The Croat had been killed during the night by frontier
guards.

In his tattered clothes the dead Croat looked like a rag
doll. His motionless, protruding eyes looked upward, their
lower lids drawn back.

Misha stood and looked at the Croat. Then he kicked
him in the face with his heel.

And started forward at a run, without looking back. He
ran till he came to the bank of a small river. This small river
was, as he knew, the frontier.

It was quite light now. There was no one around. He took
off his boots and started to wade, carrying the boots over his
shoulder so as not to wet his pounds sterling. The water
was warm and yellow. Sharp, brittle reeds broke off with a
dry, ringing sound.

Once on the Persian side, he crawled into some bushes
near the water and lay down. He washed his swollen face
and drank for a long time. His gums were bleeding. A gray
lizard sat on a gray stone watching him. The sun was rising
over the low hills.

2

In the Persian town of Asterabad he bought a gray suit and
a soft hat. He traveled by stagecoach to Teheran. There he
rented a room with an Armenian family who spoke Russian.
He assumed a new name and to begin with was very careful, for he did not know if the Russian authorities would not
try to get him back from Teheran. But from Russia there
came ever fresh news, event followed event, and gradually
Misha began to realize that the Russian authorities were not
interested in him.

His toothless mouth was unsightly, and in the fall he went
to a dentist to have gold teeth put in. It turned out that the
dentist was from Russia and even from the same town where
Misha was born. Misha told him how he and his friends on
the main street had made fools of the passers-by, and the
dentist was much amused. His own youth had been passed
on the very same street. He told Misha that before putting
in his new dentures, he would have to get rid of the roots of
the broken teeth. It was very painful, but Misha agreed.
Every fifth day he would pay a visit to the dentist and the
dentist would pull out some of the roots. By New Year's
1918 his mouth gleamed with two rows of gold teeth.

In the Persian sunlight they gleamed so brightly, Misha's
gold teeth, that everyone who conversed with Misha involuntarily screwed up his eyes. Misha was pleased, in spite
of the fact that the dentist took almost a quarter of his capital.

Having gotten his teeth, Misha stared to take a careful
look around, searching for some way of investing his money.
There were quite a few Russian business men in Teheran
and he gradually succeeded in getting acquainted with
them. They took a liking to him because he was a joker and
because they guessed that he had money. Little by little he
started to take a hand in various deals.

But his service in the prisoner-of-war camp had perverted

his imagination. He did not like slow, complicated deals which yielded insignificant returns; he was not suited to them. He wanted quick profits.

But the quick profits did not come his way.

He lived one whole year in Teheran, buying and selling all sorts of paltry nonsense, but the big chance never came, and his funds were dwindling. He left Teheran and started out through Persia, selling insurance policies. But the Persians lived in clay houses and were not afraid of fire. No one bought his policies. His money was dwindling. The only comfort came from the rumors of civil war in Russia: all evidence of his stealing would be wiped out once and for all time.

He was sick of poverty-stricken Persia. He left and went first to Baghdad, where there were British troops, and then a few months later to Syria, which had at that time been seized by France. In Alexandretta he posed as a representative of the Wrangel[1] government and started to sell various Russian documents. It was a wonderful idea and Misha's spirits soared. But unfortunately the real representatives of the Wrangel government turned up in Syria and exposed him. Misha left Syria and went to Palestine.

Wearing a white suit and a tropical helmet Misha took the best hotel room in Jaffa. It had mirrors, a bath, and a view of the Mediterranean. Precisely because his affairs were in bad shape he pretended to be rich. He had the feeling that he would be through if he did not manage to pull off a real coup in this place. And with greedy haste he looked for an opening.

This was the time when England was setting up a Jewish state in Palestine as a British mandate. Every day fresh ships brought to Jaffa fresh loads of ragged people from Rumania, Hungary, Poland, and Lithuania. From Jaffa these people were transported out to various parts of the Palestinian plains and allocated patches of uncultivated, rocky land.

---

[1] Baron Pyotr Wrangel, commander of White armies during the latter part of the Civil War.

Misha happened to see some of them, divided into groups, carrying stones. It reminded him of the Croats who in the same way had carried rails. The resemblance excited him and he turned all his attention to the immigrants.

He started to observe the activities of an American charity organization which was distributing clothing to the immigrants. The clothing had been given by New York Jews to whom it had previously belonged. Among the piles of worn, threadbare clothing there were some fine articles: dresses almost new, silk underwear, sweaters, men's suits, coats, even furs. All these things were being taken out to the Palestinian settlements and given away for nothing.

The hungry immigrant, receiving free of charge a heavy overcoat or a wool sweater and having no use for these things in the hot Arabian sun, would try to sell them. He would also try to sell the underwear because he had no money to buy food. But his neighbors also all had overcoats, sweaters, and underwear for sale. There were no buyers. No one would give even small change for the clothes.

Reckoning up what remained of his wealth, Misha rented a dirty old Ford and spent a month traveling around all the settlements between Jaffa and Jerusalem, between Bethlehem and Nazareth, between the Sea of Galilee and the seaboard valleys at one time inhabited by the Philistines. He bought up skirts, dresses, coats, overcoats, trousers, furs. When the Ford began to overflow, he drove to Jaffa, put everything he had bought in storage, and set out again in search of fresh loot. Many of the Jews spoke Russian. This helped, because they regarded him as one of them. He would tell the men the very funny story about the rabbi taking a bath. With the women he got on even better than with the men.

He loaded his bundles of ready-to-wear clothing on the first ship bound for Constantinople. He had authentic information to the effect that the price of clothing was very high in Constantinople. Turkey was at war. Turkey had entered the war in 1914; it was now 1921 and Turkey was still

at war. After the capitulation of Germany in 1918 the Turks
had found themselves obliged to fight on for a long time,
with the Greeks, with the Sultan, with the British. There
were no commodities in Constantinople and the price of
clothing was going up and up.

Happy, Misha sat on deck beneath the awning, peeled
and ate oranges, looked at the warm blue sea. There were
French girls on board—slender, with dark eyebrows, wearing pink dresses. He succeeded in attracting their attention
by feeding bread to the seagulls. The red-beaked gulls were
flying in disorderly formation astern of the ship. Misha
threw into the air pieces of soft bread and the gulls caught
them in flight and swallowed them. Misha knew only a few
phrases in French which he had learned in Syria, but the
girls understood him perfectly.

In Constantinople he unloaded his goods, which were
packed in mothballs.

Constantinople was at that time full of Russian White
Guards fleeing from the Crimea, which had recently been
occupied by the Reds. Everywhere he met people from his
part of Russia—in the restaurants, in the hotels, in the streets.
Their dejected looks gave him pleasure—he felt himself
superior to these refugees, these failures. He got to know
them, talked with them, even stood a beer to some, told
them about Papaluki and Mamaluki and all the Lukis, told
them about the rabbi taking a bath, and let fall vague hints
about his wealth.

He really was very rich—he had been offered huge sums
for his clothing. But he was in no hurry to sell. He watched
and listened.

He met a certain Armenian merchant who had only just
arrived from Tiflis. Tiflis was then held by the Menshevik
Georgian government which was at war with Soviet Russia.
This merchant dealt in just about everything and knew
what any commodity would bring in any place. It was he
who told Misha that ready-to-wear clothing was worth at
least twice as much in Tiflis as in Constantinople.

Misha at once changed his plans. His bundles of rags
would be changed into bars of gold. He broke off talks with
the Constantinople buyers, loaded his wares aboard a ship
and crossed the Black Sea to Batum.

Batum was overcrowded and uneasy. People were sleeping underneath the palms on their suitcases. The crowds
stormed aboard the ship in which Misha had arrived—everyone wanted to get out and go to Constantinople. Merchants,
landowners, officials from all over the Caucasus had
thronged into Batum: the Reds were closing in on Tiflis.

"You're mad!" people said to Misha in the cafe when they
learned that he was going to Tiflis.

But to Misha it seemed unbelievable that his brilliant un-
dertaking, now almost successfully accomplished, could suddenly fall through. He was not afraid of the Bolsheviks. In
Persia everyone had been afraid of the Kurds; in Arabia it
had been the Wahabis that they feared; but Misha knew
very well that you could sell anything and everything to the
Kurds and to the Wahabis. He loaded his treasures into two
Tiflis-bound freight cars.

He was traveling in an empty train. The trains coming the
other way were full to overflowing—there were people on
the buffers, on top of the coaches, on the engines. When he
arrived in Tiflis, there were red flags flying in some places
and workers were singing in the streets.

He spent the night in a hotel which was crammed with
people who had not managed to get away. Everyone was
trying to be as quiet and inconspicuous as possible. People
even walked on tiptoe along the corridors. There was some
firing in the streets before dawn.

In the morning he wandered along toward the station to
have a look at the freight cars containing his clothing. Red
Army units were making their way through the deserted
streets. There was a commissar in charge of the station, a
vast Caucasian wearing a shaggy black fur cap. He knew
nothing about Misha's two cars and was not in the least bit
interested in them. Misha went to look for them himself and

wandered for a long time along the different tracks. The depots and trains were guarded by men with rifles. They chased Misha away, but he kept coming back. Eventually a switchman Misha talked to told him that the freight train which had arrived the day before from Batum had left before dawn for Baku without unloading.

Misha cursed the Armenian in Constantinople who had advised him to go to Tiflis, climbed into a heated freight car, and traveled for three days through country which had just been cleared of Whites. He reached Baku. His freight cars were not in Baku. But he had written down the numbers in a notebook and was able to find out from the duty stationmaster that they had been sent on to Rostov. He spent four nights in Baku at the ticket office and managed to get a ticket for Rostov.

It was March, and for the first time in many years Misha saw snow. There was not much snow in Rostov, but in Voronezh it was only just beginning to thaw. Misha arrived in Voronezh ahead of his cars. He spent a week in Voronezh, waiting. Finally they arrived—he saw them himself on the rusty siding. He wandered about in their vicinity, filled with longing. Their firmly closed doors were sealed.

Misha pulled out the shipping receipts which had been given him in Batum by the Whites. But when the railroad officials saw the stamps on Misha's receipts, they advised him not to show the documents to anyone. Misha realized that his Palestinian merchandise was somehow no longer his. He was completely at a loss. Now he no longer thought that the Bolsheviks were like the Kurds and the Wahabis. All day he walked the streets of Voronezh, fighting down his anger and despair.

That night the freight cars left Voronezh. Misha again dashed off in pursuit. He did not know what he would do when he caught up with them, but he just could not let them go. He followed them to Kazan. They were not in Kazan. He hurried on to Sorapul, to Krasnoufimsk, to Sverd-

lovsk. Spring turned to winter, the weather became colder
and colder, there was more and more snow on the ground. He
traveled interminably in trains through mountain valleys,
through dark towering forests.

He finally caught up with his cars in Chelyabinsk. They
were standing on a siding. The dirty snow was melting
around them.

Misha dashed up the low embankment.

He reached the cars, looked inside. It was all dark and
empty. A few bits of mothball gleamed on the floor.

3

He came back to his home town, but did not find his father
there. He found nothing of what had been familiar to him
before. The stores were boarded up and those which were
doing business belonged to the co-operative. Of his friends
and relatives not one remained. He happened to meet an
old man who had worked in one of his father's fishmonger
stores. The old man told him that Misha's mother was dead,
that his father had been in prison several times because he
was a bourgeois. He had moved to Petrograd six months
earlier, not wishing to remain in his home town, where he
was too well known.

Misha sold his leather suitcase at the market, sent his father a telegram, and left for Petrograd. His father met him
at the station. Misha did not recognize his father till the latter rushed up to embrace him. So that's what he had become,
his father! Once he had looked formidable and dignified.
Once he had been corpulent and worn a mustache. Once he
had worn a frock coat, made of cloth as thick as armor, and
he had walked with his head thrown back. Of his former
dignity nothing now remained. He was very small, like a
mouse. A gray blouse outlined his stooped shoulders. His
mustacheless face was sagging and baggy. His head had a
broad moist bald spot. There were gray wisps of hair over

his ears. The veins on his temples were knotted like an old man's. The only familiar thing about him was his smell—the scarcely perceptible smell of fish.

Misha's father was glad to see him, though he seemed a little disappointed when he saw that Misha did not possess even a suitcase. They went on foot through the broad streets, bright in the strong May sunlight. When they reached the entrance and started to go up the stairs, Misha had the feeling that his father was slightly embarrassed.

His father's small apartment was not as bad as might have been expected. The rooms were crammed with furniture which was tattered and dirty, but expensive. There were a great many locked chests, cupboards, and chests of drawers, and Misha had the thought that in these chests, cupboards, and chests of drawers something there must surely be. Suddenly there was a rustling sound from the next room and a corpulent middle-aged woman in a colored gown came out to meet him. She had a white complexion and dark eyes. "Oho!" thought Misha.

It was his father's new wife. So he had married again after the death of Misha's mother. He stood hesitantly on the threshold, waiting to see how the meeting would pass off between Misha and his stepmother. But the meeting was a complete success. Misha's stepmother put her fleshy arms around his neck, drew herself close to his face, and kissed him. She had a drawling southern speech and, talking without stopping, she was telling Misha how glad they were to see him and how much his father had missed his son.

"But where are your suitcases?" she asked.

Misha was put in the back room. A dim window looked out onto the courtyard. A worn leather couch stood near the window between two cupboards and Misha at once lay down on it.

Day after day, night after night, he lay on the couch, getting up only when he was called to eat. After he had finished eating, he lay down again. He never went out into the street. Days passed, nights passed, summer came, hot stuffy air came in through the small ventilation window; still he lay and stared at the dirty curling flakes of plaster on the ceiling.

Sometimes his father came in, sat down at his feet on the edge of the couch, and talked about business. The New Economic Policy had begun, private trade had been sanctioned, and his father was beginning to be hopeful about his prospects. He had already opened a fish stall in the market—a paltry two-bit affair. But at the same time he had succeeded in re-establishing some of his old business connections with men in the fishing industry in the north, connections which the local fish merchants did not have. If he now had capital, in such a large city as Petrograd he could have developed a really worthwhile business. His father sighed. Unfortunately he had not been able to save anything. If it had turned out that Misha had brought something back from abroad . . . But since he had brought nothing, there was no sense talking about it. Since things were this way, it would be a good idea if Misha were to go to work with the Soviets. Why not indeed? It would not be a question of the pay, that would be worth almost nothing. But it would make a difference in the way the authorities acted toward the family. . . .

"Tell me, Papa, in a train how do you sit down on the bench?"

His father reflected a moment.

"With my backside," he answered naïvely.

"Well, I sit down as a passenger!"

No, Misha is no idiot. He's not fool enough to go to work here. Misha is not about to do anything here. What's the sense in doing anything in a country where the state itself directs the trade, where the land and the factories are not bought and sold? Misha felt like a prisoner. He lay on his couch and dreamed of escape.

Sometimes, when his father was not home, his stepmother would come into his room. She wore a dressing gown and slippers, but no stockings. She was round. Smiling, she would sit at his feet on the edge of the couch and try to get a con-

versation going. She very much wanted to know what he
had been doing abroad, and she asked him many questions.
But he was morose and taciturn. Then she would start to
talk about herself. She told him of her life in the town where
Misha was born. She had had a friend who had left with
the Whites and gone abroad. She had been getting ready to
follow him, but had waited one day too long and then there
was no way through. And she had married Misha's papa. It
was true that he was old, but he was kind. One day as he
listened to her talk, Misha got up from the couch, put his
arms round her, and kissed her. She screamed, tore herself
loose, and ran out of the room. He did not run after her. He
lay down again on the couch.

He lay and listened to what she was doing on the other
side of the wall in the bedroom. She was quiet at first, then
she started to walk around, tapping loudly with her heels.
Perhaps she wanted to attract his attention. But he lay silently on the couch. About ten minutes later she came quietly up to the door of his room. She was standing behind the
door. He could hear her breathing. But he did not move.
"Let her stand there," he thought.

When his father returned from the market, he would come
into Misha's room as before, but he no longer talked with
him about going to work with the Soviets. He would look
at him and sigh, and seemed all the time to be waiting for
something from Misha. Once or twice, as though casually,
he mentioned that in the north some wealthy people in the
fishing industry had launched into a new business: they
were taking people to Norway in their boats. He had known
these people for about twenty years and they knew him.
What did they require? Only the guarantee of a reliable person and the money.

At these words everything turned upside down in Misha's
stomach, but he pretended that he was completely indifferent. He was in no hurry. He would lie a bit longer on his
couch and wait. His father would become more generous
with time.

His stepmother gave up visiting his room. But she often stood outside his door. She no longer addressed him so readily as at the beginning and she was terribly embarrassed when he looked at her. Sometimes, with his father there at dinner, he would amuse himself by staring into her face without saying anything, without smiling, without moving a muscle of his face. Under his gaze she would become confused, gasp for breath, and from every pore sweat would appear on her face.

The summer was passing, and his father's business was constantly expanding. From what he said Misha soon realized that his father no longer had one stall in one market, but several stalls in each of several markets. He was already looking over a location to set up a store. The store would contain a large aquarium with live fish. Although he still wore the gray blouse and still complained that he had lost everything, his eyes had regained their confidence and more and more often Misha recognized in him his old ways and mannerisms.

"If you like, Misha, I can give you a letter of recommendation," his father said, sitting down on Misha's couch.

"Are you driving me away, Papa?" Misha asked.

His father smiled, looked him in the eye, and said nothing.

Misha refused to accept the letter unless his father would give him money. But evidently his father still thought that Misha had money. He offered only one thousand rubles—in old Czarist notes. He tried to assure his son that one thousand old notes was exactly what they charged for the crossing. Misha did not take the money and continued to lie on his couch. Then his father started to offer more. He increased his offer gradually, every two or three days. At five thousand old notes he stopped.

"I don't need paper notes abroad," Misha said. "Give me something more solid."

But he realized by now that his father would not give him anything more solid. July came to an end; it was the begin-

ning of August. If he did not leave before fall, he would have
to wait till the following summer. Misha accepted the letter
of recommendation and the five thousand.

His father grew more cheerful. Misha also grew more
cheerful. They both grew much more cheerful. Misha went
to the station to find out the departure times of the trains
for Murmansk. He came back and told his father and stepmother that the trains for Murmansk left twice a week—
on Tuesdays and Saturdays. It was Wednesday. Three days
to Saturday.

Next morning, when his father was not at home, Misha
heard the splashing of water on the other side of the wall.
He got up from his couch, went into the corridor and pushed
open the bedroom door. Her hair undone, in her colored
gown, his stepmother was standing in the middle of the
room, holding in her hands a white earthenware washbasin.
Seeing Misha, she dropped the basin and it broke into several pieces. The water splashed all over the floor. Saying
nothing, Misha kicked the broken pieces aside and advanced on his stepmother. He seized hold of her and kissed
her. She offered no resistance.

Ten minutes later, as they sat together on the edge of the
bed, he proposed that she go with him. He showed her the
letter his father had written. It was addressed to a certain
Fedor Akimovich Lapshin in the fishing village of Ust-Shan.
He told her that he had lied on purpose about the train
schedule and that the Murmansk train actually left not on
Saturday but tomorrow, Friday, at 2:40 in the afternoon—
when his father would not be at home. She was frightened,
despondent, crushed. But she agreed to everything.

He told her that abroad he must have at least some money
to start with, otherwise they would be lost. Didn't his father
have any money? But it turned out that she didn't know at
all what his father had and did not have. His father did not
let her in on his affairs and kept nothing in the house. At
first Misha didn't believe her; then he became angry. She became terribly frightened when she saw that he was angry.

She routed about in a chest of drawers and from under a pile of underwear she brought out two earrings, wrapped in paper. They were her own. He took them over to the window and examined them. His face lit up. The diamonds were undoubtedly genuine. Yes, that would be as good as money. He told her to sew the earrings into the lining of his trousers. She did so.

That evening his father was even more cheerful than the day before. He kept on patting Misha on the back and on the shoulders. He worried about Misha catching cold on the journey. And he kept on saying how sorry he was that he had nothing to give him. Misha was also exceptionally lighthearted, kept laughing and winking. In a gay mood they sat down to table—his father next to his stepmother, Misha opposite. His father put a small bottle of vodka on the table. Misha drank off a small glass and told the story of how a husband and wife went to bed, but the blanket was short. The husband pulled the blanket up to his chin and their feet stuck out. The husband looked and he saw that there were six feet instead of four.

"See here," the husband said, giving the wife a shove, "why have you and I got six feet?"

"Idiot," the wife said. "There aren't six. Count them again. There are four."

The husband counted them again—there were still six.

"You don't know how to count!" the wife screamed. "Get out of bed and count them properly."

The husband got out of bed and counted the feet.

"Quite right," he said, "there are four."

Misha's stepmother gasped for breath and her brows grew moist. His father laughed wholeheartedly. Misha himself laughed a lot. Roaring with laughter, he loudly slapped himself on the knees, while the yellow gleam from his teeth flitted across the faces of his father and stepmother.

Next day, Friday, his father left the house early. Misha heard the door slam shut behind him, but for a long time he continued to lie on his couch. He heard his stepmother mov-

ing about in the bedroom. She was crying. He remained on
the couch until half past eleven, got dressed, and went in to
see her. Frightened, she wiped her swollen eyes. On the
floor there were open suitcases, but she evidently did not
know what to pack in them. He himself opened the chest of
drawers, examined her underwear, her dresses, and gave her
advice. The packing and the discussion about what should
be packed gradually took her mind off other problems and
she brightened up. He walked about the room whistling,
while she showed him the various things and asked whether
she should take them or not. If he saw that she liked something, he advised her to take it. Both suitcases were full,
and more and more packages and bundles littered the floor.
Three times she asked him what the time was, but each
time he told her not to hurry. He said that he would fetch a
cab when it was time.

At ten minutes of two she started to get dressed. It was
after two when he went out to get a cab, leaving her alone
in the apartment with the luggage. Without hurrying he
went down the stairs, without hurrying he walked to the corner. The letter was in his pocket. The five thousand Czarist
rubles hung around his neck in a small canvas bag. The two
earrings were sewn into his trousers.

Twenty-five minutes remained until train time. Misha
took a cab and, without going back for his stepmother, left
for the station.

4

Misha walked slowly along the shore of the bay. The waves
were almost touching his feet. The huts of the village of Ust-
Shan lay around the bay in a semicircle. Out in the bay the
bare black masts of the fishing vessels rolled back and forth.
Above the masts there circled a noisy flock of gulls, like some
wheel of eternal motion. Beyond the huts were rocky, barren ridges of hills. A large sun hung low in the sky; you could

look at it without squinting. The cliffs cast long dark-red shadows.

Misha had in his time been in the Central Asian steppes, in Persia, in Arabia. He had seen the Mediterranean, the islands of the Greek Archipelago, and the Bosporus. Now he was walking on the shores of the Arctic Ocean. But now, as before, he was indifferent to what he saw around him. Wherever fate took him, he remained always the same. His surroundings might change, but Misha was unchangeable, like a small coin that passes from pocket to pocket.

Arriving at the end of the village, he looked around and made out a hut which stood apart from the others on the slope of the hill. Then he turned around to see if anyone had been following him. But all around it was deserted and he walked unhurriedly up the slope.

He was met at the doorway by a lanky youth of about seventeen.

"Who do you want?" the youth asked Misha in an unfriendly manner, barring his way.

"Does Fedor Akimovich Lapshin live here?"

"What do you want to know for?"

"I have a letter," Misha said. "From Petrograd."

"From Petrograd," the youth echoed with indifference, just as if he were hearing the word for the first time.

At this point Misha was rescued from his predicament by a deep and sullen voice which boomed out from inside the hut:

"Kondratij, let him in."

Kondratij stepped to the side, and Misha opened a door lined with heavy felt.

He was struck by a wave of stuffy air. The windows of the room were heavily curtained and let in no light. At first, Misha's eyes could distinguish only the half-opened jaws of an iron stove in which crumbling slabs of peat glowed red-hot, and the small flames of many lamps burning in the corner before the icons.

The icons covered the entire right-hand corner—from floor to ceiling. A small lamp was burning before each icon, and one large lamp—as large as a soldier's mess tin—was hanging in front of the whole array. The icons depicted heads cut off by swords, emaciated visages with the fangs of black serpents piercing their temples, the fires of hell surrounded by devils with the faces of swine and horses.

"Surely he doesn't keep his money behind the icons?" thought Misha. "No, he's not that simple. He buries his money in the earth."

When Misha's eyes had become accustomed to the dark, he saw an elderly peasant sitting on a bench. The peasant was broad-shouldered, thick-set, with shaggy eyebrows. His large beard was gray at the edges, but its black, egg-shaped center clearly showed through the gray hairs. His strong, lusterless dark eyes were fixed on Misha.

"Fedor Akimovich?" Misha asked.

The peasant examined Misha's face in silence. Then he said:

"Take off your cap in front of the icons."

"He's going to be difficult," Misha thought, hurriedly pulling off his cap. He felt that he was afraid of this peasant.

"I've brought you a letter."

Misha pulled out the letter and handed it to Lapshin. Lapshin took the letter, got up, and went over to the lamps. He stood there reading for a long time, soundlessly moving his lips. Misha waited. He wanted to smoke. He pulled out a cigarette and bent over a small lamp to light it, but did not dare. Who knows what rules they have? He carefully took the cigarette from his lips and hid it in his pocket.

Lapshin finished reading, carefully folded the sheets together, and held them up to a lamp. The flame started to creep along the paper and finally reached the brown fingers with their large, cracked nails. Then Lapshin threw the light black ashes on the floor.

"Kondratij!" he shouted.

Kondratij came in, carrying an earthenware pot. He set

the pot down on the table and put out two plates and two
tin spoons.

"Sit down," Lapshin said to Misha, and Misha obediently
sat down.

Lapshin poured the soup out into the plates. Misha took
his spoon and started to eat. Lapshin sat right opposite him
and also ate. Kondratij did not sit down.

The heat was unbearable. The soup reeked of fish fat. But
Misha swallowed it, deciding to submit to everything. When
the soup was finished, Kondratij took the pot away and
brought in a dish of roasted fish. Lapshin sucked the verte-
brae with his thick lips. Misha carefully spat out the small
bones onto the lower part of his coat.

"My papa wrote to you . . ." Misha began, feeling as
though his voice somehow did not belong to him, it was too
high-pitched, and he stopped short.

Lapshin said nothing.

After a little while Misha began again:

"I have not come empty-handed, Fedor Akimovich. I understand, of course . . ."

It was as though Lapshin had not heard.

He was sucking the bones, pulling them out of his mouth
with his fingers, and laying them down on the edge of the
plate.

"I can even pay with Czarist . . ."

Misha gasped for breath and the sweat ran down his
cheeks over his collar.

"I've got fifteen hundred . . ."

"Five thousand," Lapshin said.

Misha wanted to laugh, he wanted to say: "You're joking!"
but he said nothing and the laugh didn't come. Lapshin
continued to eat in silence, staring at his plate. "Only I won't
give him anything, until he's taken me over," Misha thought.

"Hand it over," Lapshin said, standing up.

Misha pulled out the small bag from under his shirt, ripped
it open, and handed over all the money to Lapshin.

With a single movement of his fingers Lapshin fanned out

the notes like cards, brought them together again, and thrust them into his pocket.

Then he opened the door into a small adjoining room, let Misha in, and left him there alone. The room was minute, with one small window, so small and low that you could only see out by bending down. Misha bent down, looked, but could see nothing except rocks. He lay down on the bed without undressing. "It doesn't matter," he tried to console himself. "Tomorrow I'll be there."

He lay there for many hours, able to hear nothing except the thunder of the waves as they broke on the shore. No one came into his room. He tried not to sleep, he was sure that he would not go to sleep, but he fell asleep unawares. He was awakened by a light tap at the window.

Misha got out of bed and went over to the window. He saw—very close—Lapshin's face. The edges of the black beard were gray and seemed to shine. Lapshin signaled with his hand.

Misha went outside. He caught his breath—the wind was blowing so savagely. A brown cloud was moving in across the land, concealing the huts and rocks. The wind was chasing it, pummeling it, swirling it along. At once Misha was soaked through to his shirt. It was almost dark, though at times through the flying mist Misha could see the sun hanging above the horizon.

Lapshin appeared from out of the fog. A double-barreled gun was slung across his shoulders.

He shouted something at Misha, but the wind drowned out his words, and Misha could catch nothing. Lapshin led him right along the water's edge over the pebbles. The wind was blowing from the shore and pushing them into the water. Sometimes the fog would clear for a moment and Misha could make out now the long crest of a wave, now the corner of a house.

Misha was running, trying not to lose Lapshin in the fog. They went through the village and beyond. Half an hour later, gasping from the wind, they reached the headland itself.

Kondratij was sitting in a small boat, bailing out the water with a tin scoop. Misha climbed into the boat and sat down on the thwart. Lapshin pushed the boat off from the shallows and jumped in when it was already under way.

At once the shore disappeared. There was nothing around except the waves and the swirling fog. The boat was buffeted by the wind. Kondratij and Lapshin rowed.

Misha was already completely shaken up by the waves, when he suddenly saw, quite close, the high, black hull of a fishing vessel. Kondratij caught hold of the cable and climbed aboard. Lapshin, in spite of his weight, easily climbed up the cable after Kondratij. Misha also caught hold of the cable but his feet slipped, and he could not haul himself up. Lapshin drew the cable up and dragged Misha up on deck as though he were a sack.

Almost at once the sails were hoisted and the anchor cable was hauled in. The vessel started out through the fog for the open sea. Twenty minutes later the engine started to chirr.

It was warm in the cabin near the iron stove, but the warmth made Misha sicker. He grabbed at the metal handrails and climbed up on deck. There he sat down near the mast. The wind went right through him. The waves washed over the deck and soaked his boots. But he no longer cared. He was already completely wet through.

Behind him Lapshin stood at the helm. He did not look at Misha, he was looking at the sea. But his proximity oppressed Misha. Misha shivered with cold, trying to huddle up into a smaller space.

Frozen stiff on deck, no longer able to stand the cold, Misha again went below to the stifling cabin. He lay down on a bunk built into the side of the ship. Close by, on the other side of the thin planks, the water surged. When Misha turned over onto his left side, the diamond earrings sewn

into the left side of his trousers bit into his leg. Weakened
by the buffeting and by sickness, he turned over from side
to side and listened to Kondratij who, leaving the engine
for a minute, was throwing logs into the stove and heating
up the teakettle. The hours passed.

Finally, Misha saw that the handrail near the hatch was
shining and realized that it had grown light outside. He
jumped up and made his way up on deck.

The fog had disappeared, the sun was shining, and the
contorted shadow of the mast lay across the waves. The
air was transparent and clear.

They were heading straight for the shore. And the shore
was already quite close.

This was the shore for which Misha had so longed. This
was the way out into the world where prevailed those rules
of life so dear to Misha.

Misha looked closely at the ridges of the hills, trying to
see houses and people. But there were no houses, no people. Reddish-brown and black cliffs, clefts, boulders. In
places, on the slopes, patches of dark-green vegetation.

The vessel stopped in a broad bay without casting anchor
and even without cutting out the engine. They were protected from the wind by the shore, and it at once became
warmer. Hand over hand Lapshin pulled the rowing boat
right up alongside and jumped down into it. The rifle bar-
rels across his shoulders reflected the sky's pale blue.

"Jump down!" he shouted to Misha.

Misha jumped down, seated himself, and caught hold of
the thwart with his hands in order not to fall overboard—
they were pitching and rolling so violently. In silence Lapshin rowed to the shore.

Jumping out onto the crunching pebbles and feeling the
earth beneath his feet, Misha at once started to walk away
from the shore. He wanted to be rid of Lapshin as quickly
as possible.

But Lapshin suddenly said:

"I'm going with you."

And Misha did not dare to argue.

They set off up the slope of the hill. The sun gently warmed their shoulders. Misha walked in front, Lapshin behind. The bilberry bushes were waist high, and at every step they could hear the large watery berries falling on the ground.

"I can't go any farther," Lapshin said suddenly. "Go on alone."

And he stopped.

Not bidding him farewell, Misha started on up. He had gone fifty paces, when he suddenly felt that Lapshin was still standing in the same spot.

He turned around.

Lapshin, pressing to his shoulder the butt of his double-barreled rifle, was taking careful aim.

Misha started to run uphill.

And at once he heard the rifle shot.

Lapshin had missed.

The bilberry branches felt springy beneath his feet. His whole body was waiting for the second shot and he kept running. If only he could make the crest of the hill and get over the top, where he would be hidden.

For one second, from the top of the hill, at a distance of about two versts, he caught sight of a wooden hut with an unfamiliar flag flying over its roof.

But the second shot rang out and Misha fell on his back, failing to make it over the crest.

He fell head down, feet up, his mouth open. Lapshin, thrusting his arm through the sling of the rifle, started to walk slowly toward him.

He undid all Misha's buttons and went carefully through all the pockets of his coat, jacket, and trousers. The pockets were empty, and he tore Misha's shirt to see if he had any-thing concealed on his body. But on the body too there was nothing.

Lapshin doggedly turned the body on this side and that, feeling it all over. They were both slowly sliding down the slope. The sun shone on Misha's teeth. Lapshin diligently searched him. But his fingers never encountered the earrings which had been sewn into the left trouser leg.

Giving up in despair, Lapshin struck Misha heavily on the open mouth with his heel. The teeth fell out of place. Lapshin went down on one knee, stuck his fingers into Misha's throat, and pulled out the two gold dentures. With the flap of his jacket he carefully wiped off the saliva and blood and put the gold dentures in his pocket.

Kharabarov belongs to the young generation of Soviet poets. He regards himself as a disciple of Pasternak, for which he was publicly exposed at the inaugural Congress of the Union of Writers of the RSFSR in 1958. Kharabarov, together with another young poet, Pankratov, was expelled from the Gorky Literary Institute and from the Komsomol for having exhibited a portrait of Pasternak in the university hostel and for having, horribile dictu, secretly visited Pasternak at his dacha in Peredelkino, despite frequent warnings. After the third Congress of Soviet writers in 1959, Kharabarov was reinstated, as a result of Khrushchev's conciliatory address, and he reappeared, together with Pankratov, as an emissary of the Central Committee of the Komsomol in Alma-Ata, where the Party newspaper Kazakhstanskaya Pravda published "Untrodden Path" on August 2, 1959. This poem was perhaps written in justification of the lonely path which had led Kharabarov to Pasternak's dacha. Translation by Walter N. Vickery.

IVAN KHARABAROV

Untrodden Path

I walk,
    I breathe the aroma of mint,
My feet in the grass
        leave scarce a trace:
Only here and there
        the leaves lie crumpled
And the stalks
      sway lightly to and fro.
With my ax

                        on the trees
                                I blaze my trail,
And the blazes show,
                        as I go my way:
White
        and visible from afar
They beckon new travelers—
                                on and on.
Not at once will they heal,
                        the wounds,
The wounds that my ax
                        has left behind.
But soon from the trees
                        green resin will flow,
Cover them over—
                        like quickening balm.
They will lose their whiteness,
                                the bark will grow,
Myself, I'll forget
                the path I trod.
So what!
            That's no great cause for sorrow,
If that should be,
                no great mischance.
Often, perhaps,
                I shall lose my way,
My tracks will be lost
                        in far-off places;
This is better than to tread
                        the beaten paths,
Where the puddles collect,
                        rotten with mold,
Where so many feet
                have passed before,
Where they travel
                who like
                        the easy road,

Where the dirt is trampled and pounded down
By so many feet—
                              ahead of mine.

Yuri Kazakov is one of the most promising of the younger Soviet prose writers. Born in Moscow in 1927, he first studied music and played in an orchestra. He then attended the Gorky Literary Institute and began publishing only after his graduation in 1957.

"The Outsider," which appeared in 1959, is striking for its sympathetic treatment of an utterly asocial type for whom there is no question of returning to the fold. Even at the present stage of "objectivity" in Soviet literature, it is remarkable that the author was able to describe such a "vestige of the past" (and during the official campaign against drunkenness) without going out of his way to moralize. The story was subsequently criticized in Literary Gazette *for its "ugly, distorted images" and for serving "not good but evil."* Translation by Walter N. Vickery.

YURI KAZAKOV

The Outsider

1

Worn out by the heat of the day and having eaten his fill of half-fried, half-salted fish, Egor, the buoy-keeper, is asleep in his shack.

His shack is new and empty. It does not even contain a stove. Only half the floor is finished. Bricks and unmixed clay lie piled inside the entrance. Along the walls tow hangs from the grooves between the logs. The window frames are new and without putty; the panes whine and rattle and echo back the sound of ships' sirens; ants crawl on the window sills.

When Egor wakes up, the sun is going down, a misty radiance suffuses the landscape, and the river is turning to a motionless gold. Egor yawns with an almost painful voluptuousness; for a moment animation seems to be entirely suspended, then he stretches, straining his muscles convulsively. His eyes are still more closed than open. With limp fingers he hastily rolls a cigarette and lights up. He inhales deeply, passionately, making a sobbing sound with his lips. He coughs—an act of physical pleasure—and with his rough fingernails he scratches hard on his chest and sides under his shirt. His eyes grow moist, intoxicated; his body is possessed with a pleasant, soft languor.

When he has smoked his fill, he goes to the hallway and drinks cold water as greedily as he had smoked. The water smells of leaves and roots, and has a pleasantly bitter taste. Then he picks up the oars and the kerosene lamps, and goes down to his boat.

His boat is heavy to handle, full of trampled reeds. There is water in the bottom; it is down by the stern. Egor knows that he ought to bail the boat out, but he doesn't feel like bailing, and so, with a glance first at the sunset, then up and down the river, he plants his legs apart and shoves off —harder than necessary.

Egor's stretch of river is not a large one. His job is to light the lights on four buoys, two upstream and two downstream. Every time he does this he spends a considerable amount of time figuring out whether it would be better to row up or downstream first. That's what he's doing at this moment. Now he settles himself, flails down the reeds with his oars, pushes away the lamps with his feet, and starts to row upstream. "It's all a lot of nonsense," he thinks to himself, as he begins to loosen up and get warmer, rowing with short, jerky strokes, his body moving rapidly back and forth, his gaze roving over the darkening shoreline, now turning pink, which is reflected in the calm water. Astern his boat leaves a dark mark on the gold of the water and regular swirls fanning out to either side.

The air is growing colder, the swallows fly low over the water uttering shrill screeches, the fish are jumping close to shore, and every time one jumps Egor's expression seems to convey his long-standing personal acquaintance with that particular fish. From the shore there drifts the smell of wild strawberries, hay, and dew-drenched shrubs; from the bottom of the boat comes the smell of fish, kerosene, and reeds; and from the water there rises a scarcely visible mist, and there is a feeling of depth and mystery.

Egor lights the red and white lights and fixes them in their places on the buoys, then lazily, with an effortless grace, almost without using the oars, he rows downstream and does the same thing there. The buoys burn brightly and can be seen a long way off in the gathering dusk. Meanwhile Egor rows rapidly back upstream, ties up just below his shack, washes, looks at himself in the mirror, puts on his boots and a clean shirt, rams his sailor's cap at an angle hard down on his head, rows over to the opposite bank, makes fast to the bushes, steps ashore onto the grass, and peers searchingly ahead into the sunset.

The grass is already covered with mist and there is the smell of damp.

The mist is so thick and white that at a distance it looks like flood water. Egor moves forward like a man walking in his sleep, swimming in mist to his shoulders. Only the tops of the haystacks can be seen, only the black strip of the woods in the distance beneath the soundless sky in which the colors of the sunset have now been almost completely extinguished.

Egor raises himself on tiptoe, cranes his neck, and finally, over the mist, he makes out a pink kerchief in the distance.

"O-o-o-oh!" he hails in a resonant tenor voice.

And from far away there is a faint response.

Egor quickens his pace, then bends down and, just like a quail, runs along the path. Turning off the path, he lies down, his knees and elbows smeared with green from the grass, and with pounding heart peers out toward the spot where he saw the pink kerchief. A minute passes, two minutes, but no one comes, there is no sound of footsteps, and Egor can stand it no longer; he rises to his feet and looks out above the mist. He sees only the last of the sunset, the strip of distant wood, the black tops of the haystacks; everything is a dim bluish gray. "She's hiding!" he thinks rapturously, impatient with desire. Again he dives into the mist and advances stealthily toward where the sun has set. He fills his lungs, holding his breath, the blood comes to his face, his cap begins to cut into his forehead. Suddenly, quite close, he catches sight of an indistinct, huddled shape and he trembles with surprise.

"Stop!" he yells wildly. "Stop, or I'll kill you!"

His boots clumping, he sets off in pursuit, and she runs away, with a screech of laughter, dropping something from her purse. He quickly catches her, they roll together onto some soft molehills which smell of fresh earth and mushrooms, and in the mist they lock together in a close, happy embrace. Then they get to their feet, find the object she dropped from her purse, and stroll slowly toward the boat.

As before, only their heads are visible above the mist, and to both of them it seems that they are like sleepwalkers, swimming somewhere, drunk with the ringing of the blood in their ears.

2

Egor is very young, but he's already a drunkard.

His wife too was a drunkard—an untidy slut of a woman, much older than Egor, who drowned during the fall freeze. She had gone to the village for vodka; on the way back she had started to drink and had got drunk; she had walked along, singing songs. Reaching the riverbank opposite the shack, she had called out:

"Egor, you bum, come out and look at me!"

Throwing on a sheepskin coat and putting some tattered

shoes over his bare feet, Egor had come out of the shack,
happy at her return. He had watched her as she came across
the ice, waving her bag, and he had seen her start to do a
dance in the middle of the river. He had been on the point
of shouting to her to hurry, but it was too late: as he watched,
the ice gave way and his wife went straight under. He threw
off the sheepskin coat and the old shoes, and ran out barefoot onto the ice, wearing only his shirt. The ice cracked,
heaved gently, and gave beneath him. He fell down, and
crawled on his stomach as far as the patch of open water.
He took one look at the dark, swirling water, gave out a
wail, screwed up his eyes, and crawled back. Three days
later he closed up the shack and went to spend the winter
in his own village, three versts away on the opposite bank.

But one day, during the next spring floods, he ferried
young Alenka from Trubetskoi across the river. When she
started to get out her fare money, Egor said suddenly and
hastily:

"That's all right . . . That's all a lot of nonsense . . . But
sometime come and visit me: I live alone, and it's dull. And
there's some clothes to be washed, a man can get lousy without a woman. And I'll give you some fish."

When two weeks later Alenka, who was on her way back
to her village from somewhere, walked into his shack one
day toward evening, his heart started to pound so hard
that it frightened him. And for the first time in his life Egor
really put himself out for a woman; he ran outside, brought
kindling, and got a small fire going in the bricks. He put on
a sooty teakettle and started to ask her questions about her
life. He would suddenly fall silent in the middle of a phrase,
embarrassing Alenka to the point of tears and embarrassing
himself. He washed and put on a clean shirt in the hallway.
When he took her back across the river, night had fallen,
and he went with her a long way through the fields on the
far side.

Now Alenka visits him often and each time she stays in
the shack for about three days. When she's with him, Egor

is cool and bantering. When she's not there, he's bored. He doesn't know what to do with himself; nothing he does turns out right; he sleeps a lot, and he has bad, disturbing dreams.

Egor has a prominent Adam's apple. He is strong but rather sluggish and slightly clumsy. His face is large, flabby, inexpressive, sleepy, with a hook nose. The summer sun and the wind have tanned his face till now it is almost black, and his gray eyes look blue. He's an odd, wayward character, as he himself knows to his sorrow. "I was a poor job to begin with," he complains, when he's drinking. "I was fathered by the devil, and my mother was a drunken she-goat!"

This spring he suddenly decided to stay by himself in the shack for the first of May. Why he didn't go into the village, as he'd originally intended, he doesn't know himself. He lolls about on his broken-down, unmade bed, whistling softly from time to time. There is a high-pitched cry from the opposite bank:

"Ego-o-or!"

Gloomily Egor emerges and goes down to the water's edge.

"Ego-o-orka, they say you've got to come . . ."

A moment's silence, and then Egor shouts back:

"Who says?"

"Old Va-a-sia and old Fe-e-dia . . ."

"Why didn't they come themselves?"

"They can't come, they're drunk . . ."

Egor looks depressed.

"Tell them I have to work, have to wo-ork!" he shouts, though of course he has no work to do at all. "Right now they're having a good time in the village!" he reflects bitterly and he visualizes his drunken relatives, his mother, the tables heaped with cold dishes, the pies, the continuous music, the yeasty taste of the home-brewed beer, the girls in their best clothes, the flags on the houses, the movie at the club; gloomily he spits into the water and climbs the steep slope to his shack.

". . . O-o-o- . . . come over . . ." calls the voice from

the opposite bank, still trying to lure him over, but Egor is not listening.

But the whole world leaves him cold—or makes him laugh. He is exceptionally lazy and has a lot of money, which comes easy to him. There is no bridge in the vicinity and Egor runs the only ferry service, charging a ruble for the trip or—when he's in a bad mood—two rubles. The work's too easy, fit only for an old man, and it's made him into a spoiled good-for-nothing.

But sometimes Egor gets vaguely uneasy, usually in the evening. As he lies beside the sleeping Alenka he recalls his service with the navy, in the north. He remembers his buddies with whom, of course, he long ago lost touch. He remembers their voices, their faces, and even the things they said, but it's all blurred and he doesn't try very hard. He wonders how they are now and what they're doing. He wonders where they're living and if they remember him.

Egor recalls a low, gloomy shoreline, the Arctic, the eerie northern lights in the wintertime, the small, stunted, blue-gray pine trees, the moss, the sand; he remembers the lighthouse in the night, its dazzling, smoky, flickering light, casting its rays over the dead forest.

He thinks of all this impassively and, as it were, from a long way off. But sometimes he suddenly begins to tremble strangely and odd, crazy thoughts come into his head. He imagines that the shoreline is still the same and the slate-roofed huts are still in their place. The lighthouse flashes in the night, and in the huts there are sailors and double-decker bunks. The radio is crackling away, men are talking together, writing letters, there is cigarette smoke in the air. . . . Everything is there, just the same as it was, but he's not there; it even seems as though he had never lived there, never served in the navy, and that all this is an illusion, a dream!

At these times he gets up and goes down to the shore where he wraps himself in his sheepskin coat and sits down under a bush. There, he strains his ears and stares out into the darkness at the stars reflected in the water and at the distant motionless bright lights of the buoys. At such moments there is no one to see him, no need of pretense, and his face turns sad and brooding. He is weary at heart, he yearns, he yearns to go away somewhere, he yearns for a different sort of life.

From the direction of Trubetskoi there rises slowly and then slowly dies away the deep, muffled sound of a three-tone whistle. A few minutes later a steamer comes into view, brightly lit up, paddles churning fast; it hisses steam and again comes the sound of the whistle. The noise of the churning paddles and the whistle give a hollow and quavering echo in the woods along the shore. Egor watches the steamer and his yearning is stronger still.

He can see a long way ahead; young women, smelling of perfume, traveling no one knows where, lie asleep in their cabins. Near the engine room there is the soft, sweet smell of steam, polished brass, and engine heat. The decks and guardrails are covered with dew, the yawning men on watch stand on the bridge, the helmsman turns the wheel. A few passengers, wrapped in their overcoats, are sitting on the upper deck, looking out into the darkness, at the buoy lights, at the occasional fishermen's lamp fires, at the glow from some factory or power station: and all this seems to them beautiful and marvelous and they feel the urge to go ashore at some small landing stage, to remain behind in the stillness, in the dewy cool of the night. And there's bound to be someone aboard who has gone to sleep on a bench, his jacket pulled up over his head, his legs curled up; just for a moment he is awakened by the whistle, the fresh air, the jolt as the steamer comes alongside the landing stage. . . .

Life is passing Egor by! Why is there this ringing in his heart and over all the earth? What is it that beckons to him and disquiets him in the still evening? And why does his heart ache so? Why does he find no pleasure in the dewy meadows and the still water, no joy in the freedom of this life of easy and casual work?

After all, the countryside, his countryside is beautiful: the dusty roads he traveled on foot since he was a child; the villages, each one a world of its own, with its own home-grown expressions and turns of phrase, its own girls; the village where he had so often gone in the evenings, where he once kissed, hid in the rye, where he fought till the blood ran and he or the other man dropped unconscious; the blue-gray smoke of the campfires above the river and the buoy lights; and spring with the violet-colored snow on the fields, the immense turbid flood waters, the cold sunsets covering half the sky, the piles of last year's dead leaves in the ravines! Autumn too is beautiful in its desolation, with its light rain, the fragrance of the night winds, and the shack which is so cozy at that time of year!

So why does he wake up? Who calls to him in the night as though the stars were booming over the river: "Ego-o-or!" He has an eerie feeling. A shiver of fear runs through him. Far-off places, the city with its noise and the world at large call to him. He longs for work, for real work—for work that will make him dead tired, make him happy!

And dragging his sheepskin coat behind him, he goes back into the shack, lies down beside Alenka, wakes her, piti-fully and greedily snuggles up against her, pressing himself close, aware only of her, like some child on the point of tears. His eyes tight closed, he rubs his face up against her shoulder, kisses her neck. Weak with joy, with burning love, and with tenderness for her, he feels on his face her answer-ing kisses, swift and tender. Now he no longer thinks of any-thing or wishes for anything, wishing only that it could be like this forever.

Then they whisper together, though there is no need for whispering. And, as always, Alenka tries to persuade Egor to steady down, to quit drinking, to get married, to go some-where else, to get himself a regular job, so that people will respect him and he'll get his name in the papers.

And half an hour later, now relaxed, lazy, and mocking, Egor is already mumbling "Nonsense!" as usual, but he mum-

bles absently somehow, inoffensively, secretly wishing that
she would go on and on whispering to him, go on and on
trying to persuade him to start a new life.

3

People often pass the night in Egor's shack. They are going
up or down river in motor boats, in canoes, and even on
rafts. And every time the same thing happens: they cut the
engine down on the river and then someone climbs up to
Egor's shack.

"Hi there, inside! Where's the master of the house?" the
stranger says with an assumed heartiness.

Egor doesn't answer. He snores ever so gently as he fingers
a willow fishing basket.

"Good evening!" The heartiness has gone out of the voice.
"Would it be all right if we spent the night in your place?"

Egor still doesn't answer. He even stops breathing, so en-
grossed is he in the fishing basket.

"How many of you are there?" he asks after a long pause.

"They're only three of us . . . We're not fussy, we
wouldn't trouble you . . ." the stranger says in timid hope.
"We'd pay, of course . . ."

Apathetically, slowly, pausing from time to time, Egor
questions the stranger. Who are they? Where are they going? Where have they come from? And so on. And when
there's nothing left to ask, Egor, with apparent reluctance,
gives his permission:

"All right, you can spend the night."

Then the other strangers get out of the boat, stow away
the gear, look for a good place for the boat, and haul it up
on shore. Then they turn it over, and carry their knapsacks,
cans, pots, and the outboard motor into the shack. Indoors
there is now a smell of gasoline, sweat, and boots. It is growing stuffy. Egor livens up and shakes hands with them all.
He's in a good mood now; he knows there is going to be

drinking. He gets busy, talking all the time, mostly about the weather. He shouts orders at Alenka, and builds a big, bright fire near the shack.

And when the vodka is poured, Egor half closes his gleaming eyes. He breathes very slowly and very quietly, worried in case he doesn't get enough. Then he picks up the glass in his strong, tanned hand, with its broken fingernails, and says in a firm, cheerful tone of voice: "Here's to friendship!" and drains his glass, with a stony face.

He gets drunk quickly, happily, and without effort. He gets drunk—and he begins to lie, fluently, with conviction, with enjoyment. He lies mainly about fishing, because he is for some reason convinced that the strangers are interested only in fish.

"Fish," he says, carefully and almost reluctantly, it seems, taking a bite of food, "we've got all sorts of fish in this river . . . Of course, there's less nowadays, b-but . . ."—he titters, pauses, and lowers his voice—". . . but if you know how to go about it . . . Yesterday, by the way, I got a pike. Actually it wasn't a very big one—only fifty-four pounds . . . When I was out at the buoys in the morning, I heard it jump close to shore. I threw in my line right away, and while I was working on the buoys, the fish took the hook: the hook went straight down into his belly!"

"Where's the pike now?" Egor is asked.

"I took it right away to town and sold it," Egor replies without batting an eyelid, and goes on to describe in detail what the pike was like.

And if anyone has doubts—and they always do—he's waiting for it. He flares up, and stretching out his hand for the bottle as if it belonged to him, he pours himself a triple shot and drinks it down quickly. Only then does he, with wild, drunken, absent eyes, look the doubter in the face and say:

"Would you like to go with me tomorrow? You want to bet? What kind of motor do you have?"

"It's an M-72," the man replies.

Egor turns around and looks for a while at the motor which is propped up in the corner.

"Is that it? That motor's a lot of nonsense," he says scornfully. "Slavka has a Bolinder. It's mine. I brought it back for him when I left the navy. I put it together myself. There's a real tiger for you: twenty kilometers an hour! Upstream too . . . Well, how about it? My motor against yours? Winner take both? I'll stake the Bolinder against your bit of nonsense! All right? One guy took me on like that, and lost his gun. Shall I show you the gun? It's a Tulka, made specially. It's a real tiger, wonderfully accurate. Last winter with that gun I"—glassy-eyed, he ponders for a second—"shot three hundred and fifty hares! How about that?"

The strangers are somewhat jarred and taken aback by his talk. Just to get under his skin a bit, they immediately ask him about the stove:

"Say, fellow, do you live without a stove?"

"A stove?"—Egor is shouting now—"Who can build one? Can you? Build one, then! There's the clay and the bricks, everything you need. Build it, and I'll give you a hundred fifty for sure! How about that? Build it, then," he goes on stubbornly, knowing that it can't be done and that he's won again. "Build it, then!"

At this moment he notices that there's still some vodka left and that his guests are amused. He goes out into the hallway, puts on his navy cap, unbuttons his shirt collar to show his navy T-shirt, and comes back.

"Request permission," he says with drunken, exaggerated deference and goes on to report: "Boatswain's Mate of the Northern Fleet, at your service. Requests permission to congratulate you on the occasion of the anniversary of the festival of communism and socialism. All forces of the camp of peace are called to the struggle with the enemy, and in honor of this occasion give me a drink!"

He is given a drink. Meanwhile Alenka, deeply ashamed for Egor, begins to prepare the beds for the night. There are hot tears in her eyes as she waits with impatience, almost with rage, the moment when Egor will astonish the strangers. And astonish them Egor does.

Now quite sodden and inert from drink, he suddenly sits down on the bench, slumping against the wall. He twitches his shoulder blades and shuffles his feet as he settles himself in the most comfortable position. He clears his throat, lifts his head, and—begins to sing.

And at the first sounds of his voice they all stop talking. Everyone looks at him in fear and amazement! He doesn't sing the popular songs of the day, though he knows them all and is constantly humming them; he sings in the old Russian way, drawing out his words, almost reluctantly, a little hoarsely; he sings the songs he has heard in childhood, the songs the old people used to sing. He sings softly, almost playfully, almost coyly; but his soft voice is so strong, so compelling, so truly Russian—almost the Russia of the days of the ancient epics—that in an instant all else has been forgotten: Egor's discourtesy and stupidity, his drunkenness and his boasting. Forgotten too are the long journey and the weariness. It is as though past and future had come together, and there is only this extraordinary, resonant voice that writhes in the air and fogs the mind. And you just want to go on listening forever with your head on your hand, your eyes closed, neither breathing nor holding back the tears!

"You should be in the Bolshoi Theater! That's where you should be!" they all shout at once, when Egor stops singing. Excited, their eyes shining, they all want to help him, to write somewhere, to the radio, the newspapers, to phone someone. . . . They all feel joyful and festive, and Egor, glad of their praise, tired and now rather subdued, is once more his condescending and mocking self. Once more his face is expressionless. He vaguely imagines the Bolshoi Theater, Moscow, the lights between the columns, the bright hall, the orchestra tuning up—he has seen it all at the movies. He stretches himself lazily and mutters:

"That's all a lot of nonsense . . . theaters and all that . . ."

And the others are no longer annoyed with him, so great

now in his glory, so strong and mysterious is he to the strangers.

But this is not all of Egor's glory.

4

This is not all of Egor's glory, but only a quarter of it. His real glory is when, as he himself says, "the urge comes over him." The urge comes over him about twice a month, when he is feeling particularly fed up and bored.

At these times he sulks and drinks from early morning. But he drinks slowly, and from time to time he says lazily:

"Well, then . . . Shall we go, then? What about it, eh?"

"What about what?"—Alenka pretends not to understand.

"Shall we sing? . . . Shall we sing a duet, eh?" Egor says dully, and he sighs.

Alenka laughs scornfully and doesn't answer. She knows that the time hasn't come yet, that he still hasn't yet got the urge. She tidies up the shack, goes down to the river to wash some clothes, and comes back again. . . .

Finally the time comes. This is usually toward evening. And now Egor no longer begs for a duet. He gets up. Unkempt and gloomy, he looks out of one window, then out of the other. He goes outside, has a drink of water, then puts a vodka bottle into his pocket and picks up his coat.

"Are you going far?" Alenka asks innocently, but she is beginning to tremble all over.

"Get going!" Egor answers crudely and walks awkwardly through the doorway.

His face is pale, his nostrils distended. The veins stand out on his temples. Alenka, coughing slightly as she knots a woolen scarf around her neck, walks alongside him. She knows that Egor will first go out onto the cliff, and will take a look up and down stream. Then he will think awhile as though he didn't know where would be best, and will then make for his favorite place, down by the upturned flat-bottomed boat which lies, full of holes, by the birches at the water's edge. And there he will sing with her, but not at all the way he sang to the strangers. For then he sang rather casually, a little playfully, not using anything like the full strength of his voice. . . .

Egor does indeed stand on the bank for a minute thinking, then he goes silently down to the flat-bottomed boat. Here he spreads out the coat, sits down, his back against the side of the boat. He spreads his legs, tucking them in slightly, and stands the bottle between them.

The sunset is beautiful. The mist over the fields is like flood water. The strip of wood in the distance is black and so are the haystacks. The birch branches overhead are motionless. The grass is wet with dew. The air is still and warm, but Alenka feels shivery: she huddles close to Egor, while with a trembling hand he picks up the bottle and takes a swallow, grimacing and clearing his throat. His mouth is full of sweet saliva.

"All right . . . " he says, twisting his neck and coughing, and he whispers a warning: "Be sure you come in after me! . . ."

He fills his lungs with air, straining, and begins to sing— mournfully, in a high tenor, pure and tremulous:

> Down by the sea,
> The deep blue sea . . .

Alenka closes her eyes. Shaking, almost in pain, she waits the moment, then she joins him in a low, resonant, true voice, in perfect unison:

> A swa-an swims with his ma-ate . . .

Alenka no longer hears her own low-pitched, subdued, passionate voice! She is aware only of the gentle, grateful pressure of Egor's heavy hand on her shoulder, she hears only his voice. Ah, the sweetness and the pain of the song! Meanwhile Egor, his voice now soft, now swelling to full force, now husky and now metallically resonant, is pouring out in song his wonderful words, words so strange, yet so

familiar, for they spring from the heart of the Russian people and reach back into the Russian past:

> A swan swims, he glides so ca-almly,
> Never rippling the fine yellow sand . . .

How well she knows all this and how it hurts her, as
though she had lived some time long, long ago and sung like
this and listened to Egor's enchanted voice! On what far-off
sea had she once drifted? It had been with him, with Egor!
With him she had walked through the meadow in the sunset,
beneath the stars, through the mist, had walked as in a
trance, drunk without wine!

> Came the gray eagle . . .

Egor groans and weeps, surrendering in deep anguish
to the sound of the singing, straining his ears, turning slightly
away from Alenka. And his Adam's apple trembles and
his lips are sorrowful. Oh, the gray eagle! Why, why did he
have to swoop down on the white swan, why did the grass
bow its head and darkness cover the earth, why did the stars
fall, and why was the sea churned up? O, let there be an end
to these tears, to that voice, an end to the song!

And so they sing, aware of nothing except the feeling that
in an instant their hearts will break, in an instant they will
fall dead upon the grass—and no fresh water will revive
them. For them there will be no resurrection after such happiness and such pain.

And when they finish singing, exhausted, stricken, happy,
when Egor silently lays his head in her lap, breathing heavily, she kisses his pale cold face and whispers breathlessly:

"Egor, darling . . . I love you, my angel, my glory . . ."

"That's a lot of nonsense . . ." Egor is about to answer,
but he says nothing. His mouth tastes sweet and dry.

Tendryakov is one of the younger Soviet prose writers of the "neo-realist" school which has established itself since Stalin's death, despite considerable opposition from the socialist realist purists. This story, which appeared in Novy Mir in 1960, is perhaps one of the most interesting Russian novellas to appear in recent years; Tendryakov describes Soviet life with a kind of Chekhovian objectivity which would have been unthinkable ten years ago. In the Soviet context, it is remarkable for its use of the jargon of the Russian underworld, for its lack of moralizing about a situation which may well have some symbolic reference to the political conditions in which it was possible for one ruthless man to demoralize and terrorize the people around him, and for its ambiguous ending.

The title is inspired by Pushkin's "Queen of Spades"; "three, seven, ace" is the winning yet fatal sequence of cards which Herman, the hero of the story, ultimately fails to draw.

The story has been cut by the editors. The first pages describe a lumberjacks' camp, a remote wilderness of Russia, and the furious rapids along the great timber-floating river which runs through it. Sasha Dubinin is the tough, hardheaded, yet benevolent foreman of twenty-five lumberjacks who live in nearly complete and austere isolation from the neighboring villages. Dubinin is greatly admired for his strength and courage by his men, and especially by the youngest, twenty-year-old Leshka Malinkin, who imitates all his gestures. One evening Leshka heroically saves a stranger from drowning in the river rapids. The stranger's documents identify him as a certain Nikolai Bushuyev who has just been released from prison. On his chest are tattooed the words: "Years go by but bring no luck." The presence of this ex-convict in camp does not worry Dubinin but it greatly agitates Petukhov, the camp miser, who fears for his savings which are locked in a trunk in the lumberjack's hut. Translation by David Alger.

VLADIMIR TENDRYAKOV

Three, Seven, Ace

Next morning, after the men had left, Dubinin looked into the hut. The bed on which the uninvited guest had slept was made.

"Early bird," thought Dubinin. "Gone already. On his way, is he? Well, I've got his identity card. He won't go far." He walked back unhurriedly.

The house in which he had his office was the only two-story house in the settlement. The office was on the ground floor, next to a room shared by the mechanic Tikhon and his wife Nastya, the maid. Above it was the club room with its desk, its bookshelf, and its table covered with a faded red cloth. Here the men gathered in the evenings to play dominoes and listen to the radio.

As he passed the stairs Dubinin heard a man singing in a low voice and playing a guitar:

> *Why are some men lucky,*
> *All their dreams fulfilled,*
> *While others' lives are wretched,*
> *Joy and laughter killed . . .*

Dubinin went up. The stranger sat, still unshaved but wearing a clean shirt borrowed from someone with broader shoulders than his own, its collar pitifully loose around his stringy neck; he was nursing the guitar which had hung unused over the desk for years.

> *Why do some avoid*
> *The cruel blows of fate . . .*

At sight of the foreman he stood up hastily.

"A very good morning, boss," he barked with forced playfulness.

A narrow face, evasive eyes; the smile bared a gap between the small, tight teeth.

Dubinin lowered himself into a chair.

"Sit down, what's-your-name . . . Nikolai Bushuyev. We'll have a talk."

"That's right, Nikolai Petrovich Bushuyev in person. I was making for Tormenga, further down the river, but here I am, landed on you by accident. Sorry I didn't let you know in advance so I could be met. . . ."

"Stop joking. Where have you come from?"

"I had a job at the saw mill. . . ."

"Ran away?"

"The boss is a bastard. Doesn't treat you like a human being. Once you've been inside, he says, you're a crook, a criminal—you're through. We didn't get along."

"That really all?"

"Why should I mess up my life again for a swine like him? Better get away from temptation . . . I had a couple hundred owing to me and I didn't even take that."

"What were you in for?"

"They say there was a good reason. I don't argue with them—they ought to know."

"Murder?"

"God forbid!"

"Stealing?"

"Don't let's go into the details, chief. What I will say is, I've turned over a new leaf."

"Sure?"

"Believe it or not. It's a long time since I was twenty. I don't somehow feel like playing cops and robbers any more."

"Where are you from? Why did you take on this job instead of going home?"

"My home's under my hat."

"And you never miss it?"

Bushuyev lowered his eyelids over his oddly light, glistening eyes, and for a second his pale, bristly face grew still, closed, expressionless. Dubinin's chance question had stripped it of its assumed cheerfulness.

"What's the good?" he said after a moment. "I know what it's like to go home with empty pockets."

"I've been told that people work—where you were—and take their earnings with them when they come out."

"I had a bit, but I lost it at cards to a man in the train. . . ."

Dubinin, stolid in his chair, his coat unbuttoned, cap pulled low over his head, watched his visitor with his usual morose calm.

"And where will you go now?" he asked.

"Tormenga . . . There's bound to be work at the loading base."

"Are you trained for anything?"

"Jack-of-all-trades, that's me. I've chopped timber, dug foundations, dug up stumps . . ."

"So you're not trained . . ." Dubinin shifted in his chair and turned aside. "How about this," he said, looking past his guest, "you can stay here. You'll have to work, like everyone else. A lumberjack makes a couple of thousand a month on an average. You've got no family, you'll spend about five hundred on your food and clothes. By the end of a year you'll have saved up fifteen to eighteen thousand. After that, if you like it, you stay on; if you don't, you go where you like. I'm offering you this for your own good, because I'm sorry for you. I'm not begging you to stay and I'm not forcing you, so don't imagine I am."

"Why should I want to go? I don't mind, it's all the same to me where I kill time."

Dubinin struck the table with his stumpy hand clenched into a small fist, covered with red hairs and heavy, like a stone from the river bed.

"Kill time? No, my friend, you'll have to work. You don't

get paid for killing time. And don't imagine you can get away with anything. This is the backwoods, the police are a long way off, we make our own rules. You've seen our boys? They'll know how to take care of you. And there's nowhere to run to—there's nothing but marsh and forest all around, even the village people don't like to go too far in. There are only three ways out—one to the sawmill where I don't suppose they'll make you very welcome, one to the village where you'd stick out like a sore thumb, and the third is down the river past the loading bases. All I have to do is lift the receiver and you'll be held till further notice. So get that into your skull—don't try any tricks. If I take you on, it's not because I trust you specially, it's because I'm not afraid of you—you can't do much here. That's how it is."

Dubinin got up.

Nikolai Bushuyev slept in the hut. Every morning he walked down to the boats with the rest of the men, an ax stuck into his belt and a gaff in his hand. When Dubinin asked the boys what his work was like they shrugged their shoulders: "All right, he pokes around."

Leshka Malinkin slept in the bed next to Bushuyev's, and worked in the same gang with him. You cannot be indifferent toward a man for whom you have committed an important, not to say heroic, act (Leshka had saved his life and that was no joke). He managed to be next to him at work, to teach him, help him, shift the stumps his weaker neighbor found too heavy.

The guitar, which had come out of a sum of money put aside for popular culture and which had hung in the club-room for so long, was moved into the hut, and here Bushuyev, lolling on his bed of an evening, would strum and sing of love betrayed, of crimes of passion, and of sorrows of captivity:

> *Some guy in his satin tie*
> *May be kissing you by the gate . . .*

One evening he took down the guitar, plucked at the strings, and then damped them.

"To hell with it—I've sung and played enough."

He added an obscene rhyme, took a tattered pack of cards out of his pocket, shuffled it expertly, and offered it to Leshka Malinkin:

"Have a game?—just for fun."

Leshka wriggled in embarrassment.

"I don't know how to play."

"I'll teach you. Beginners are lucky. Don't be scared, I won't fleece you. Here, I'll start the bank with a ruble. You can stake ten kopecks if you like."

Afterward, nobody could tell how Bushuyev happened to have a pack of cards. When they brought him in out of the rapids there was nothing in his pockets except sodden documents and fifteen rubles in small notes.

Bushuyev made himself at home on Leshka's bed and patiently taught him.

"Don't you get excited, kid. Cards don't like you if you get excited. Want a card? All right. Here it is. Look at that, you've won again. I told you you'd be lucky to start with."

Leshka held good cards and grew pink with excitement. Stupnin came and stood close by; he blinked his yellow-fringed eyelids and shook his head.

"It's a sinful business. How much in the bank? Only eighty kopecks! Well, all right, I'll have a card—just out of curiosity."

He took it, looked at it doubtfully, and drawled:

"There's a business! Give me two more. Fancy that! Well, get busy, take yours. . . . My trick!"

Others from the nearby beds joined the players and surrounded them. Petukhov watched the cards, his lips tight.

"Ten kopecks here, ten kopecks there, before you know it a good red ruble is gone. It's ages since I've touched a card."

"Better keep away now," Bushuyev agreed. "Cards don't take to misers."

Toward ten o'clock they finished the last bank and counted

the winnings: Leshka had won twenty rubles. Stupnin and
the rest had won and lost trifling sums. Bushuyev paid. . . .

The very next evening five of them settled down to a
game of cards on Bushuyev's bed—just to kill time; besides
Bushuyev himself there were Leshka, Stupnin, and two others—a lanky boy called Kozlov and a redhead, Savateyev.
Curious onlookers crowded around, including Petukhov, who
always got agitated when he saw money changing hands.

The stakes were small. Now one man, now another got
his bit of luck. Leshka was winning steadily again. He took
the bank. Petukhov grunted:

"Some people are born lucky."

Stupnin sighed:

"There's a business. . . . Well, you can play for kopecks
if you like, I'm going the whole hog. Fortune favors the
bold."

Little by little the stakes rose, until not only ruble and
ten-ruble notes rustled on the crinkled coverlet but twenty-
fives and even hundreds.

Leshka was winning, so was Stupnin. From time to time
Bushuyev calmly took more money from his pocket and
flung it down with a careless gesture.

"What's that? Call this a game? I remember games, my
children, when there was ten thousand in the bank."

Others joined in. It was after payday, everyone had
money, and they all felt they could allow themselves a little
leeway—they could afford a bit of fun.

Only Petukhov, lips primly tight, watched the cards, followed every movement of the players' hands as they stuffed
their winnings in their pockets, and shook his head in disap-
proval though he never left their side. No one took any notice of him.

When Stupnin, jubilant and steaming red, grabbed the
bank in his huge paw, Petukhov gave Leshka a nudge.

"Move over a bit. My legs aren't made of iron."

"You don't mean you want to take a hand?" asked Bushuyev.

"Why not? Think I'm not as good as you are?"

"You'll lose your shirt. Cards don't take to misers."

"I'm staking a ruble," Petukhov repeated with stubborn anger.

"Well, well, that's quite a skirtful from a careful girl like you."

Bushuyev dealt nimbly.

Petukhov's card was swallowed up in his huge red hand with its broken nails; his eyes riveted on it, his lips pursed as though about to whistle in surprise. Bushuyev smiled his needling smile, blinking his deceptively transparent eyes and showing the gap in his strong teeth.

As soon as Petukhov sat down the game changed. Until now the players had joked, sniggered, exchanged idle comments, and not minded when they lost; although the stakes had risen you could still feel that they were playing for fun. With Petukhov's coming the stakes rose no higher. On the contrary they fell, but jokes ceased at once and suddenly everyone was grave, not looking straight at the crumpled notes but shooting them sidelong shamefaced glances.

Bushuyev was still smiling complacently, but every now and then he bit his lower lip, and at such moments his lean, drawn face had something sharp and swooping in it like the look of a cat ready to spring at a sparrow.

Petukhov, his shoulders hunched and strained, held the bank, but somehow he soon lost it. Bushuyev, raking in the pile of crumpled notes, threw him a glance.

"Out you go. Your five rubles are gone."

But the five rubles Petukhov had started with had gone unnoticeably, without pain. All they left him was the feeling of having missed his chance. . . .

The game went on and the voices sounded in turn restrained, expectant, alert, surprised. The game went on, the money rustled. Petukhov got off his bed, pulled his suitcase out, and undid the lock.

Straightening his shoulders, a sort of sour disdain in his expression, he came back.

"Here, you bastard, here's the money. Now deal."

Bushuyev gave a short laugh.

"That's a big wad of money! Hoping that five-ruble note will rake you in a fortune?"

"Just you go on grinning. I'll stake what I want. Let's have the cards."

"Staking the lot?"

"I'm staking one ruble."

"Why bother to get change?— You'll lose it all anyway. . . ."

"How much in the bank?" Petukhov asked tonelessly, the card in the palm of his hand damp with sweat.

"Want it all?"

"None of your business. How much is there, I asked you?"

"I haven't counted."

"Count it."

"Leshka," Bushuyev nodded carelessly. "See what the bank's worth. I don't seem to remember."

Leshka, frowning, kneeled and counted clumsily, taking the money from the pile note by note and putting it down.

Everyone else was silent. Petukhov wiped his sweating face with his sleeve.

"Seven hundred and forty-five rubles."

Petukhov passed his sleeve again over his face and mumbled through dry lips:

"All of it."

"No tricks, grandpa." A muscle quivered in Bushuyev's cheek. "You put down seven hundred and forty-five rubles right here in this corner where everyone can see, then I'll believe you."

"I'll put it down all right. What d'you mean?" Petukhov objected, his voice not quite certain.

"Well, do it then. Don't hold up the game. Get out your trunk." For once Bushuyev's eyes were wide open.

Petukhov knew he must get up. That was what Bushuyev expected; so did all those wary, silent men.

"Well . . ."

He got up heavily. His legs were numb, hard to move, he had pins and needles in his feet. He crumpled the card in his sweaty hand. The card was all right. But no card was enough. Suppose he drew a six at once? Bushuyev had boasted he could see right through the cards. But what about the cards? Nobody had checked them.

He crossed over to his bed, dragged out the suitcase, felt the heavy, well-made lock, the small steel shaft gripped by solid rings. He had riveted the rings himself. All desire to go on gambling had left him at the first touch of the padlock. But now the suitcase was open and his hand groped under the clothes to where several packages, all his earnings for the past three months, lay discreetly in a corner. He had been meaning for a long time to get out on a Sunday and hand it over to the bank in town, but here it still was—five thousand in hundred-ruble notes and about three hundred in small change. Now he must take one thousand out and count seven hundred and forty-five! And all for whom? For that jailbird! This was his own sweat and blood! He never gave a penny to his wife, he never ate in the canteen. And now, seven hundred and forty-five rubles for this tramp!

"All right." He turned his head stiffly without looking up. "To hell with your bank. I'll stake fifty rubles."

"That's more like it," Bushuyev drawled mockingly. "You had me worried for a moment."

Petukhov thought he heard a note of relief in Bushuyev's voice. Was he worried about the bank? That pile of money at his side—he's come in for the whole thing. But me, I'm in for fifty rubles; a measly fifty rubles. The rest will be squandered on that crook's drink and a gay life—and it's a good card.

The suitcase was open. His hands groped through the clothes for the bundle of notes.

"Come on. Get going. What are you stuck over there for?"
Bushuyev was pressing.

"The whole thing!" His voice blasted out: "There's the
money, you bastard."

Petukhov took out the wrapped-up savings, peeled off a
thousand, and slammed the case shut. Then he spent a long
time looking for the ace of hearts which had dropped behind it.

And while he was looking his confidence ebbed away.

The whole thing . . .

Card in one hand (a good card—come on, God, help me,
help me!); in the other, a bundle of hundreds. Money he
had sweated for, toiled for, skimped and saved—gone hungry for.

"See, you louse? Believe me now?"

"Sure." Bushuyev's answer was terse, serious. "Sit down."

They were all hushed. From all sides wide-eyed stares
were riveted on the center. They waited. But Petukhov was
swamped in despair. How had it happened? Bushuyev
would slaughter him. His thieving face was taut; it had
shown some wrinkles before, now it was dead serious.

Bushuyev had already flicked him a card. He took it. Pack
it in? Too late. Once he had taken a card he couldn't pack
it in—it wouldn't only be Bushuyev who would mind.

The king of diamonds.

Bushuyev's eyes narrowed on the sights.

"Another?"

The whole circle could be heard breathing.

"Let me take it," Petukhov asked hoarsely.

His clumsy, fat rough fingers drew a card from the pack.
Please, God, please! Petukhov could not see. Sweat ran
from his brow, stung his eyes.

"Well?" Bushuyev's whole body seemed to be in the word.

The king and the ace, and—bust.

Bushuyev laid his narrow, almost refined, hand on the
kitty. Without a word he dragged it over to his own pile.

"Keep the change"—he threw Petukhov a few notes.

Petukhov obediently took them.

Genka Shamayev, back from his usual jaunt across the river, for the first time found the hut awake. They were all seated on the floor under the light in a fog of tobacco smoke. Shamayev went to his own bunk, pulled back the blanket. "I see you're really at it. You'd get hell if Sasha found out." Nobody paid him any attention. Petukhov went on to lose the rest of his thousand.

A sullen morning: clouds clawing the fir-tree tops along the water's edge; drizzle. As they came out of the warm stuffy hut, their belts buckled over their jackets and water-proof capes. the men shrank involuntarily. Sleep was still in their faces; there was no talking. As always in the morning, the noise of the water at the Big Head seemed louder and more insistent.

Head bent, eyes downcast. Petukhov went with the others toward the boats. His face had become puffy overnight. His step was leaden, he dragged his gaff behind him.

Bushuyev was standing by the boats where the men shuffled around waiting for the latecomers. An old waterproof cape borrowed from the lanky Khariton billowed out over his jacket. And though Bushuyev was to all intents just like the others, with his belt, his ax stuck in it, his hook in his hand, still he managed somehow to look as if he was not in earnest, did not mean business.

Petukhov, head bent, edged toward him, poked at the ground with his boot, blurted out guiltily:

"Listen pal, it wasn't . . . it was kind of a joke last night . . . very funny . . . I know I sort of asked . . . listen, give me my money back and let's forget it."

Bushuyev's face twisted into a sneer, his eyes puckered.

"You're kidding, grandpa. Rivers don't go backward."

"Listen here, give it back, I said. Or else . . ." Petukhov closed in, threateningly.

"Steady now. Clear off!" Bushuyev squared up.

"Lousy bastard. I'll smash you!" Petukhov raised his gaff. Bushuyev leaped back, grabbed his ax.

"Come on, hand it over. I'll split your thick skull open."

Shamayev turned to them, stocky in his short coat and thigh-length rubber boots. A dry tuft of hair stuck out from under his forage cap.

"Stop fooling around. I'm in on this." Striding over to Petukhov he grabbed the hook. "Serves you right, you fool —you'll keep your nose out of it next time. Get to the boat."

Petukhov calmed down and did as he was told.

Until now life in the camp had been quiet and monotonous; days had followed nights with no alarms, no excitements. Even the distractions were monotonous—listening to the radio and a game or two of dominoes. Such entertainment as this did not stave off sleep for long. And in the morning—the boats, the logs, dinner, and so endlessly on.

But this was really something—a solid ring of people on the floor, tense faces, excited shining eyes, clipped words, money, the shrinking piles of notes, money going from one pocket to another, the grip of near success, the disappointment . . . and Petukhov blowing the whole load in his suitcase! Wasn't that really something? You had to admit it was a damn sight more entertaining than dominoes at bedtime.

Evening fell and the whole hut gathered in a circle, some to play, others to watch, to get worked up on the sidelines. Only two didn't take part: Shamayev, and Petukhov who was lying, still dressed, face down on his bunk.

The stakes rose immediately. Stifled exclamations reached his ears. He lay clenching his fists in hate. He couldn't touch Bushuyev now—all the others would stand up for him. The thousand was gone—he wouldn't get it back.

But the voices tore into his very being.

"Pass."

"Let's have another."

"Hell—there goes the bank."

Even the short tense silences gripped him. Somebody

would have the luck, but he, wronged and forgotten, lay alone. It never entered anyone's head to feel sorry for him. But suppose he tried again? No risky stuff this time— play it clever, careful, cautious. He'd get his money back soon. He'd gone bust on big stakes—might manage with small ones.

Petukhov slid from his bunk, carefully pulled out his suitcase, got the money, took out a hundred note.

He roughly shouldered the others aside—claiming the right of one offended to the tolerance and sympathy of others.

"Move over!"

He sat down, trying not to meet anyone's eyes, and took a card.

At the end of the stone dam behind the settlement Dubinin was laying bait. He went to check his lines each evening, and now he was returning with a bucket splashing with perch.

He walked straight along the dam, striding on the great boulders. It was a stone barrier almost the height of two men, stretching a quarter of a kilometer from the canteen to where it slid diagonally into the tempestuous river.

Two years ago Dubinin's section had been the toughest on the whole length of the river. The Big Head threw up the timber onto a stony shoal and there, several times each summer, great blockages piled up. At peak flow you had to work twelve hours a day. By autumn the men were exhausted. After that they had decided to build themselves a dam to keep the logs off the shoals. . . . The dam was remarkable enough but it was just a side show. The men were as used to it as to the ceaseless noise of the Big Head. Dubinin was possessed by a vague sort of pride for his charges: "They're a good hard-working bunch, you've got to admit—they earn their grub, all right."

At the end of the dam a cobbled slope ran up to the canteen wall. Behind a corner of the canteen a lighted window

showed from the hut. It was pretty late but they hadn't
turned in.

The feeling of pride and quiet confidence that everything
was all right, that life was fine, all vanished. "They're at the
cards again."

Some deadbeat scum was lording it over a score of grown,
healthy, thinking, self-respecting men. And for him, Dubinin
the foreman, the most powerful man on the site, whose every
word was listened to, it wasn't so easy just to say: "That's it,
boys—stop the nonsense."

So everything was fine, everything fixed—was it? Everybody satisfied, everything quiet—a sight too quiet. Sleep
and work, work and sleep.

Dubinin could make them haul boulders in biting frost—
that was necessary. He could order the raftsmen—normally
no abstainers—not to drink on the site. That was necessary.
It was in that one word "necessary" that Dubinin's whole
strength lay. But try taking away their cards—they'd be up
in arms right away.

"Who do you think we are—your slaves? How do you
like that: 'Now, now, boys—no cards.' Does the work suffer?
No. Well then, don't butt in."

But it wouldn't end there. Wherever there were cards,
drinking and trouble were not far away. "All right, let it go.
When trouble comes. I'll be here; that's when I'll call a stop.
Just let them try anything. . . ."

Tobacco smoke hung in layers above the figures huddled
on the floor. Many of them shot frightened glances at Bushuyev; it was not possible to win like that without cheating.
He couldn't fool them, they'd fix him. The joking had
stopped, the laughter had vanished, in the thick smoky air
something evil was building up—everyone was waiting for it
to break.

Bushuyev squatted by the money, his vest hanging loose.
Every so often he stuffed some of the money into his pockets,
but the piles at his knees soon grew again. When Bushuyev
got up and went for a drink all heads turned to follow him,

ten pairs of eyes suspiciously followed his every move. Bushuyev leisurely filled an aluminum cup with water from the tank, drank thirstily, returned to his place, and squatted down again.

Petukhov shuffled the pack with trembling hands, an unaccustomed desperation on his face, his eyes red. The suitcase had been pushed right into the gangway. It was open and the crumpled clothes showed white.. Petukhov was losing his last ruble.

"The whole thing," Bushuyev called relentlessly as he had already so often that evening.

The whole thing. Petukhov's head sank into his shoulders, his hands shook. He threw out a card. Bushuyev calmly took it, gave it a fleeting look, and stretched out his hand toward the pack.

"Let me take one."

Petukhov's hands trembled. So did the pack, so did his slack lips.

Someone behind Bushuyev exclaimed in a hostile voice: "He's got it!"

Petukhov abruptly flung the cards to the floor, lunged across the scattered money at Bushuyev, and shouted:

"You're cheating. I'll strangle you, you bastard."

Bushuyev sprang to his feet. Clumsily turning among the huddled bunch of dumbfounded figures, his face purple, his teeth bared like a wild animal, Petukhov roared:

"I'll slaughter you, smash you to bits, you swine!"

Now on his feet, heavy, clumsy, he swayed over Bushuyev, whose narrow shoulders were enveloped in his flapping shirt. He had him cornered, now he would squash him, crush him, cripple him. But Bushuyev ducked nimbly and dived at Petukhov. A short butt with his head brought Petukhov heavily to the floor.

It all happened quickly. Nobody had time to take it in. Nobody seized Petukhov, nobody restrained Bushuyev.

Bushuyev leaped to his bunk, flung off the mattress, and an ax appeared in his hands.

In the sudden silence the muffled roar of the waters at the Big Head pressed through the windows.

Till then all they had felt toward Bushuyev was distaste. An intense one for sure, kindled by obscure suspicion, but the moment they saw the ax in his hand they understood that he was their enemy. He recognized it too; not for nothing had he concealed an ax in his bunk for a year.

"Now," Bushuyev brandished the ax, "anyone who wants to . . . I've got nothing to lose. . . ."

His white shirt hung outside his trousers, his sharp collarbones stood out under the open collar. His long neck was scraggy as a chicken's leg; his eyes were an empty pale light in his pallid black-bristled face.

It was one against all the rest. All those men were stronger than he. There was a whole crowd of them, more than a score. And what if he did have an ax? There were axes in the corridor; it would be easy enough to dash through the door and pick them up.

The noise of the rapids seeped through the tightly closed windows. Nobody moved. They stood, they shuffled, they looked at Bushuyev. Fists were out of the question. In the twinkling of an eye the ax would be up and there was no doubt that this man wouldn't think twice about bringing it down on the first head that came his way. No conscience, no law would restrain him. Even Petukhov, mad with hate and despair, hesitated to grab an ax and brain him. More than a score of hefty men stood bewildered before one weak, narrow-chested specimen. They stood in silence. The noise of the river went on. . . .

For the past few days Leshka had gone around in a daze —the piles of money, the wins, the losses, people breathing hard down the back of his neck. He found it vaguely disturbing and frightening. He would have been glad enough to get out of it but he wasn't strong enough. And Sasha wouldn't think much of it either. He was getting out of his depth. His heart sank as he wondered how it would end.

And now there was Petukhov's hoarse cry, the scuffle, and Bushuyev, ax in hand, lying on his bunk.

Leshka shared the hatred which the others felt for this stranger. He had expected Stupnin and Petukhov, who were both strong men and never figured to be afraid of anything, to go for Bushuyev and pin him down. But no one did. They had all stood, as bewildered as himself. The sight of this man with his narrow glinting eyes was terrifying. They cowered before him.

Leshka went apprehensively to his bunk, which was flush against the one where Bushuyev was sprawled smoking. He started hurriedly to undress. If only he could get his head down quickly, turn his back on Bushuyev, and forget him. Scarcely had his head touched the pillow, however, when he felt something hard bulging under his pillow. He thrust his hand inside, but Bushuyev's intent stare made him turn.

"You," Bushuyev hissed, barely audibly, "go outside."

Leshka stared open-mouthed, not understanding.

"Go outside, I said. Like you were going for a piss. Wait for me there. Go on."

Bushuyev casually turned back, letting the smoke drift to the ceiling. Leshka was still at a loss.

"Get!" hissed Bushuyev through a cloud of smoke.

Leshka didn't dare disobey. He got into his rubber boots and holding up his pants he made for the door. Nobody paid any attention.

The moon behind the forest was almost full. From the dark river poured the muffled detached noise of rushing water. Leshka started his vigil in the shadow of the wall, shivering in his underwear from the night cold, trying to stop his teeth from chattering, and looking around every minute. He felt as if eyes were somewhere watching him suspiciously. He strained to listen for the sound of approaching footsteps in the noise of the water.

He had a long time to wait. The bloated moon, slightly shaved on one side, lit the wide yard and the cistern in the center. A dim light shone from the office window. Sasha sat there. Suppose he dashed over to him, said Bushuyev was up to no good? He wouldn't let him get away with it.

Leshka shuffled and shivered, and couldn't bring himself to move.

There was a scraping on the porch step and Bushuyev appeared with his shirt outside his pants, gripping his ax. His free hand grabbed Leshka by the chest, dragging him forward and wrapping him in a stench of tobacco. He whispered hoarsely:

"Under your pillow. There's ten grand. Take it home to your village on Saturday. Hide it till I come and see you. Maybe soon, maybe not—but I'll come for sure. You're from Yaremnaya, third house on the right. I know it all, see? Double-cross and you're dead. If you do it right you get two grand to play around with. Get it, sucker? It won't occur to them that you've got the money. Let 'em search me."

Bushuyev spat through his teeth.

"Get going."

Leshka's teeth chattered.

"Give the money back," he begged, "the boys are pretty wild."

"Don't you teach me, snot-nose."

"Th-then go now—take the money and go."

"Listen, you chattering runt, how do I go without my papers? Sasha's got them. Now get moving, or the others will start thinking. And remember, one squeak and I'll kill you. . . ."

Leshka lay on his bunk with his eyes tight shut, feeling infinitely small, helpless, and stupid before the ocean of life which surrounded the small island he knew—the tiny settlement squeezed by the forest against the river. It was his first disillusionment, his first dismay, his first fear—an overgrown child's first naïve glimpse of reality.

Petukhov could not settle down. He stumbled against the headboards going toward Bushuyev's bunk, angrily felt the jacket hanging above it, picked up the pillow, thumbed it, raised the mattress.

"He's after the money." Leshka froze. "Now he'll tell me to get up." The money pressed against his forehead through the pillow. "What shall I do? Tell him? What about Bushuyev? What will they do to him? Throw him out, hit him, beat him up even—but he'll still be alive and well. And he even knows my village, knows the house. He'd dig me up from under the ground."

He still lay with the money pressing against his forehead. The Petukhov who was tearing Bushuyev's bed apart was not the Petukhov he knew. He used to be an ordinary sort of man—a bit meaner than the rest. But now his face was fierce and determined, his eyes red. If Petukhov found out that he was lying on the money he might hurl himself on him and strangle him. He was a complete stranger, mystifying. And yet they had lived side by side for over a year.

Leshka held his breath under the blanket and watched as Petukhov finished tearing at the bunk, cursed, and went away.

Dubinin cleaned the fish, wrapped it up in nettles, and stood the bucket outside the door, where it was cool; then, without taking off his coat, he sat down in his office and began thinking to the ceaseless grunting of the telephone. . . .

The first time he had met Bushuyev he had told him that it was hard to leave the district. But was it? Instead of walking or going by rowboat he could take the outboard. It was always near the bank and Tikhonov never took the motor out. If he started in the evening, he could leave all the sites behind by morning. At the end there would be the sorting base—hundreds of workers, easy to get lost among them—and then the railroad and the highway. He'd be able to laugh about it afterward; he'd have twisted the fools around his finger.

Silent and mysterious, the wooded slope rose above the river, separating the small settlement from the rest of the world. The river was black, except in midstream where the

moonlight boiled and rushed together with the current
which it could not leave.

Dubinin took the motor out of the boat, put it on the
bank, and stood for a long time among the boulders, looking
at the moonlight feverishly trembling on the stream, listening to the roaring rapids and the patter of spray on the deck.

What could he do? Reason with him? Find the right
words? How? He was not good at talking. Just fling him
out? Get rid of him, push him onto others, let them work it
out among themselves—that would be too much like Bushuyev.

Dubinin shouldered the heavy motor and watching his
short shadow crawl over the stones, he climbed the slope
toward the dim light of his office window.

Some ten yards before he got to it he saw a shadow flit
across the window. What could it be? At this time of night?

Bent slightly under the weight of the motor, he approached cautiously.

Humped over the desk, Bushuyev was going through the
drawers. His ax lay on top of the desk.

What was he doing? What did he want? Suddenly he
realized—the identity card.

It wasn't in the desk. It was in the rucksack hanging on
the wall next to the telephone, just behind Bushuyev's back.
He didn't notice it.

Dubinin must have made a careless step, Bushuyev
glanced sharply at the window; his face was screwed up,
frozen, his eyes darted like those of a hunted beast.

They met on the dark porch.

"Sasha. It's you? I was coming to see you." No fear, no
embarrassment.

Dubinin grabbed his arm and pulled him out.

"Come on."

"Where?"

Dubinin did not answer.

THREE, SEVEN, ACE [225

The broad yard looked even more deserted by moonlight. Halfway to the bunkhouse, the old iron cistern loomed black. Light in the hut windows though it was long past midnight, and Bushuyev in his office for some reason with the ax under his arm—all this suggested to Sasha that something had happened, that it was time to act.

Bushuyev stopped before he reached the cistern.

"Where are you taking me?"

"Come on. Don't talk."

"Wait a minute. Do you want me to give back the money? Well, why don't you say so?" His voice was conciliatory.

"You'll give it back. But first we'll have a talk with the boys."

"It will be easier to talk once the money is on the table. They'll be more inclined."

"You'll put the money on the table all right."

"But I've hidden it." Still held by the arm, Bushuyev looked back.

"Where?"

"Oh well, I give up. Come on, I'll show you."

"Lead the way."

Bushuyev led him in the direction of the river, away from the canteen and the bunkhouse, toward the dam.

"Remember, Sasha," he went on in the same conciliatory voice, "You asked me if I wanted to go home. I haven't been home for seventeen years, not since the beginning of the war. Well, the idea took hold: why not go back, take a wife with a house of her own? Any girl will take you if you have money. Why not live like everybody else? I'm sick of knocking around, I'm sick of drifting."

"You should have done some honest work and then gone home. We'd have given you a sendoff."

"And another thing, Sasha my friend, I'm sick of your forests. Living here isn't freedom. Damp, clouds, rapids—to hell with it. At home there are fields all around, big spaces, it's warm. I didn't want to fleece your boys, the fools asked for it. Nobody could resist it. I'm sick of looking at these banks and at the dimwits who live in this hole. . . ."

"All right, wise guy, that's enough talk. Where did you hide the money?"

"Wait a minute. We're in a hurry today, aren't we? I'm in no hurry.

"Don't rush me." Bushuyev tore his arm out of Dubinin's grasp and faced him, white shirt hanging outside his pants. With his rubber boots on, the lower part of him was big and clumsy, his shoulders narrow, his neck strung out.

Behind him the stones and stakes of the dam slid into the transparent moonlit shadow. The noise of the Big Head was close, you could feel its damp breath.

Bushuyev got a better grip on his ax.

"You wanted to talk with a lot of people around, but I'd rather do it like this. It's cozier. This is fine, nobody around." Bushuyev looked at the foreman mockingly.

"Where's the money, you son of a bitch?" Dubinin made a step toward him.

"Get back, you. Your boys won't see any money."

"Don't think you can frighten me with your ax."

"Now, now, mister foreman, don't get het up. Let's have a talk. You tell me where my card is and let me go without any noise, I'll be kind too; I won't touch you."

"Drop your ax!" Dubinin clenched his fists.

But Bushuyev raised the ax and hissed:

"Bare fists, eh? Want to die? I'll bash you in and throw you in the river. There's plenty of room. Give me back my card, you louse. It's not with your papers, you must have it on you. Give it back, you swine!" Dubinin leaped back, bent down, and tried to pick up a stone.

"So that's it, is it!" Bushuyev came on him. "Defend yourself with a feather, will you? I'm not frightened. Just you try something, you'll see!"

Dubinin had completely forgotten the sheath knife in his belt. He pulled it out. But a knife is no more help than fists against a man with an ax. With the knife in his hand,

Dubinin backed toward the river, anxious lest he stumble on the rocks and fall down.

His foot slipped on the slimy pebbles. The river was at his back; there was nowhere to retreat.

"You've had it now! Give me the card or else . . ."

Dubinin threw himself forward. He just had time to swerve and cover his head with his hands. The ax blade must have been blunt; it caught his sleeve and slit it from wrist to elbow. Dubinin's hand fell useless to his side.

Bushuyev's face, contorted into a wild-eyed grin, was close upon him. Once again the ax swung up. Dubinin threw himself underneath it. If he could get in close enough the ax would not be dangerous. He tried to clasp Bushuyev's body to him but his shattered arm would not obey. Bushuyev twisted sideways, still holding the ax above Dubinin's head.

Without another thought, frightened only of the raised ax coming down, Dubinin struck Bushuyev with his knife. He struck him in the chest again and again.

The ax fell with a dull ring on the stones. Bushuyev stiffened, stretched out his neck, and fell soundlessly back.

Apart from the roar of the rapids there was not a sound. The crushing boulders reared above. Bushuyev lay, his legs stretched out, his white shirt flapping around him, the blunt toes of his rubber boots sticking up. The water rumbled on.

Dubinin looked at his knife. Dark stains showed on the blade which shone in the moonlight. He threw it down. He stumbled toward Bushuyev, bent over him, and suddenly jerked back. Bushuyev's eyes were open, his neck throbbed, a black stream of blood flowed from his mouth, his breath came in jerks. Dubinin bent down again and tried to raise his head but his fingers felt something sticky on the back of the head. Bushuyev's fall had only seemed soft and noiseless. In fact his skull had been broken against the stones. A dark, oily stain was spreading on his shirt. Dubinin straightened himself up.

He went back home. The tops of his rubber boots scraped

against each other. Still the sound of water, the sand squelching under his feet, the rubber boots scraping at each step, the moon looking down . . .

Back in his office Dubinin picked up the telephone. The line that only a little time ago had seethed with conversations was now frighteningly still. His left hand was helpless. He had to tuck the receiver under his chin in order to turn the handle with his right hand.

A man called Osipov, whom he did not know, was on duty at the regional militia post.

"Dubinin of the Fifth River District speaking . . . D-U-B-I-N-I-N. I've just killed a man . . . Yes, me . . . There's nothing to tell, you'll see for yourselves . . . Send the boat for you tomorrow morning? All right. . . .

He hung up, sat down on his chair, and gingerly put his wounded arm on his lap.

Around eleven the next day, Tikhon, the mechanic, fetched three persons by boat: the Prosecutor, a woman doctor, and the district militia officer.

All the inhabitants of the small settlement stood waiting for them in a silent crowd; they followed them to the dam where Bushuyev's body still lay on the stones beside the water.

The doctor, middle-aged and with a faded, homely face, cut Bushuyev's shirt from hem to collar, examined his wounds, carefully feeling his chest with her fingertips, lifted his head and looked at the broken skull. The Prosecutor picked up the knife and frowned at it, and asked the militia man to take charge of the ax.

Back in the office, the doctor undid her coat, pushed her shawl back from her hair onto her shoulders, sat down at Dubinin's desk, and busied herself with her forms. Peace radiated from her industrious figure, filling the room which was half office, half bachelor dwelling. Looking at her, Dubinin felt as though what had happened was not so frightening after all.

The Prosecutor was young. His large gristly ears propped up his cap and underneath it his face was round and full-cheeked with a heart-shaped mouth. His manner with Dubinin was coldly polite.

"You knew about the winnings of the deceased?"

"Yes."

"And had you no idea where the deceased kept the money?"

"If I had I wouldn't have gone with him to look for it."

As Dubinin answered he guessed what was in the Prosecutor's mind and was appalled: he suspected him of having killed Bushuyev for his money. He all but lost his temper and shouted: "Who do you think you are, you snot-nosed runt?" Then he realized that when he was the Prosecutor's age he had had no more intelligence or charity. The Prosecutor had been sent to fetch a criminal. And since Dubinin was the criminal, the Prosecutor, even as he got into the boat, had made up his mind. No shouting, no argument would dissuade him; there was nothing to do but to endure.

Dubinin answered briefly and obediently.

"We'll question the others and we'll look for the money," declared the Prosecutor. "If we don't find it, I'm sorry to say that I'll be obliged to arrest you. Please sit on the porch and don't go away without my permission."

Dubinin went out.

Bushuyev was brought to the door of the office. He lay beside the porch, his chin pointing at the sky, his blood-stained shirt cut open exposing his flat chest with its inscription: "The years go by but bring no luck."

The conversation with Bushuyev, the money, then, in the early morning, shouting and murder—all this had completely dazed Leshka. He felt like sobbing, like tearing his hair, like crying for his mother. He could understand nothing. Everything was dark.

All night the money lay under his pillow. That terrible

money! He longed to shout: "Here it is, take the damn stuff
away from me!"

But what would they do? . . . Petukhov would go after
him: "There I was looking for it, and you lay nearby and
said nothing!" And what a strange and changed face Petukhov had. . . . And not only Petukhov—they would all
go after him, they would say he had conspired with the
thief, that he had sold out his friends for money.

And Sasha? A murderer! He did not dare say the word
aloud, he hardly dared think it—it made his blood run cold.
What was it like for him? And it was all his fault. He had
pulled Bushuyev from the rapids (if only he had known!)
he hadn't had the nerve last night to run to Sasha and tell
him all about it. . . . Now there was the money . . . If
Sasha got to know of it . . .

Sasha would turn his back on him, they would all turn
their backs on him, they would drive him out of the district,
the village would hear that he was a thief. Bushuyev's
threats were nothing to that. It was all frightening, and con-
fusing. What was he to do?

Straightening out his bunk, Leshka got the money from
under the pillow. No one noticed. The money was tied up in
a dirty handkerchief. Leshka started to stuff it into his
pockets, but the pockets bulged and he felt still more frightened—anyone could see it now. Leshka went to the wooden
outhouse and undid the bundle. He divided the money into
two bundles and stuffed them into his rubber boots.

Together with the others he met the Prosecutor, together with the others he went to the scene of the murder;
he stood beside the office porch and not for a single moment
did he stop wondering what he was to do. Should he hide the
money among the stones and later on pretend that he had
found it? Or still better, fix it so that someone else would
find it, say Petukhov? But the very thought that he would
have to hide it like a thief made him shake with fever. He
felt like throwing it into the river and forgetting all about it.
The men gathered in the hut, and for the first time the

words were spoken: "They suspect Sasha." Leshka felt faint.
He sat hiding his face, trying not to look at the boots where
the money was hidden. Somehow he had never thought that
Sasha could be accused. He was blaming himself enough as
it was, and now there was this idea that Sasha had committed murder for the money. What was all this? He must
tell everything, he must produce the money, he must save
Sasha. . . .

The militia man came in. He asked the men not to dis-
perse; The first man he summoned to the office to be ques-
tioned by the Prosecutor was Shamayev.

"The courts are just, they are sure to understand. I'll ask
them not to tell. The money has been found, that's all there
is to it. No one is to blame except Bushuyev. Why should
anybody care where it was found?"

He was summoned immediately after Petukhov and this
alarmed him. Petukhov did not trust him; he could have said
anything to the Prosecutor. The Prosecutor would get sus-
picious, and when he saw the money . . . Just try and get
out of that one!

"I'll tell anyway, I don't care" Leshka told himself, step-
ping carefully, his boots stuffed with thousand-ruble notes.

Near the porch lay the body of Bushuyev in its blood-
stained shirt. Dubinin sat on the doorstep and next to him,
leaning against the doorpost, was the militia man.

Dubinin sat erect, looking sideways at the clamoring waters of the Big Head and holding his wounded arm. To
Leshka at this moment he appeared small and lonely. Sasha
was no longer the foreman, he was as helpless as himself.

It was the stranger who was now the master of the district,
the man with the shiny peak to his cap, with bright buttons
on his chest and, underneath the cap, eyes which looked
calm and cold.

His first words to Leshka were frightening: that he must
speak nothing but the truth; if not he, would be held responsible under the criminal code. There was something about
statutes. What code? What statutes? Leshka did not know

but he imagined something terrible. All he wanted was to be understood, to be pitied, and to be forgiven.

The eyes looked steadily from under the shining peak. He'd never believe it. He would say that he was in with Bushuyev. And what about Sasha? Suppose even he didn't believe? How could Leshka prove he was telling the truth? Bushuyev was the only one who had known the truth. For the first time he was sorry that Bushuyev was dead, that he was gone and even the man with the shining peak couldn't make him talk, couldn't make him tell the truth.

The Prosecutor wouldn't believe . . . Sasha wouldn't believe . . . The boys wouldn't believe . . . When he was asked if he knew where Bushuyev could have hidden the money, he answered:

"I don't know."

Once again he walked past Dubinin, past the militia officer, and past Bushuyev's chin pointing at the sky. He passed them with his head bowed. He stepped as cautiously as before, conscious at every moment of the money which lay inside his boots, and turned not toward the dining room but to the river. He walked on, afraid to look back, expecting someone to shout! "Hey you! Where are you off to?" But no one called.

One after the other Dubinin's friends walked past—those he had lived with, those he had lived for. They threw him a pitying, puzzled glance and hastily looked away. One after the other—into the office and out.

At his back stood the silent militia officer; on the ground the man he had killed with his own hands.

He wasn't guilty. He couldn't have done anything else. And when he turned and looked at the logs diving over the Big Head, at the rearing wooded bank, at the low, peaceful clouds, he believed that he wasn't guilty. But he forced himself to look down at the waxen chest, the sagging head, the bloodstained, tattered shirt, the stiffened yellow hand on the trodden grass.

Yes, he had done it in self-defense, he had done nothing

but use his knife against a man armed with an ax, and if he hadn't killed him, he would be lying by the porch himself. But all the same there was the head, the rusty bloodstains on the shirt, the clenched hand—there was no forgiveness for inflicting death. . . . Tikhon, the mechanic, who usually cursed his fate before every journey, now only fussed and sighed: "Oh Lord, Lord."

The engine wouldn't start.

"Oh, Lord, Lord."

Finally the engine spluttered. The Prosecutor, the doctor, and the militia man climbed into the boat.

The men stood on the shore in a silent crowd. Dubinin nodded to them:

"Don't worry, boys. It'll work out."

"Sasha," Shamayev stepped forward, "I want to tell you . . . Hold it, Tikhon, don't push off . . . If we have to turn the earth upside down, we'll prove that you're innocent."

"It'll be all right."

Leaving a puff of a bluish smoke drifting above the water, the boat turned into mid-stream and began to dance on the Big Head, now crouching in a trough, now pointing up its bow; it passed the Small Head and vanished. No one said a word.

Silently, looking down at their feet, they went to the hut; silently they dispersed to their bunks.

Only Petukhov was missing. He roamed the riverbank, in the dusk, turning up the stones, peering under the bushes, still hoping to find the money.

Shamayev was the first to speak.

"So we gambled away a man. And what a man. Old Sasha!"

"All right, don't rub it in. We feel bad enough already."

"Come on, boys, better think about how we can get him out of this mess."

"The lousy part of it is the money. If we could find that, he'd be cleared right away."

"Suppose we raise the money and say we found it."

"We could. It wasn't marked."

"That's not very smart. They'd be sure to catch on. We'd only make things worse."

"You're all being too clever. The money didn't fly away with Bushuyev's soul. It's here somewhere. We'll turn every stone in the district, every log and every splinter in the hut —we're sure to find it."

There was a sound of subdued sobbing. They all raised their heads. It was Leshka, sobbing into his pillow.

The Big Head roared outside. Leshka sobbed openly, without embarrassment. The rest were silent; they looked at each other. Only Stupnin said, uncomfortably:

"Well, that's a business."

The publication, in the winter of 1960, of the first installment of Ehrenburg's memoirs in Novy Mir was the political and literary sensation of Moscow. Ehrenburg's tortuous intellectual career has earned him the reputation of an arch-double-dealer, denouncer, and cynical opportunist. Now he is concerned with showing that this is perhaps an oversimplification. Throughout his memoirs he reasserts in emphatic form the patently "revisionist" ideas on literature and art for which he has fought since Stalin's death.

This excerpt has been taken from a section of the memoirs in which Ehrenburg reminisces about various artistic figures in the twenties. In some ways it is the most extraordinary document to appear in the Soviet press since Stalin's death. It throws open the whole question of the true nature of Mayakovsky who, after Stalin's canonization of him in 1935, was obligatorily regarded in the works of critics and in textbooks as a "reinforced-concrete" proletarian poet. Ehrenburg shows—as is obvious from Mayakovsky's lyrical work—that far from being made of concrete, he was a vulnerable, sensitive, neurotic, and in many ways helpless person for whom the Revolution proved only a tragically short-lived solution to his inner anguish.

For young Soviet intellectuals who have been reared on the myth of Mayakovsky, as on many other myths about the avant-garde of the twenties, this comes as a revelation. Until now the only real Mayakovsky was to be seen in the heroic bronze statue on Mayakovsky Square, from which Ehrenburg, as he tells us, always averts his gaze.

Ehrenburg has also given the young Soviet intellectuals a completely new idea of those avant-garde painters, like Malevich and Tatlin, who were associated with Mayakovsky, and who have long been forbidden in the Soviet Union. For Stalin's inscrutable political reasons, these painters were not permitted to enter into Soviet mythology, but became "un-persons," cast out of Russian cultural history in the thirties, in order to make way for the socialist realist painters of the type of Gerasimov. Now young people are being told that these painters were an essential "link" in Russian artistic tradition. Ehrenburg's rehabilitation of them is admittedly cautious; he seeks to show that

*even at the time he had doubts about their extreme modernism.
He therefore dwells on their avid political support of the
Revolution—support much in contrast with the academic artists
of the time, many of whom emigrated, but who, by a supreme
irony, were to be restored to favor by Stalin.*

*One interesting aspect of Ehrenburg's rehabilitation of early
Soviet art may escape the Western reader. There is an increasing
realization, even in the most conservative Soviet official circles,
that a great modern state which wishes to compete with its rivals
for world power cannot impress its image on those it seeks to
influence without to some extent adopting those achievements
of modern art which are taken for granted in the West. The design of a Soviet book cover, of a woman's scarf, or even of a
humble matchbox may mean much in terms of the Soviet image
abroad. As Ehrenburg suggests in his memoirs, the adoption of
the principles of modern design depends upon some recognition
of the avant-garde of the twenties. Parts 1 and 2 of the Ehrenburg memoirs are being published in the United States by Alfred
A. Knopf in 19   . Translation by John Richardson.*

ILYA EHRENBURG

People, Years, and Life

I do not remember who introduced me to Mayakovsky. The
first time we met we sat in some café or other and talked
about the cinema, then he took me home—a small room at
the San Remo rooming house in Saltykov street, near the Pet-
rovka. Not long before I had read his "As Simple as Mooing."
I had imagined him exactly as he was—a big man with a
heavy jaw and eyes which were alternately sad and hard.
Loud-mouthed, gauche, and always spoiling for a fight, he
was a cross between an athlete and a dreamer, a medieval

mountebank who prays on his head, and an implacable iconoclast.

On our way to his room, he mumbled the epitaph written
by François Villon while awaiting the gallows: "I'm François, though not glad of it, / A doomed rogue this confesses,
/ Whose neck will surely know quite soon, / The weight his
ass possesses."[1]

No sooner had we arrived than he said: "I will now read
you . . ." I sat on a chair while he stood. He read me his long
poem "Man," which he had finished not long before. The
room was small and there was no one else but me, but he
read as though declaiming to a crowd in Theater Square. I
looked at the awful wallpaper and smiled. Boot-tops were
indeed becoming harps.

Mayakovsky amazed me. He somehow combined poetry
with revolution, and turbulent streets of Moscow with that
modern art which the habitués of the Rotonde dreamed of. I
even felt that he could help me find the right path. It turned
out differently: Mayakovsky was for me a tremendous event
in poetry and in the life of our century, but he had absolutely
no direct effect upon me, remaining close and yet infinitely
distant at the same time.

This may be the mark of genius, or it may have been simply Mayakovsky's character. He used to say that poets ought
to be "different," and was himself the sponsor of LEF, New
LEF, and REF;[2] he wanted to enlist the support of many people and bring them together, but the only people around him
were his followers, and sometimes his epigones. He told me
how he used to talk to the sun at his country house near Mos-

---

[1] This Russian jingle is a deformation of Villon's: "Je suis François, dont
ce me poise, / Né de Paris emprès Pontoise, / Et d'une corde d'une toise,
/ Sçaura mon col que mon cul poise."
[2] Mayakovsky's "ultra-revolutionary" literary organizations which fought
for the introduction of Mayakovsky's style, derived from futurism, as the one
style adequate for the epoch of technology. New LEF (Left Front) and
REF (Revolutionary Front) made some concessions to increasing conformism
demanded by RAPP. In 1929, Mayakovsky left REF and announced his ad-
herence to RAPP.

cow,[3] but he was himself a sun, around which his satellites orbited.

I met him in Moscow in 1918 and 1920, in Berlin in 1922, in Paris, and again in Moscow, and then again in Paris (the last time we saw each other was in the spring of 1929, a year before his death). Sometimes our encounters were fleeting, and sometimes long and significant. I would like to say something of what I think of Mayakovsky; I know that this will be one-sided and subjective, but can the testimony of a contemporary be otherwise? It is easy to recreate an image of a man from a great number of different and sometimes contradictory accounts. The trouble is that Mayakovsky, though a passionate destroyer of various myths, himself became a mythical hero with extraordinary rapidity. It is as though he were fated to become something different from what he was. There are eye-witnesses who have recorded some of his savage jokes. There are the school textbooks. And last but not least there is his statue. There is the teenager who learns bits from "Good!" by rote and there is the housewife in the streetcar who asks anxiously: "Are you getting off at Mayakovsky?" How difficult it is to speak about people. . . .

Until the mid-thirties, Mayakovsky was the subject of passionate argument. Whenever his name was mentioned at the First Congress of Soviet Writers,[4] some applauded wildly while others were silent. At the time I wrote in *Izvestia:* "We did not applaud because somebody[5] wanted to canonize Mayakovsky—we applauded because for us Mayakovsky's name stood for the rejection of all literary canons." I could never have imagined that a year later Mayakovsky would actually be canonized. I did not go to his funeral. Friends tell me that the coffin was too short. It seems to me that in fact it was Mayakovsky's posthumous glory which was not only too short, but more important, too constricting.

---

[3] The subject of a famous Mayakovsky poem, "An Extraordinary Adventure."
[4] 1934.
[5] That "somebody" was to be Stalin, who proclaimed in 1935 that "Mayakovsky was and remains the best and most talented poet of our Soviet epoch. Indifference to his memory and to his work is a crime."

I want first of all to talk about the man. He was by no means a "monolith"; he was huge and complicated, with tremendous willpower, and a bundle of sometimes contradictory sensations.

Anna Segers[6] called her novel *The Dead Are Always Young.* First impressions are almost always eclipsed by later ones. In this book I have tried to talk about the young Alexei Tolstoy, who was one of the first writers I ever met. But often when thinking of him I see a corpulent man, with his fame, with his loud laughter and tired eyes—just as he was in the last years of his life. Then I look at a photograph— standing next to Mayakovsky is Alexander Fadeyev, young and dreamy, with tender eyes. I find it very difficult to remember Fadeyev in this way. Now I see those cold eyes, full of self[7] will. . . . But Mayakovsky remains young in my memory.

To the end of his life he retained certain traits, or rather certain habits from his early youth. The critics do not like to dwell too long on Mayakovsky's so-called "futurist" period, although his later epic verse cannot be understood outside the context of his early poems. But I am not now talking about poetry, but about the man. Mayakovsky, of course, soon gave up not only the yellow smock[8] but also the slogans of the early futurist manifestoes. But he retained the spirit which motivated the "A Slap in the Face of Public Taste" in the way he behaved, in his jokes and in his replies to questions at his public readings of his verse.

I remember the Poets' Café in the winter of 1917-1918. It was on Nastasinsky Street. It was a very strange place. The walls were covered with weird paintings and just as weird inscriptions. "I like to watch children dying" was a line from an early, pre-Revolutionary poem by Mayakovsky which

[6] A leading and notoriously conformist East German writer.
[7] Fadeyev, who committed suicide in 1956, was Secretary of the Union of Soviet Writers during the worst postwar years before Stalin's death, and as such was responsible for the most savage of the literary purges following Zhdanov's denunciations in 1946.
[8] His costume as a futurist.

graced the wall to startle newcomers. The Poets' Café was
not a bit like the Rotonde; here no one talked about art,
argued, or beat his breast; there were only actors and spec-
tators. The visitors to the cafe were, as they said in those
days, "unslaughtered bourgeois," black marketeers, writers,
"respectable citizens" out for a good time. Mayakovsky was
hardly their idea of a good time. Although they couldn't make
out much of his poems, they sensed there was a close connection between his strange words and the sailors[9] walking
along Tverskaya Boulevard. But they all understood Mayakovsky's jingle about the bourgeois who gorges himself on
pineapple just before the end.[10] There were no pineapples
on Nastasinsky Street, and even humble pork stuck in their
throats. What amused the visitors was something else. For instance, David Burlyuk,[11] smothered in powder and with
lorgnette in hand, would go up onto the stage and read his
verse "I like pregnant men . . ." Goltschmidt also created a stir in the audience; on the posters he was billed as
the "real-life futurist" but he wrote no verse. Instead he
gilded two curls on his head with a special powder, had
extraordinary strength, broke wooden beams in two with his
bare hands, and bounced trouble-makers out of the café.
Once the "real-life futurist" decided to erect a monument to
himself on Theater Square; it was of plaster, not very big and
by no means futuristic—it was a statue of Goltschmidt in the
nude. The passers-by were indignant, but did not dare tamper
with the mysterious monument. But later it was smashed to
pieces anyway.

These are all things of the past. Two years ago two American tourists—David Burlyuk and his wife—came to Moscow. In America, Burlyuk draws, makes a fairly good living,
and has gone respectable; the lorgnette and the "pregnant

---

[9] The most revolutionary element at this period, and the terror of the bourgeoisie.
[10] "Eat pineapple, eat grouse, the end has come, you bourgeois louse!"
[11] The futurist painter who "discovered" Mayakovsky. He later emigrated
and now lives on Long Island.

men" are no more. To me futurism now seems far more ancient than ancient Greece. But for Mayakovsky, who died
young, it was, if not a living thing, still close to his heart.

I went to the Poets' Café rather often and once I even performed and was paid by Goltschmidt.

I remember an evening when Anatole Lunacharsky[12] came
to the café. He sat down modestly at a rear table and listened. Mayakovsky asked him if he would like to speak. He
refused. Mayakovsky insisted: "Repeat what you told me
about my poetry." Lunacharsky had to speak. He talked about
Mayakovsky's talent, but criticized futurism and spoke in
passing of the futility of self-advertisement. Then Mayakovsky said they would soon put up a monument to him at the
very spot where the Poets' Café then stood. He was only a
few hundred meters off—the monument was erected not far
from Nastasinsky Street.

Was this conceit or arrogance? The question has often been
put by Mayakovsky's contemporaries. Take, for example, the
way he celebrated the twelfth anniversary of his career as a
poet. He often called himself the greatest of poets. He demanded recognition during his lifetime—this was very much
in the spirit of the times, and part of that debunking of
"idols" complained of by Balmont[13] which was aimed at
drawing attention to art at all costs.

"I like to watch children dying . . ." Mayakovsky could
not even stand the sight of a horse being maltreated. A friend
of mine in the café once cut his finger on a knife and Mayakovsky hurriedly turned away. Arrogant? Yes, of course, he
was quick to answer his critics and to insult his literary
enemies. I remember the following exchange: Member of the
audience: "Your poetry is not fiery, stirring, or catching."
Answer: "I am neither a stove, a spoon, nor a disease."
Autographing books he always inscribed "For internal use
only." All this is well known. Other things are less well
known.

---

12 Then Minister of Education.
13 The Decadent poet Konstantin Balmont.

I remember Mayakovsky reciting one evening in the Café Voltaire in Paris. Lydia Seifullina[14] was there. It was the spring of 1927. Someone called out "Read us some of your old poems!" Mayakovsky, as usual, got out of it with a joke. When the evening was over, I went to an all-night café near the Boulevard Saint Michel with Mayakovsky, Seifullina, Elsa Triolet[15] and others. There was music and someone danced. Mayakovsky joked, mimicked the poet Gregory Ivanov[16] who had been at his reading, and then fell silent for a long time, looking around gloomily like a lion in a cage. We agreed that I would go see him the next morning, as early as possible. In his tiny room at the Hotel Istria, where he always stayed, the bed had not been slept in. He was in a bad mood and immediately, without greeting me, asked: "Do you think my early verse was better?" [17] He had no self-confidence: it was his studied pose that misled people.

I think that the pose was more a matter of calculation than of temperament. He was given to romanticism, but he was ashamed of it and held himself in check. "Who has not been a philosopher at the sight of the sea?" (he once said, pondering in a bitter mood about his life), and then immediately he added ironically, "it's just water." In his article "How to Make Verse" everything seems logical and simple. In actual fact Mayakovsky knew well the stresses and strains which creative effort inevitably involved. Here he talks in detail about how he "stored up" rhymes for future use, but he "stored up" other things—inner agonies—which he did not like to talk about. Just before his death he wrote in a poem that "love's boat has smashed against the daily grind." This phrase was a concession to the romanticism which he had so often ridiculed; in actual fact his life was smashed against

---

[14] A naturalistic Soviet novelist.

[15] Russian-born French communist writer who is the wife of Louis Aragon and the sister of Lily Brík, Mayakovsky's mistress in Russia.

[16] *Émigré* Acmeist poet.

[17] Mayakovsky's early verse was almost entirely concerned with his personal torments. After the Revolution his work became increasingly political in content.

poetry. Addressing posterity, he said things he did not want to say to his contemporaries: "But I subdued myself, setting my heel on the throat of my own song."

On the surface he was all strength, health, and *joie de vivre*. But at times he was intolerably depressed; he was a terrible hypochondriac and always carried a cake of soap in his pocket, and whenever he shook hands with someone who was physically repulsive to him, he immediately went away and carefully washed his hands. In Paris cafés he drank hot coffee through the straws supplied for cold drinks, so as not to touch the cup with his lips. He made fun of superstition, but he was always consulting signs and omens. He loved gambling, flipping coins, and double or quits. In Paris cafés there were automatic roulette wheels; you could put five sous on red, green, or yellow; if you won, you received a metal token with which you got a cup of coffee or a glass of beer. Mayakovsky would stand for hours at these roulette wheels. When he left Paris he gave Elsa Triolet hundreds of tokens. He had no use for them, he had only wanted to guess which color would turn up. He put only one bullet in the cylinder of the revolver—again a game of double or quits. . . .[18]

Whenever Mayakovsky talked to women, his voice changed: usually harsh and incisive, it became soft. I read in a book by Victor Shklovsky, "Mayakovsky went abroad. He met a woman and there may have been a love affair. I am told that they were so like each other and got along so well that the people in the cafés smiled appreciatively when they saw them."[19] Mayakovsky's poem to Tatiana Yakovleva, the one mentioned by Shklovsky, has recently been published. And I have kept the manuscript of *The Bedbug* he gave to "Tata" (Tatiana Yakovleva), which she had

---

[18] The method Mayakovsky chose to commit suicide in 1930—Russian roulette—has until now never been hinted at in a Soviet publication.

[19] While in Paris in 1928 Mayakovsky fell desperately in love with a young White Russian *émigrée*, Tatiana Yakovleva. When he wished to return to France to visit her the following year, he was refused a visa by the authorities.

thrown away. No, she was not like Mayakovsky, although, like him, she was tall and good-looking. I do not want to indulge in what Mayakovsky rightly called "gossip," and have only mentioned this episode (by no means the most significant one in the poet's life) to show how little he resembled the bronze statue erected to him of the heroic St. Vladimir of popular legend.

When Mayakovsky was eighteen years old, he entered an art school—he wanted to become a painter. In his poetry his perception of the world is that of a painter; his images are visual, and not derived from his fantasy. He liked painting and had a feeling for it, and he also liked the company of artists. He didn't hear the world, he saw it (he used to say jokingly that an elephant had stepped on his ear).

I have mentioned elsewhere an evening at the Tsetlin's when Mayakovsky read "Man." Vyacheslav Ivanov[20] nodded his head approvingly from time to time. Balmont was clearly bored. Baltrushaitis[21] was as usual inscrutable. Marina Tsvetayeva[22] smiled, while Pasternak kept glancing lovingly at Mayakovsky. Andrei Bely listened ecstatically, and when Mayakovsky had finished reading, jumped up in such excitement he could hardly speak. Nearly everybody shared his enthusiasm. But Mayakovsky was annoyed by someone's cold, polite remark. This is how he always was—he seemed never to notice his laurels, but always to be seeking the thorns. In his verse he wages a constant battle with the enemies, real and imagined, of the new poetry. What was the real meaning of his taunts? Was he perhaps arguing with himself?

I have read some articles on Mayakovsky written abroad, whose authors try to prove that the poet was destroyed by the Revolution. It is difficult to imagine anything more ab-

---

[20] Symbolist poet who emigrated to Italy in 1924.
[21] Yurgis Baltrushaitis, a Lithuanian poet who also wrote in Russian.
[22] The poetess who became an *émigrée* in the early 'twenties. She committed suicide after her return to Russia in 1939.

surd. Without the Revolution there would have been no
Mayakovsky. In 1918 he rightly called me a "frightened intellectual"; it took me two years to understand what it
was all about, but Mayakovsky understood and accepted
the Revolution at once. He was not only carried away—he
was completely absorbed by the building of a socialist society. He never made any concessions in anything and, when
certain people tried to bring him to heel, he snapped back:
" 'Turn your faces to the village.' That's the slogan they've
launched. To your lyres, my poet friends! But understand,
I've only one face—a face not a weathervane. You can't mix
ideas with water; water's for turkeys to wet their feet. A
poet without ideas has never even lived. What do you think
I am? A parrot, or a turkey?" He was never in conflict with
the Revolution; that's an invention of people who will stop
at nothing in their struggle against communism. Mayakovsky's trouble was not the clash between poetry and Revolution, but the attitude of his LEF to art: "Let the poets moan,
dribbling at the mouth, twisting their lips in contempt. I,
striking out my soul, shout about what's needed in the time
of socialism." At the time, one of the newspapers changed
the words: "I, without humbling my soul," instead of "I,
striking out my soul," but Mayakovsky restored the original
text, which gives us the clue to his poetic and human
achievement.

Mayakovsky liked Léger; they had something in common
in their understanding of the role of art in contemporary society. Léger was enthralled by machinery and urbanism. He
wanted art in his everyday life, and did not go to museums.
He painted good pictures which, in my view, are decorative
and do not in any way diminish our love of Van Gogh or
Picasso, but which undoubtedly reflect modern times. For a
number of years, Mayakovsky waged war against poetry not
only in manifestoes and articles; he also tried to destroy
verse with verse. The LEF magazine published a death sentence on art—on the "so-called poets," "so-called artists"
and "so-called directors." Instead of traditional art, painters

were advised to concern themselves with the aesthetics of
machinery, textiles, and pots and pans; directors were advised to organize folk festivals and demonstrations and say
good-by to the footlights, while poets were advised to leave
lyrics alone to write for newspapers, and compose texts for
posters and advertisements.

It wasn't so easy to give up poetry, even though Mayakovsky was a strong-willed man. But there were times when he
desisted from his own expressed policy. In 1923, when LEF
was still denouncing lyricism, Mayakovsky wrote his "About
This." [23] It was not understood even by the people close
to him, and was run down by both his allies and his enemies
in literature, but nevertheless it enriched Russian poetry.

As the years went by, he relented in his renunciation of
the art of the past. At the end of 1928, New LEF reported
that Mayakovsky had stated publicly, "I pardon Rem-
brandt." I will remind readers once again that he died
young. He lived, thought, felt, and wrote in his own way—
he was above all a poet. I remember the enthusiasm with
which he spoke of the new industrial beauty of America in
those distant years when the electrification of our country
was still only an idea, when on the dark, snowbound Theater Square lamps shone with the sign: "Children are the
flowers of life." I met him when he came back from America. Yes, Brooklyn Bridge is a great thing, of course, and
they've got so many machines over there. But how barbarous
and inhuman it is! He cursed and said how pleased he had
been to see the tiny gardens of Normandy. LEF's program
assumed rejection of Paris—where every house is a broken
fragment of the past—and glorification of the ultramodern
industrialized America. But Mayakovsky damned America,
and not ashamed of seeming sentimental, declared his love
for Paris. What is the reason for this contradiction? LEF
lasted only a few years, while Mayakovsky was a great poet.
In his programmatic verse he scoffed at the admirers of

---

[23] A long, lyrical poem, with suicidal overtones, in which Mayakovsky de-
spairs of the infidelity of his mistress.

Pushkin and people who visited the Louvre, but he was also enchanted by lines from Onegin and by old paintings.

He realized right away that the October Revolution had changed the course of history; yet he saw the details of the future schematically, like a poster rather than a painting. Nowadays we would hardly be attracted by the hygienic idyll of the last act of *The Bedbug*. To Mayakovsky the art of the past seemed not so much alien as doomed. His iconoclasm was like a taking of the vows—"a feat of self-denial." [24] He waged war not only against various critics and against the authors of sentimental ballads, but against himself as well. He wrote: "I want to be understood by my country, but if I am not—what then? I'll pass through my native land like a shower of slanting rain," and then crossed out these lines, thinking them too sentimental. But his native country did understand him, and also understood the beautiful verses he discarded.

I remember him in the autumn of 1928. At that time he stayed more than a month in Paris. We often met. I see him in a somber mood in a little bar called *La Coupole*. He ordered White Horse whisky, drinking little of it but writing a ditty which went, "White Horse whisky is a good old mare, with a white mane and white tail." Once he said to me: "Do you think I have an easy time of it? . . . I could write better verse than anybody." To the very end he was devoted to his concept of himself.

There has been much conjecture about why he committed suicide—some say it was difficulties over the exhibition,[25] others that it was the attacks of RAPP, and others that it was a love affair. I don't like this sort of guessing game: I can't view the life of a man I knew as I would the plot of a novel. . . . I will say only one thing: people often forget that a poet is an unusually sensitive person, otherwise he wouldn't be a poet. Mayakovsky called himself an "ox" and

---

[24] *podvig*.
[25] "Twenty Years of Work," an exhibition of Mayakovsky's writings and posters which took place a few months before his suicide.

spoke of his poems as "hippopotamuses," and at one gathering said he had had the hide of an elephant and that it was bulletproof. In actual fact he did not even have ordinary human skin.

According to Christian legend, the heathen Saul, once he had become the Apostle Paul, began to cast down the graven images of gods and goddesses. The images were perfection itself, but Paul succeeded in overcoming his sense of the beautiful. Mayakovsky cast down not only the beauty of the past, but himself as well; that is the greatness of his "feat of self-denial" and also the key to his tragedy.

In St. Petersburg there was a writer called Andrei Levinson, who was considered a connoisseur of choreography. In 1918 he published a lampoon of Mayakovsky in the magazine *Life of Art.* He was answered by many artists and also by Lunacharsky. Levinson emigrated to Paris. When he got the tragic news of Mayakovsky's death, he wrote a vile and slanderous notice in *Les Nouvelles Littéraires.* Together with several French writers I composed a letter to the editors of this literary newspaper in which we expressed our indignation. The letter was signed by all decent French writers of the most divergent views; I don't remember anybody refusing to sign. I took the letter to the editor, Maurice Martin du Gard (he was an insignificant figure, nothing like the great writer Roger Martin du Gard). The editor calmly read through this extremely sharp letter and then said: "I would like to ask you to make one small change." I answered that the text could not be modified. "I am not asking for that, but perhaps you could change the phrase "We are outraged that a literary journal" to "we are outraged that *the greatest* of literary journals." He didn't mind being slapped on the face, but he wanted us to make clear that it was a big face. This would have been a great theme for Mayakovsky. . . .

Mayakovsky's fortunes in the world at large have been extraordinary. Not long ago some writers from black Africa talked to me about him; he had even reached them there.

He orbits the world. His verse is of course difficult to translate and much of what he claimed to be the form of the
future is now the form of the past. But as man and poet he
is young as always. Neither Aragon, nor Pablo Neruda, nor
Eluard, nor Tuwim, nor Nezval has ever written an imita-
tion of Mayakovsky. But they all owe much to Mayakovsky—
he taught them not new verse forms but how to make a
courageous choice in life.[26]

We must be able to distinguish between the modern and
the fashionable, between the pioneering spirit and various
"novelties" which appear old-fashioned twenty-five years
later. . . . In 1940 nine-tenths of the budding poets broke
up their lines in Mayakovsky's manner, but they are now
imitating other examples; fashions change. Mayakovsky was
beaten about the head with volumes of Pushkin, Nekrasov,
and Blok. Should we now pummel the young with volumes of
Mayakovsky?

I have said that Mayakovsky could have helped me figure many things out. I remember a conversation we had one
night in February, or maybe March, 1918. We had left the
Poets' Café together. Mayakovsky was asking all about Paris,
Picasso, and Apollinaire. Then he said he liked my poem on
the execution of Pugachev. "You should be happy, but
you're whining. That's bad!" I readily agreed: "Of course
that's bad!" Politically he was right, as I soon realized, but
we always thought and felt differently. In 1922 he told me
he liked *Jurenito*.[27] "You understand many things better
than other people. . . ." I laughed: "Actually I don't think
I understand anything yet. . . ." We often met, yet never
came really close together.

I have often thought about Mayakovsky. Sometimes I
disagree with him, but I am always full of admiration for his

---

[26] I.e. the choice of becoming a communist, which was made by all the
poets mentioned, in various circumstances.
[27] *Julio Jurenito*, a picaresque novel by Ehrenburg published in 1922, whose
hero is modeled on Diego Rivera, and which pokes fun at all political
systems, including the new Soviet regime.

poetic achievements. I never look at his statue. It stands still, but Mayakovsky is on the move—through the newly built districts of Moscow, through old Paris, through the whole of our planet; he moves, not with his stocks of novel rhymes but with his new thoughts and feelings. . . .

Every morning the townsfolk carefully studied the still damp, crinkled decrees pasted on the walls to find out what was allowed and what was forbidden. Once I saw a crowd of people in front of a placard which bore the title "Decree No. 1 on the Democratization of the Arts." Somebody was reading out loud: "Art's permit to reside in those woodsheds and outhouses of human genius—palaces, galleries, salons, libraries, and theaters—is hereby annulled together with the Czarist regime." "Heavens, they're taking away our outhouses!" squealed a woman. The man in spectacles who had read the "decree" aloud explained to her: "It doesn't say anything about outhouses, but the libraries will be closed down and the theaters, of course. . . ." The poster had been composed by the futurists and bore the signatures: "Mayakovsky, Kamensky, and Burlyuk." These names meant nothing to the passers-by, but they all understood the magic word "decree."

I remember May Day, 1918. Moscow was decked out with futurist and suprematist paintings. Crazy squares wrestled with rhombuses, and faces with triangles instead of eyes spotted the peeling façades of colonnaded Empire mansions. (The art which is now called "abstract" and is much discussed both here and in the West, was at that time served up to Soviet citizens in unlimited quantities.) That year, May Day coincided with Good Friday. Worshippers thronged the street near the chapel of the Iberian Virgin. Trucks which had once belonged to the Stupin Company drove by draped with abstract canvasses. Actors on the trucks were performing various scenes such as "The Exploits of Stepan Khalturin" or the "Paris Commune." An old woman, looking at a cubist painting with an enor-

mous fish-eye, was wailing, "They want us to pray to the
devil. . . ."

I laughed, but my laughter was cheerless.

I have just reread an article I wrote in the summer of
1918 for the paper *Monday* entitled "Among the Cubists."
In it I talked about Picasso, Léger, and Rivera. I said that
the works of these artists could be regarded either as "lu-
natic decorations of a house about to collapse, or as the
foundation of a new structure, hitherto undreamed of even
in the dreams of artists."

It's no accident, of course, that Picasso, Léger, and Rivera
became communists. It was not the academically inclined
artists, but the futurists, cubists, and suprematists who
were on Red Square in 1918. What was it that disturbed me
about the triumph of these artists and poets, who reminded
me (though only outwardly) of the greatest friends of my
early youth?

Above all, it was their attitude to the art of the past.
Everyone knows that Mayakovsky developed and changed,
but remained at the same time a passionate iconoclast:
"You find a White Guardist, and put him against the wall.
But what about Raphael? What about Rastrelli?[28] It's high
time that bullets spatter the walls of museums. Shoot up
that old rubbish through the maws of 100-inch guns. Deaf
to White Guard blandishments, you've mounted your guns
at the edge of the forest. And why isn't Pushkin taken by
storm?" I could not understand this. Often, wondering along
the streets on Moscow, I have repeated Pushkin's verse to
myself and lovingly recalled the old Italian masters. When
first arriving in Moscow, almost the first thing I did was to
race to the Kremlin. I was staggered by fifteenth-century
painting; until then I had no idea of the Russian renaissance.

Arguments about the values of the past soon died down.

---

28 Count Bartolommeo Rastrelli, the Italian-born rococo architect who designed most of St. Petersburg's palaces and government buildings during the
reign of Elizabeth Petrovna.

Mayakovsky wrote a poem about Pushkin and materials on Mayakovsky have now been published in the Academy of Sciences "Literary Heritage" series.[29](I have already mentioned the magazine *The Thing*; among its staff members were many representatives of our "left-wing art"— Mayakovsky, Malevich, Meyerhold, Tatlin, and Rodchenko. In an article on the aims of the magazine I wrote: "It is now ridiculous and naïve 'to throw Pushkin overboard.' There is a continuity in form and classical examples have no terrors for the modern masters. We can learn from Pushkin and Poussin . . . *The Thing* does not deny the past in the past, but calls for the modern in the modern. . . .")

Mayakovsky is not a difficult poet: his poems were always met with roars of laughter. Before the Revolution people used to make fun of the pictures of the futurist (Malevich, Tatlin, Rodchenko, Puni, Udaltsova, Popova, and Altman). After October the epigones of classical poetry and art began to pack their bags. Both Bunin and Repin went abroad. The futurists, cubists, and suprematists stayed behind. Like their Western counterparts, and the prewar habitués of the Rotonde, they hated bourgeois society and saw the way out in revolution.

The futurists decided that people's tastes could be changed just as rapidly as the economic structure of society. The magazine *The Art of the Commune* wrote: "We definitely lay claim, and would probably not refuse if allowed, to use the power of the state to put our ideas of art into practice." This was of course more of a dream than a threat. The Moscow streets were decked with suprematists and cubists mainly because the academically minded artists were in the opposition (political not artistic). The results were nevertheless lamentable. The trouble was not the old woman who thought that a cubist painting was the devil, but the

---

[29] The volume on Mayakovsky, published in 1958, which contains, among other biographical materials, some of his love letters, was soon withdrawn from sale and its editors accused of "defamation."

artistic reaction which followed the brief appearance in the streets of "left-wing art."

Discoveries in the field of the exact sciences are provable, and whether or not Einstein is right can be decided by mathematicians and not by the millions of people who remember nothing but their multiplication tables. New art forms have always reached people's awareness slowly and by tortuous paths, being at first appreciated and accepted only by a few. In any case, it is not possible to prescribe, inculcate, or foist tastes on people. The gods of the ancient Greeks used nectar, which the poets called ambrosia; but if nectar had been forcibly passed through a tube into the stomachs of the Athenian citizens, they would have probably ended up vomiting all over the town.

Anyhow, all this is now ancient history (not only arguments on who is going to bedeck the squares of Moscow, but also on "left-wing art"). Once again I will break the rules which oblige a writer of memoirs to keep chronological order. I'm trying to understand what happened to me and many poets and artists of my generation. I don't know who entangled the threads—our opponents or we ourselves— but I will try to unravel them.

First of all, I would like to talk about myself. I was soon carried away by what was then called "constructivism" but I admit that the idea of "dissolving" art in life both inspired and repelled me. In 1921 I wrote a book called *E pur si Muove*, which was rebellious and naïve, and something like the proclamations of LEF (LEF pointed out that "the Ehrenburg group's conclusions coincide with ours to a great extent"). I was seeking to show that "the new art ceases to be art." At the same time I was laughing at my own ideas; in the same year, I wrote *Julio Jurenito*; my hero reduces propositions of *E pur si Muove* to absurdity. Jurenito says: "Art is a hotbed of anarchy, and artists are heretics, sectarians, and dangerous rebels. So art must be prohibited without hesitation in the same way that distilling hard liquor

and importing opium are prohibited. The cubist or suprematist pictures can be used for various purposes, such as proto-
types for kiosks on the main streets, designs on fabrics, and
models for new footwear, and so on. Poetry is changing to
the language of newspapers, cables, and business conversations. . . ." I was not double-crossing—double-crossing,
after all, always proceeds from either fear or deliberate
calculation. I simply didn't believe very much in the death
of art proclaimed by so many, including myself.

Futurism was born at the beginning of our century in provincial, technically backward Italy. There at every corner
you could see magnificent monuments of the past, while the
shops sold German knives, French saucepans, and English
cloth. Factory chimneys had not yet begun to elbow their
way into the polite society of ancient towers. (The north of
Italy can now compete with the most industrialized countries, but you won't find any more futurists in Italy who demand the burning of all museums, while the former futurists
Carra and Severini are inspired by Giotto's frescoes or the
Ravenna mosaics.) The enthusiasm of Mayakovsky, Tatlin,
and other representatives of Russian "left-wing art" for industrial aesthetics during the first years of the Revolution is
quite understandable; at that time not only lumps of sugar
but even matches were being sold singly on the Sukhar-
evka.[30] In *Mystery Bouffe* Mayakovsky dreamed of the future as follows: "The airy giants of transparent factories and
apartment houses will tower into the sky. Trains, streetcars
and automobiles stand woven in rainbows . . ." (When the
artist depicts nature or human emotions, his works do not
grow old. Nobody would say that a woman of the twentieth
century is more beautiful or more perfect than Nike of the
Acropolis, created twenty-five centuries before; nobody
laughs at Hamlet's anguish or Romeo's love for Juliet. But
the painter has only to take to machinery and his Utopias
are surpassed or refuted by time. Wells was an extremely

---

[30] Moscow's famous "flea market."

educated man, and he thought that he foresaw the future, but the discoveries of modern physics have made his Utopian novels ridiculous. How could Mayakovsky foresee that streetcars would soon share the fate of horse-drawn buses or that trains would become an archaic means of communication?)

Picasso's cubist paintings were not born of a longing for machinery, but of a painter's desire to free himself from superfluous details in his depiction of man, nature, and the world. Nowadays few people are interested in the books of Metzinger, Gleizes, or other theoreticians of cubism, but the canvases of Picasso, Braque, and Léger are alive; they delight us, upset us, and move us. Picasso considers himself the heir of Velasquez, Poussin, Delacroix, and Cézanne, and he never saw electric trains or jet aircraft as the legitimate heirs of art.

It stands to reason that art has always gradually become part of everyday life, changing buildings, clothing, vocabulary, gestures, and household utensils. Medieval poetry with its chivalrous cult of womanhood helped people to find forms for the expression of their feelings. The canvases of Watteau and Fragonard became part of life, altered the layout of parks, men's suits, and dances, and have had an effect on divans and snuffboxes. Cubism has helped modern city-dwellers to free themselves from over-ornamented houses; it has had an effect on furniture, even on cigarette packages. The utilitarian use of art or its decorative use cannot be the aim of the artist, but it is a natural by-product of his creative flights. The opposite process is evidence of creative sterility. An abstract ornament is quite in place on fabric or on pottery, but when it claims the title of a work of art in itself, this is not the resurgence of art but its decline.

I was recently at a retrospective exhibition of Malevich in Brussels. His early work ("Jack of Diamonds" period) is very good. In 1913 he painted a black square on a white background. This was the birth of abstract art, which forty years later cast a spell on thousands of Western painters. It seems to me to be ornamental first and foremost. Picasso's paintings represent a world with so many thoughts and feelings that they arouse either delight or genuine hatred; but the pictures of the abstract painters remain designs on fabric or wallpaper. A woman may put on a scarf with an abstract design, her scarf may be pretty or not, it may suit the woman or not, but it will never make anyone think about nature, man, or life.

The headlong development of technology demands from the painter a more profound understanding of man's inner world. This was quickly realized by those advocates of "left-wing art," who were the champions of industrial aesthetics. After seeing America, Mayakovsky stated that industry would have to be muzzled. He was thinking, of course, of the part played by the painter, but he was not denying the necessity for technical progress (at that time, in 1925, there was extremely little modern machinery in Moscow); Mayakovsky realized that unless a humanistic muzzle was placed over the face of industry, it would bite man. Meyerhold, having forgotten about biomechanics, was absorbed in *The Forest* [31] and *The Inspector General,* and had visions of producing *Hamlet.* Tatlin took to conventional painting, while Altman painted portraits; Puni became a small landscape painter. In the meantime the nectar and the stomach tube had passed into different hands which were much more suited to such operations.

Our museums have a splendid collection of "left-wing art" from the first years after the Revolution. It's a shame that these collections are not open to the public. You can't remove a link from a chain. I know some young Soviet painters who "discover America" in 1960 and do (or rather try to do) what Malevich, Tatlin, Popova, and Rozanova did in their time. If they could perhaps see the history of the development of these painters, they would not try to return to 1920, but would find something new in tune with our times. Our

---

[31] A classic nineteenth-century realist play by Alexander Ostrovsky.

young poets know Khlebnikov's verse and appreciate him still, but do not try to imitate him blindly. Why is Tatlin "more dangerous" than Khlebnikov? Maybe because the monopoly of one trend [32] has become particularly entrenched in the field of plastic art. . . .

Naturally, the representatives of our "left-wing art" during the first years of the Revolution were mistaken in many ways. The mistakes of artists, writers, and composers are discussed often and with avidity; this is hardly due to the fact that they alone make mistakes. . . . But now, looking back, I think with gratitude even of that canvas which scared the old woman near the Chapel of the Iberian Virgin. Much has been done, and a concentrate is always diluted. Noble traces of "left-wing art" can be seen in the works of a number of writers, painters, producers, film producers, and composers of the ensuing decades.

Throughout my life I have never been an ardent supporter of any one school of painting. I compared the young Maya-kovsky with St. Paul, who cast down the graven images of the false gods. Before he embraced the new faith, Paul was called Saul. In 1922, when I was defending constructiv-ism and editing the magazine *The Thing*, Victor Shklovsky called me Paul Saulovich[33] in his book *Zoo*—this was spiteful but just. Through the whole of my life I have kept my love for many works of art of the past—the novels of Stendhal, the stories of Chekhov, the verse of Tyutchev, Baudelaire, and Blok. It has not stopped my hating imitations or liking Picasso or Meyerhold. Paul must have a patronymic, and it's better to sculpt a new statue than to destroy, even for the highest reasons, a statue that has already been made. To the sculptor who chiseled the effigies of the Indian gods and goddesses in Ellora, Brahma, Vishnu, and Shiva were gods; to us they were images created by the genius of man whose passions are close to ours and whose harmonies are clear to us.

---

[32] I.e. socialist realism.
[33] A mock patronymic meaning "son of Saul."

Idols have outlived their time not only in religion but also in art. Iconoclasm has died together with the adoration of icons. But could the desire to say something new in a new way really disappear on that account? I recently read the words "modest innovation" in a periodical; at first they amused me, then they saddened me. An artist must be modest in behavior, but by no means moderate, tepid, or limited in his creative endeavors. Surely, it is more seemly to write squiggles in one's own way than to copy something of the past in neat handwriting. I feel that *kolkhozniks* depicted in the manner of the academic school of Bologna will give pleasure to few, and that it is not possible to convey the rhythm of the second half of the twentieth century with that plethora of relative clauses which Leo Tolstoy used so brilliantly.

Evtushenko was born in 1933 in Irkutsk province, where his Ukrainian peasant grandfather was exiled under the Czarist regime. He came to Moscow in 1948, and attended the Gorky Literary Institute. One of the most outspoken of the younger poets, he is idolized by the restive young intelligentsia, and has thus far resisted the temptation of being co-opted into the Soviet establishment.

Like many Soviet intellectuals, he is evidently troubled by the persistence of anti-Semitism in the USSR. Babi Yar, the ravine near Kiev where some 34,000 Jews were shot by the Nazis in 1941, is a symbol both of the wartime agony of Soviet Jews and of their present plight. Khrushchev, when he was First Secretary of the Ukrainian Communist Party after the war, publicly announced that a memorial would be erected at Babi Yar to the victims of the massacre, but the place remains to this day a desolate garbage dump. The publication of Evtushenko's poem in Literary Gazette on September 19, 1961, opened the first polemic on the inflammatory topic of Soviet anti-Semitism: the Nazi massacre of Jews is scarcely a more popular subject in the Soviet press than present-day anti-Semitism which has, up to now, not been acknowledged at all. Evtushenko was denounced for overconcern with Jews, for singling out Jews as particular victims of Nazi genocide policy, and for slandering the Soviet people. These attacks seem to have made Evtushenko more of a hero than ever among young people, who wildly and pointedly cheer him whenever he appears in public.

A line of "Babi Yar" was apparently excised before publication. In a public reading of the poem before its publication, it has been reported that Evtushenko included a line which stated that anti-Semitic sentiments among Russians "still arise on the vapors of alcohol and in conversations after drinking." Translation by Max Hayward.

EVGENI EVTUSHENKO

Babi Yar

There are no memorials at Babi Yar—
The steep slope is the only gravestone.
I am afraid.
Today I am as old as the Jewish people.
It seems to me now that I am a Jew.
Now I am wandering in Ancient Egypt.
And now, crucified on the cross, I die
And even now I bear the marks of the nails.
It seems to me that I am Dreyfus.
The worthy citizenry denounces me and judges me.
I am behind prison bars.
I am trapped, hunted, spat upon, reviled
And good ladies in dresses flounced with Brussels lace
Shrieking, poke umbrellas in my face.
It seems to me that I am a boy in Byelostok,
Blood flows and spreads across the floor.
Reeking of onion and vodka
The leading lights of the saloon
Are on the rampage.
Booted aside, I am helpless:
I plead with the pogrom thugs
To roars of "Beat the Yids, and save Russia,"
A shopkeeper is beating up my mother.
O my Russian people!
You are really international at heart.
But the unclean
Have often loudly taken in vain
Your most pure name.
I know how good is my native land

And how vile is that, without a quiver,
The anti-Semites styled themselves with pomp
"The union of the Russian people."
It seems to me that I am Anne Frank,
As frail as a twig in April.
And I am full of love
And I have no need of empty phrases.
I want us to look at each other,
How little we can see or smell,
Neither the leaves on the trees nor the sky.
But we can do a lot.
We can tenderly embrace in a dark room.
Someone is coming? Don't be afraid—
It is the noise of spring itself.
Come to me, give me your lips.
Someone is forcing the door.
No, it is the breaking up of the ice . . .
Wild grasses rustle over Babi Yar.
The trees look down sternly, like judges.
Everything here shrieks silently
And, taking off my cap,
I sense that I am turning gray.
And I myself am nothing but a silent shriek,
Over the thousands and thousands buried in this place.
I am every old man who was shot here.
I am every boy who was shot here.
No part of me will ever forget any of this.
Let the "Internationale" ring out
When the last anti-Semite on earth is buried.
There is no Jewish blood in mine,
But I am hated by every anti-Semite as a Jew,
And for this reason,
I am a true Russian.

Arzak is the pseudonym of a Soviet writer who, judging from his accomplished Russian style, is probably an experienced professional. This nightmarish satire on the Soviet regime's contempt for public opinion would seem much less far-fetched to a Soviet reader than to a Western one. The reactions of the various characters to a particularly outrageous announcement by the government is a by no means implausible study in the mentality of a people whose political reflexes have for so long been conditioned by terror.

Arzak is also the author of a gruesome short story, The Hands, which concerns a former Cheka member whose nerves are shattered in the early days of the Revolution during the execution of a priest. As a joke, his comrades load his gun with blanks and he is overcome with superstitious horror when the priest seems immune to his bullets. Like "This Is Moscow Speaking" it has thus far been published only in Polish translation by Kultura, Paris.

The poets to whom the various verse extracts in this story are ascribed appear to be fictitious. Translation by John Richardson.

NIKOLAI ARZAK

This Is Moscow Speaking

"Mew!" whimpers the little kitten.
"Mew!" it cannot yet meow properly.
Oppressed by boundless solitude,
It wanders dejectedly among the benches.

Reclining on the benches beside it
Are people, crude, all-powerful, and big,
The cars around growl like dogs,

It is afraid. What lies ahead?

Independence has suddenly befallen
Its pitiful, feline intellect.
"Mew!" whimpers the emancipated cat.
"Explain to me! Show mercy!"

No matter, it will be matured by
        wearisome wanderings.
It will be adorned with claws and fangs
Its yellow teeth will flash
Like the glass of broken vodka bottles
It will master "Meow." It will proclaim
        in a strong voice
That it will take on any thug;

But for the moment, its heart is in pieces,
For the moment, it's "Mew! Mew! Mew!"
            —Ilya Chur, "Moscow Boulevards"

1

When I now try to reconstruct in my mind the events of the
past year, I find it very difficult to put my memories in order
or to give a coherent and consistent account of everything I
saw, heard, and felt; but the day when *it* began I remember
very well, down to the minutest detail, down to the merest
trifle.

We were sitting in the garden at the *dacha*. We had all arrived the night before to celebrate Igor's birthday; we had
drunk a great deal, made a lot of noise into the early hours,
and finally gone to bed in complete certainty that we would
not wake up until midday; the suburban tranquility, however, woke us up at seven o'clock. We got up and all began
doing all sorts of absurd things; we ran about the lanes in
our shorts, did exercises on the beam (no one was able to
pull himself up more than five times), and Volodya Margulis even doused himself with water from the well, although

everyone knew that he never washed in the mornings, making the excuse that he would be late for work.

We sat around and argued vehemently on the best way to spend a Sunday. Swimming, volley-ball, and boating were naturally among the activities mentioned, and one misguided enthusiast even suggested a cross-country walk to the church in the next village.

"It's a very nice church," he said. "A very old one, I don't remember which century. . . ."

But everybody laughed at him—no one felt like walking four miles in the heat.

We probably looked rather strange—men and women in their thirties undressed as though for the beach. We tactfully tried not to notice all sorts of unexpected things about each other, both amusing and depressing: hollow chests and incipient potbellies in the case of the men, and hairy legs and no waists in the case of the women. We had all known each other for a long time, and were familiar with each other's suits, ties, and dresses, but no one had imagined how we would look without clothes, in a state of nature. Who would have thought, for instance, that Igor, who was always so elegant and dignified, and so successful with his female colleagues at the college, would turn out to be bandy-legged? Examining each other was as interesting, amusing, and shame-making as looking at dirty postcards.

We sat with our backsides glued to the chairs, which looked so absurd on the grass, and talked about our forthcoming athletic feats. Suddenly Lilya appeared on the terrace.

"Boys," she said, "I just don't understand it."

"And what exactly are you supposed to understand? Come and join us."

"I just don't understand it," she repeated, smiling sadly. "Over the radio . . . they broadcast it over the radio . . . I only heard the end . . . it will be broadcast again in ten minutes' time."

"The latest reduction—the twenty-first so far—in the

prices of horsecollars and harnesses," said Volodya, mimicking an announcer's voice. . . .

"Let's go inside," said Lilya.

We all trooped into the room where a square plastic loudspeaker was hanging modestly on a nail. In reply to our puzzled questions Lilya did nothing but sigh.

"Steamboatlike sighs," joked Volodya. "That's a good metaphor, isn't it? As good as something out of Ilf and Petrov."

"Lilya, stop pulling our legs," began Igor. "I realize you find it boring washing the dishes by yourself . . ."

At this moment the radio began speaking.

"This is Moscow speaking," it said. "We are now broadcasting a Decree of the Supreme Soviet of the Union of Soviet Socialist Republics, dated July 16, 1960. In view of the increased well-being . . ."

I looked around. Everybody was standing quietly listening to the reverberating baritone of the announcer; only Lilya bustled about like a photographer trying to take a picture of children, and made beckoning signs in the direction of the loudspeaker.

". . . in response to the wishes of the masses of working people . . ."

"Volodya, give me a match," said Zoya. They all hissed at her. She shrugged her shoulders and, dropping the unlit cigarette into the palm of her hand, turned away toward the window . . . .

". . . Sunday, August 10, 1960, is declared . . ."

"Here it comes!" cried Lilya.

". . . Public Murder Day. On that day all citizens of the Soviet Union who have attained the age of sixteen are given the right of free extermination of any other citizen with the exception of persons mentioned in the first paragraph of the annex to this Decree. The Decree comes into force on August 10, 1960, at six A.M. Moscow time, and expires at midnight. Paragraph one. Murder of the following categories is prohibited: (*a*) children under sixteen; (*b*) persons dressed in the uniform of the Armed Forces or the Militia, and (*c*) transport workers engaged in the execution of their duties. Paragraph two. Murders committed prior to or subsequent to the above-mentioned period and murders committed for purposes of gain or resulting from sexual assault will be regarded as a criminal offense and punished in accordance with the existing laws. Moscow. The Kremlin. Chairman of the Presidium of the Supreme . . ."

Then the radio said:

"We will now broadcast a concert of light music. . . ."

We stood and looked at one another in a daze.

"Extraordinary," I said, "most extraordinary. I can't see the point."

"They'll explain it," said Zoya. "The newspapers are bound to have an explanation."

"Comrades, it's a trick!" Igor was prancing around the room looking for his shirt. "It's a trick. It's the 'Voice of America' broadcasting on our wave length!"

He hopped up and down on one foot, drawing on his pants.

"Oh, sorry!" he ran out into the terrace and buttoned up his fly. No one was amused.

"The 'Voice of America'" said Volodya thoughtfully. "No, it's not possible. It's not technically possible. After all," and he looked at his watch, "it's half past nine. There are broadcasts going on. If they were operating on our wave length we'd hear both broadcasts. . . ."

We went outside again. Half-naked people began appearing on the terraces of neighboring *dachas*. They huddled together in groups, shrugging their shoulders and waving their arms in confusion.

Zoya lit her cigarette at last. She sat down on a step resting her elbows on her knees. I looked at her hips in the tight-fitting bathing suit, and at her breasts half revealed by the low-cut top. Despite her plumpness, she was very attractive. More so than any of the other women. As always, her expression was calm and rather sleepy. Behind her back they used to call her "Madame Phlegmatic."

Igor was fully dressed and, contrasted with the rest of us, looked like a missionary among Polynesians. Ever since Volodya had categorically asserted that the radio announcement could not have been a trick played by transatlantic gangsters, he had become subdued. He evidently regretted the fact that he had dismissed the broadcast so lightly, but in my opinion he had nothing to worry about. There were not supposed to be any informers among us.

"What are we getting excited about, anyway?" he said cheerfully. "Zoya is right. There'll be an explanation. Tolya, what do you think?"

"Damned if I know," I mumbled. "There's still almost a month left before this, what's it called, Public . . ."

I broke off. We stared at each other again in dismay.

"I know," said Igor with a shake of the head, "it's all connected with international politics."

"With the presidential elections in America, is that what you mean, Igor?"

"Lilya, you ought to have kept quiet about the whole thing, damn it!"

"Let's go for a swim," said Zoya, getting up. "Tolya, bring me my bathing cap."

It seemed that the confusion had shaken even her, or she wouldn't have called me "Tolya" in front of everyone. But apparently no one noticed.

As we were going toward the river, Volodya came up to me, took me by the arm, and said, looking at me sadly with his biblical eyes:

"You know, Tolya, I think they're plotting something against the Jews. . . ."

2

Who would be able, who could stand it,
If they hadn't arranged
For the sale of masks to wear at home
For every day, for every hour?

Disguise yourself as an elevator man or poet,
Enthusiast or dandy,
Knock at the window for a ticket.
Shout! but don't forget
"No admittance without masks."
                  —Ilya Chur, "Tickets Are Being Sold"

And so here I am writing all this down and wondering
exactly why I needed to make these notes. I shall never be
able to have them published here; there's no one to whom I
can even read them or show them. Should I send them
abroad? No: first, it's not possible in practice, and second,
what I intend to describe has already been reported in hundreds of newspapers abroad, and the radio has filled the air
with it for days and nights; no, they've already done it to
death abroad. Anyway, to tell the truth, to be printed abroad
in anti-Soviet publications is not so good.

I'm pretending. I know why I'm writing. I want to find
out for myself what happened. And, more important, what
happened to me. Here I am, sitting at my desk. I'm thirty-
five. I'm still working in this ridiculous technical publishing
house. My appearance has not changed. Nor my tastes. I
like poetry just as much as ever. I like to have a drink. I like
women, and on the whole they like me. I fought in the war;
I killed. I was nearly killed myself. Whenever women suddenly reach out to touch the scar on my hip, they draw
back their hands and say in a shocked whisper: "Good
heavens, what's that?" "It's a wound," I say, "from a dum-
dum bullet." "Poor boy," they say, "did it hurt very much?"
Generally speaking, everything is as before. Any one of my
acquaintances, friends, or colleagues might easily say: "Well,
Tolya, you haven't changed a bit!" But I know only too well
that Public Murder Day grabbed me by the scruff of my
neck and made me look into myself! I know that I had to get
to know myself all over again!

And there's another thing. I'm not a writer. In my youth
I wrote poetry, and I still do on special occasions; I've written
a few reviews of plays. I thought that I would gain a foothold

in the literary world that way; but nothing came of it. Nevertheless, I still write. No, I don't suffer from graphomania. Those who do (and in my profession I often come across them) are convinced of their own genius, but I know I have little or no talent. But I really want to write. After all, what is the great thing about the position I'm in? It's that I know in advance that no one will read me, and I can write without fear whatever comes into my head! If I want to write:

> And like black Africa the piano
> Bares its negroid teeth

I do. But no one will accuse me of expressing pretentious or colonialist ideas. If I want to write and say that in the government they're all rabble-rousers, phonies, and mostly, sons of bitches, I do so . . . I can afford the luxury of being a communist when alone with myself.

If I'm to be completely frank, however, I still hope that I'll have readers—not now, of course, but in many, many years' time when I shall no longer be alive. In Pushkin's words, "at some time the industrious monk will read my diligent, anonymous work . . ." and it's nice to think about it.

Well, now that I have revealed myself to my imaginary readers, I can continue.

We just weren't able to have any fun that day. Our jokes fell flat, we got bored playing games, didn't have anything to drink, and broke up early.

The next day in Moscow I went to work. I knew in advance that there would be an inevitable commotion about the Decree and that some would express their opinions while others would keep quiet. But to my surprise almost everyone kept quiet. True, two or three people asked me what I thought about it all. I muttered something to the effect that I didn't know and we would have to wait and see, and the conversation ended there.

A day later a long editorial entitled "In Preparation for Public Murder Day" appeared in *Izvestia*. It made very little

mention of the reason for the measure, but repeated the
usual jumble of expressions, such as "increased well-being"
. . . "tremendous advances" . . . "true democracy" . . .
"only in our country" . . . "as one man" . . . "for the first
time in history" . . . "visible signs" . . . "bourgeois press"
. . . It further stated that no damage should be done to public property and that therefore arson and bombings werc
prohibited. The Decree, moreover, did not cover persons
serving sentences in jail. So there you are. The article was
read and reread, but no one understood it any better, although people became somehow calmer. The actual style of
the article, its routine solemnity and prosaic pomposity,
probably reassured people. There was nothing special about
it. After all, we had "Artillery Day" and "Soviet Press Day,"
so why not "Public Murder Day"? . . . Bus and train services
would be operating and the police were not to be harmed—
that meant everything was in order. Ten or so days passed
like that. Then something began which is difficult to describe
in words. There was a kind of strange agitation and unrest.
No, I can't find the right words! Everyone became fidgety
and began rushing around. In the subways, in movie houses,
and on the streets people kept going up to each other, smiling
obsequiously, and striking up conversations about their ailments, fishing, the quality of nylon stockings—in short, about
anything at all. And provided they were not suddenly interrupted by their listeners, they shook their hands for a
long time, looking gratefully and searchingly into their eyes.
Others, particularly the young people, became rowdy and
insolent, everyone in his own way. People sang in the streets
and declaimed poetry in loud voices, mostly Esenin, much
more than usual. Incidentally, on the subject of poetry, *Literature and Life* published a selection of poems devoted to
the forthcoming event by Bezymenskiy, Mikhalkov, Sofronov,
and others.[1] Unfortunately, I can't find a copy of this issue

---

[1] Contemporary Soviet poets well known for their capacity to turn out verses
on topical themes.

recently, despite my efforts, but I remember by heart part of
the Sofronov poem:

> The lathes of Rostov's Agricultural
> Machinery Plant were humming,
> The factory whistles were singing,
> And our great Party
> Seized the Trotskyists by the collar.
>
> I was seventeen at the time,
> I was far from maturity,
> I couldn't tell people apart,
> So my aim when hitting them was poor,
>
> Perhaps I sang more tunefully then,
> But I was not calm and brave;
> Feeling pity, I left some alive,
> Others I could not finish off . . .

An absolutely astronomical number of jokes went around;
Volodya Margulis hurried from one friend to another; telling
them and hooting with laughter. Having exhausted his entire
supply on me, he reported that Igor had said at a meeting in
his college that August 10th was the result of the Party's wise
policy, that the Decree reconfirmed the development of the
creative initiative of the popular masses, and so on, and so
on in the usual vein.

"You know something, Tolya?" he said. "I knew Igor was a
careerist and all that, but I didn't expect this of him."

"Why not?" I asked. "What's so special about it? He was
told to make a speech, and he did. If you were a Party member like Igor, you would have reeled one off, too."

"Me? Never! First, I wouldn't join the Party for anything,
and, second . . ."

"First, second! Stop shouting! Are you really any better
than Igor? Didn't you jabber about nationalism[2] at school
during the Doctors' Plot?"

---

2 The Zionist nationalism with which the Jewish doctors were charged
in the notorious affair of 1952.

I said it, and was immediately sorry I had. It was a sore point with him. He couldn't forgive himself the fact that he had believed the newspapers for a while.

"I'd rather hear how you're getting along with Nina," I said more amiably. "How long since you've seen her?"

Volodya brightened up.

"You know, Tolya, it's not easy to love," he said. "It's not easy. I called her yesterday and said I wanted to see her, but she answered . . ."

And Volodya began describing in detail what she had answered, what he had said to her, and what they both said.

"Tolya, you know me; I'm not the sentimental type, but I almost burst into tears. . . ."

I listened to him and wondered how people manage to create problems out of nothing. Volodya was married and had two children. He taught literature in a school better than anyone in the area and was in every way a bright fellow. But oh, his love affairs! It's true his wife was a bitch; you'd leave a wife like that for any woman. Well, O.K., who cares how often he did it? But what was the point of all the suffering, the transports of passion, and the small-town Hamlet act? And such expressions as "moral obligations," "divided loyalties," and "she believes in me" . . . Besides, "she believes in me" is said both of his wife and the latest heartthrob. No, I look at all this much more simply. I don't need play-acting, diplomacy, or obligations to make it all honest. Do we like each other? Great. Do we want each other? Wonderful: what more do we want? What about adultery? Who cares? If I marry, I won't be worried by Volodya's kind of problems, I'll simply say in advance: "I'm married, you know, I don't intend to divorce, and I like you very much. Does that suit you? Great: where and when shall we meet? It doesn't suit you? Too bad; good-by; think it over . . ." That's what I'd do, though not quite so crudely. And I think that's much better than talking a lot of nonsense about incompatibility between you and your wife, and saying, "Of course, I admire my wife, but . . ." I have never yet really wronged a woman, and only because I've never let them have any illusions about me. . . .

Volodya talked for another half hour about his complicated love life and went away. I showed him out, but he immediately rang the bell again, put his head through the half-open door, and said in a whisper so the neighbors wouldn't hear:

"Tolya, if there is a Jewish pogrom on August tenth, I'm going to fight. This isn't going to be another Babi Yar[3] for them. I'll shoot the swine. Just wait and see!" And opening his jacket, he showed me the butt of an officer's pistol sticking out of his inside pocket; he had kept it since his army days.

"They won't take me easily. . . ."

When he had finally left, I stood for some time in the middle of the room.

Who were "they"?

3

No, Alcinous, you are wrong: there
is indeed infinity in nature,
The stupidity and baseness of people
are an illustration of it.
     — Cyril Zamoysky, "Experiments and
     Sermons"

"Tolya, you simply don't want to be serious about it! Just try to understand one simple thing . . ."

My neighbor was soaping a dirty dish with a mop. His stomach, covered with gray hair, was tightly enmeshed by a net undershirt; it protruded from his pants and rested on the edge of the sink. He was terribly excited although I had not objected to a single word.

". . . no, no, don't get me wrong! Although some people may be, I'm not an admirer of newspaper clichés. But facts

---

[3] Scene of Nazi massacre of Jews near Kiev in 1941.

are facts, and you've got to face them: public awareness
has definitely increased! Ergo, the State has the right to con-
duct an extensive experiment and hand over some of its functions to the people! After all, we have the voluntary militia
squads, Komsomol patrols, people's voluntary police for the
maintenance of public law and order! And that's a fact which
means something. But obviously, even they make mistakes—
lapses, you might call them—they've slashed the tight
trousers of the dandies and girls have had their heads shaved,
but that's bound to happen!4 Production costs! You can't
make an omelet without breaking eggs! And the Decree is
nothing else but the logical continuation of a process already
begun—the process of democratization. Democratization of
what? Democratization of the organs of executive authority.
But the ideal, and don't misunderstand me, is the gradual
assumption of the executive authority by the masses, at the
lowest level, so to speak. No, I don't mean lowest level, that
wasn't right, we don't have any low levels. Well, you know
what I mean . . . and believe me, an old lawyer, hundreds,
thousands, tens of thousands of people have passed through
my hands—believe me, the people will first and foremost
settle the score with hoodlums, spongers, and the dregs of
society . . ."

I was hoping against hope he would drop the slippery
plate, and he finally broke it against the sink. His wife came
hurrying in, looked disapprovingly at the pieces and then at
me, and said in an even voice:

"Peter, go into our room."

"That spell in the concentration camp didn't do that fool
any good," I thought as he left, and I went off to answer the
bell.

Zoya came in.

We went through to my room, and Zoya, sighing with re-

---

4 The formation of vigilante groups (*druzhiny*) who assist the ordinary
militia to fight "hooliganism" is a notable feature of the post-Stalin era.
There have been frequent cases of these groups molesting young people who
dress in Western style.

lief, threw off her shoes. I like to watch women taking off
their shoes: the shape of the leg changes and immediately
becomes intimate, domestic, and somehow unsophisticated.

"It looks as if you're wearing white slippers," I said, pointing to her untanned feet. "Show me where else you're still
white."

"I want to have a talk with you," she replied. "All right,
then, later on . . ."

I kissed her.

"Lock the door," she said.

. . . We lay side by side a little way from each other.
Zoya's skin was cool, despite the heat; her lightly tanned body
had three white bands around it—on her breasts, hips, and
feet. She lay beside me, spread out freely and unashamedly,
beautiful and resplendent like a clown at a circus, and I felt
that I loved her very much. I wanted to wink just as freely
and unashamedly at some imaginary observer and, perhaps,
accomplice, and say to him: "You see, my friend, what kind
of a woman I've got!" I lay there and wondered whether
what was happening between us could be called "life"—
struggle, conquest, mutual capitulation, acceptance and vehement rejection, a deep sense of oneself and complete loss
of self alienation and union—all in one, all at the same time.
And at that moment I didn't care that she was married,
or that I was not the only one who possessed her clever, sub-
missive, ever waiting flesh, or that she had a husband who
caressed her on a legal basis, or that in a month's time my
sister would be back from vacation and Zoya would no longer
be able to come and see me, and that we would have to loiter
in attics and doorways, like stray cats, or that I would again
be surprised and even slightly shocked by her ability to give
herself to me in the most unlikely places, and that I would
be very grateful to her for it; but now I didn't care about any
of that. I lay there and waited for her to speak.

And she did.

"Tolya," she said, "it will soon be Public Murder Day."
She uttered these words very simply and in a business-

like way as though she had said: "It will soon be New Year's,"
or "It will soon be May Day."

"And what about it?" I asked. "What has that got to do
with us?"

"Aren't you fed up with hiding?" she asked. "Now we can
change everything."

"I don't understand," I murmured. But I was telling a lie,
I understood perfectly.

"Let's kill Paulie."

That's what she said: "Paulie." Not my "husband," or
"Paul," but "Paulie." I felt my lips stiffen.

"Zoya, are you in your right mind? What are you saying?"

Zoya slowly turned her head and rubbed her cheek against
my shoulder.

"Tolya dear, don't be upset. Just think calmly. After all,
there won't be another chance. I've thought it all out. You
can come to us the night before. You can say that you want to
spend that day with us. Paulie and I haven't planned to go
anywhere. And you and I can do it together. Then you can
come and live with me and we'll get married. I wouldn't involve you in it, and would do it all by myself, except that
I'm simply scared of not being able to carry it off."

She talked, while I lay and listened, and every word seized
me by the throat like a momentary spasm of choking.

"Tolya, why don't you say something?"

I coughed and said:

"Get out."

She didn't understand.

"Where to?"

"To hell," I said.

Zoya stared at me for a few seconds, then got up and began
to get dressed. She put on her brassiere, then her panties, and
then her petticoat. I watched her disappear under the clothing. She threw on her dress, pushed her feet into the shoes,
and began arranging her hair.

Having done so, she took her handbag and unlocked the

door. On the threshold she turned around and said, not too
loudly:
"Sissy."
And she left. I heard the front door click.
I got up and dressed. I carefully rearranged the bedclothes.
I swept up the room. I made a large number of movements,
concentrating on each one. I wanted very much to avoid
thinking.

4

I hate them so much I have spasms,
I scream and I tremble; oh, if only all these whores
Could be collected and exterminated at once!
        —George Bolotin, "Trumpets of Time"

Nevertheless I had to think. It may seem stupid, but what
staggered me most of all was the word "sissy" which Zoya
had hurled at me. I wasn't a coward; I had learned that much
at the front, and once or twice since the war too. But Zoya
had decided I was a coward. But it wasn't cowardice, it was
simply unthinkable to take Paulie and kill him—uncomplain-
ing, meek, unsuspecting Paulie. Yes, we had been deceiving
him. If he'd known about our love affair he would have felt
very bad, of course. We spent his money on drink, we
laughed at him behind his back and to his face. That was
true, but to kill him? Why? What for? After all, if things
had reached that point, if it was only a question of marrying
me, she could have divorced him. It meant . . . it meant
that murder was not simply a way of ridding oneself of an
unloved, stupid, and elderly husband. It meant that murder
had for her some meaning, incomprehensible to me. Perhaps
she hated him and wanted to get even? Of course, she wanted
to get even for falling in love with him at the age of nineteen,
when all he could talk about was "the miracle of modern
science" and other such banalities and tell Jewish and
Armenian stories . . . She couldn't help hating him. And

once she did, of course, she might kill him. That much I understand. Hatred gives one the right to murder. In hatred I might myself . . . mightn't I? Well, obviously, I might. I might definitely. Whom do I hate? Whom have I hated in my life? Well, schooldays don't count, but what about when I was grown up? College. I hated one of the teachers who purposely failed me four times in my exams. Well, to hell with him, that was a long time ago. The bosses of different departments in which I'd worked. Yes, they were crooks. They certainly made my blood boil. They should be punched in the face, the bastards. Who else? The writer K.,[5] who writes novels in the spirit of the Black Hundreds. Yes, I remember I used to say that I'd kill him if I knew that nothing would happen to me. That swine deserves to be taught a lesson! So that he'd never take up the pen again. . . .

And what about the fat-faced masters of our destiny, our leaders and teachers, true sons of the people, receiving messages of congratulation from collective farmers of the Ryazan region, from metal workers in the Krivoi Rog region, from the Emperor of Ethiopia, from a teachers' congress, from the President of the United States, from attendants in public toilets. The best friends of Soviet gymnasts, writers, textile workers, color-blind persons, and madmen? What should be done with them? Should they be forgiven? What about 1937? What about the postwar insanity when the country was possessed of the devil, thrashed about in the throes of a fit, and became hysterical and began devouring itself? Do they think that once they have desecrated the grave of the Mustached One,[6] that's all that's required of them? No, no, no, they must be treated differently. Do you remember still how to do it? The fuse. Pull out the pin. Throw. Lie flat on the ground. Lie down! It's exploded. And now, a leap forward. As you run, spray around you at belly level. A burst of

---

[5] This refers to Vsevolod Kochetov and his novel *The Brothers Ershov*. See Introduction, p. xxxii, and footnote 12, p. xxxvii.
[6] Stalin. The desecration of his grave is to be understood figuratively; the story was written before Stalin's body was removed from the Lenin Mausoleum.

machine-gun fire! . . . They're lying over there—cut to shreds and riddled with bullets. It's slippery. One's legs slip. Who's this? He's crawling along, dragging his guts along the plaster-strewn floor behind him. And who's this man, bedecked with medals, who accompanies the Chief on trips? Why is he so thin? Why is he wearing a padded coat? I saw him once before, crawling along a grade, spilling his blue and red stomach into the dust. And these people? I've seen them! Only then they had on belts with the inscription *"Gott mit uns"* on the buckles, caps with red stars, knee boots; Russians, Germans, Georgians, Rumanians, Jews, Hungarians, peajackets, placards, medical corps, spades; over the body runs a Studebaker, two Studebakers, eight Studebakers, forty Studebakers, and you lie there flattened like a frog; we've had all that before!

I got up from the bed, went to the window, and wiped my sweaty forehead with the curtain. Then I went into the kitchen, washed in the sink, and put on my jacket. I couldn't stay at home another moment.

I went along the street, scorched by the August sun; coming toward me were housewives with net shopping bags; some boys were making a deafening buzz with their bicycles; sweaty old men were wandering along the sidewalk, stopping at every stall selling mineral water. I reached the corner of the Arbat and Smolensk Square and stopped. I felt like visiting someone. But who? It was summer and everybody was away at their *dachas,* and those who weren't were probably at the Silver Copse,[7] or somewhere else where they could swim. And I felt like a drink. I remembered that an artist friend of mine called Sasha Chuprov lived not too far along the road leading to the Kiev station. Even if he wasn't at home, I could still sit there for a while, since the door of his room was never locked.

I stopped in at a large grocery store on the corner and wandered through, looking for the liquor section. I went up

---

[7] A riverside beach near Moscow.

to various counters and watched the salesgirls working. In their uniform they all looked the same, but they behaved differently— in a businesslike and correct way in the sausage section, apathetically and superciliously in the fruit and vegetable section, coquettishly and subserviently in the candy section, and in a confused and disorderly way in the grocery section. In the liquor section, which I finally found, they were condescending and just a little familiar. I stood and gazed at the revolving stand with bottles, rising up in a cone beside a column. It was here that emotions were stored. Poured into different bottles and sealed with wax, they were given random labels such as "brandy," "vodka," and "Georgian wine;" but in actual fact the bottles were filled with melancholy, gaiety, unbridled anger, charming gullibility, touchiness, and bravery. The emotions were biding their time. In due course they would be released from their glass prisons; they would hear stupid farewell toasts and would run riot in hands clutching drunkenly at tablecloths; on lips feverishly kissing; in lungs taking in extra air so that they could sing "Moscow Nights" in the proper way. "Time is on our side," they were thinking as their many colors glimmered in the electric light. "Our cause is right, our day will come . . ."

I bought a bottle of brandy (Georgian, as I didn't have enough for a better brand) and a lemon, and left the shop.

Chuprov turned out to be at home.

"So it's you, old pal," he said gloomily. "Come in . . ."

The spacious light room was incredibly messy.

An open sketchbook lay on the floor; there were rolls of paper on and underneath the table and on the windowsill. The owner himself, fully dressed, was rolling about on the bed, trying to rest his feet on the rail.

"What's the matter?" I asked.

"Those bastards," he answered. "I've worked and worked and it's all been a goddamn waste of time."

"What have you been working on?"

"You know what, posters."

Chuprov painted left-wing[8] pictures and was known as being avant-garde in liberal circles. But there was no one to whom he could sell his nonconformist canvases which were so tainted by the pernicious influence of the West. He was afraid to approach foreigners, and he had to eat, so he painted posters of girls with shining faces against a background of the Kremlin walls; of miners in full underground regalia, marching confidently toward a bright future; of young engineers in overalls with calipers in their breast pockets and the *History of the Communist Party* under their arms. He was paid well, though not very regularly.

"Why, haven't they accepted your work?" I asked. "Didn't you have a contract?"

The point was he didn't. He had thought there'd be no other posters for them to choose from and so had decided to take a risk for the occasion. He had painted a nonconformist poster, in his own free manner. "Can you imagine? I took it to them, and there . . ."

"Wait a minute, for what occasion?"

"Where have you been all this time? For Public Murder Day. I don't suppose they'll manage without posters. Anyway, listen and don't interrupt. So I took it along. And the chief, that bureaucrat—he's one of the old school—says to me: 'Chuprov, you've come to the wrong place. This kind of stuff may be all right for *Life*,[9] but it's no good to us.' And he went on and on about 'events in the life of our country . . . the Party is showing us the way . . . great ideas require efficient implementation . . . so as to inspire . . .' Then he said: 'Look at this' . . . and he showed me a poster by Artemev and Kranz. And you should have seen it, old pal! And I'm not saying this because he rejected my poster and took theirs. You know what I think of such work. For me it means bread and that's all. But after all, there's a limit! If you do it, do it properly, no potboilers! But those jerks had drawn some

---

[8] See Introduction, footnote 12, p. xxxvii.
[9] The American magazine.

kind of stuffed dummies—you couldn't tell whether they
were dead or alive, with a tower crane in the background and
that's all. And that's what's called a colorful poster! Well,
anyway, I don't give a damn for their money; I managed to
get enough over the May Day holiday, but I'm sorry for the
sake of the work put into it for the idea! When will they ever
understand that it's now the middle of the twentieth century and that art must progress at a new . . . er . . . er . . .
new tempo, mustn't it?"

Chuprov fired all this off in one salvo and then swore ob-
scenely. The ash of his cigarette broke off and fell onto the
pillow.

"Listen, Sasha," I said cautiously, "what about this rejected
poster of yours? . . . May I have a look at it?"

"I suppose so. Take a look. It's over there by the wall."

I cleared a space on the floor and unrolled the poster.

Against the background of a rising or maybe a setting sun
stood the conventional boy and girl; the sun was behind them
and their red shadows lay across the poster; in the bottom
left-hand corner the shadows merged with a red-black puddle lapping against the corner of a conventional house; in the
bottom right-hand corner lay a body with arms outstretched
and one knee drawn up.

"Well, how do you like it?" asked Sasha.

I thought for a moment and then said:

"There's lots of expression in it."

I was risking nothing: I knew for certain that Sasha had
never read Huxley.

"Really?" Sasha was radiant.

"Yes," I continued, "but I think the corpse is too garish."

Sasha jumped up from the bed and sticking out his lip,
looked at his work.

"You're probably right, old pal," he said. "And do you
know why it is? I ought to have done it in a more conventional way, not quite so realistically, not quite so true-to-life,
don't you think? . . ."

We drank the brandy. Sasha told me about his plans and I

listened and thought how Zoya was responsible for it all and
if it hadn't been for her I wouldn't have given the cursed
Public Murder Day a thought. Why should it concern me?
Damn the Day . . . and Zoya was a bitch. Paul should be
told. No, that wasn't necessary now. Now that I had given
her up, she would be afraid. She was a bitch, a murderer.
Everything had been so nice, we had enjoyed it so much, but
now I would never touch her again. And she wouldn't give
herself to me, anyway. It was because of her that I had to
sit there and listen to the drunken Chuprov pouring out his
heart. Nonconformist! Avant-garde! If tomorrow they announce a "Queers' Day," he'll reach for his brush and paint
a graph of the rise in homosexuality since 1913. I don't want
to kill anyone any more. I don't want to!

"What don't you want?" asked Chuprov.

"I don't want to drink any more."

"There isn't any more to drink. And why don't you want to
drink? It's the right moment. Wait a minute, I'll run down
and get a bottle . . . or I know what. If you like, I'll intro-
duce you to a friend, an old man. My, what an old man! He
writes poetry. Let's go; you'll be grateful to me. You've never
seen anyone like him."

"Let's go."

I got up, feeling sick.

"Let's go, Sasha! Let's go, Alexander Chuprov! Let's go,
you genius of an artist! Is the old man also a genius? Will he
explain everything?"

"Everything! He can explain everything—he's a waiter!"

5

They lie in wait in any doorway,
They exude a smell of carbolic acid,
They're in the grass springing up from the earth,
In old books, dozing on the shelf.
Everywhere you can hear a deadened whisper,
And any phrase conceals a wicked end.

They're in the water flowing in the shower,
And in the hoarse gurgling of the toilet bowl.
                              —George Bolotin, "Devils of Death"

While we were buying the vodka, trying to find a taxi, and
driving somewhere near the Danilov market, I managed to
sober up a bit. "Why and where am I going?" I wondered.
"What the hell's this old boy to me? Well, anyway . . ."
Anyway, I had to get through Sunday somehow or other. So
why not with this old boy? Things were really great: I'd
parted from my woman. I'd separated from my mistress. I'd
quarreled with my girl friend. So why not with an old man?
    Sasha stopped the cab and paid the fare.
    "You sit here for a moment and I'll go and find out whether
we can see him. I won't be a second. . . ."
    I sat down on a bench and lit a cigarette. The streetcars
were clanking behind me. Young fathers were wheeling baby
carriages along the side streets. Freshly scoured soldiers were
strolling along with girls, conversing with decorum and not
yet allowing their hands to wander—it was still light. I raised
my eyes.
    New eight- or ten-story apartment houses stood in open-
ordered ranks, parallel to the boulevard; their light brick
faces with clear eyes looked benevolently and encouragingly
at the young greenery of the gardens. But the old buildings
of the thirties stared hard between the gaps in this showy optimism with gloomy awareness of their own superiority. With
their corners facing the boulevard in wedge-shaped formation, they advanced from the depths of the courtyards without really budging an inch. There was such confidence in
their righteousness and such unshakable faith in an idea that
it seemed that had the Architect[10] who created them risen
from his grave and pointed with his finger, these gray wedges
would have moved forward, sweeping the showy new card-
board buildings from their path. They would have leveled to

---

[10] Stalin.

the sidewalk all the self-service elevators, the Finnish-style furniture, the volumes of Hemingway, and all the fashionable people secretly thumbing their noses.

Chuprov suddenly appeared beside me as though he had sprung out of the ground.

"Come on," he said, "the maestro's at home."

I followed him, bumping against the bottles stuffed into his jacket pockets.

We were met by a little old man with twitching eyebrows in a spick-and-span one-room apartment. Over his knitted track pants he was wearing a pair of old-fashioned pajamas tied with cords, resembling a guardsman's tunic; from under the pajamas peeped a black shirt with big white buttons like the stops of an accordion.

"Very pleased to meet you," he said. "Please come in, sit down, and excuse the disorder. I lead the life of a bachelor as my wife likes to spend her time at the *dacha*."

We went into a large, long room. The furniture was new and the tablecloth on the solid round table was carefully covered with transparent plastic; on the divan lay pillows, ranging, like peas in a pod, from large to small. One wall was completely covered by a gray curtain.

"My friend Tolya is very interested in your poetry," said Chuprov. "Would you read some to us?"

"Don't be so eager, Sasha. You're always in a hurry, always rushing somewhere. And may I ask where? Everything takes its time. Don't speed up time, which is flying anyway. You will manage. Let me just have a drink with your friend Tolya, talk about one or two things, and we will put out our feelers, like ants. We can look at the poetry later—it's right here. 'Verse is good for the digestion,' as a very old friend of mine used to say. What do you think, Anatole, do you agree with me?"

"Don't call him Anatole, call him Tolya!"

"No, my dear Sasha, I cannot. This is the first time I have met the young man. I accept everything that happens today, I welcome everything, and, as they say, I congratulate them, but I cannot agree with this new-fangled custom. I've been called Gennadi Vasilevich since I was fifteen. And rightly so! For when you address a man respectfully, it exalts him and elevates him, so to speak, above the sinful earth. Don't you think so, Anatole Nikolaevich?"

"Call me anything you like," I said. "Sticks and stones will break my bones . . ."

". . . but names will never hurt me," said the old man, finishing the saying. While he talked, he was laying the table rapidly and neatly. Wineglasses, forks, plates, some radishes, pickles, sliced bread, and sausage appeared on the table as though by magic. And his words—rounded, cozy and old-fashioned, like forks with bone handles—came just as rapidly. He poured out the vodka and we had a drink.

"You are quite right about the sticks and stones, Anatole Nikolaevich. The opposite is also observed, incidentally. Some people are just dying to call others names and use the sticks and stones as well. . . ."

"People are like wild beasts," said Chuprov gloomily. He had evidently remembered the rejected poster.

"There's no point in speaking disparagingly about wild beasts, Sasha. Haven't you noticed what people like talking about most when they're in a good mood? Wild animals and their young. And why? Because everyone likes them. People argue about everything, about books, let's say, or pictures or statues, and obviously about politics. But they never argue about wild animals. This spring I read an article in a magazine about zoos in different countries. It was written by the director of the Moscow Zoo. You may wonder why I would be interested in the fact that a tapir was born in Italy? But I read about it and I was delighted. And everyone's like that. Wild animals will soon be the only link, the only point of contact between people. Wild beasts, my young friends, are not simply animals, they are the bearers and keepers of the spiritual essence!"

These remarks were so out of character with what had gone before that I couldn't help raising my head from the plate. The old man observed this and stopped speaking. Sasha immediately broke into the pause:

"Let's drink to the tapir! Hoorah!"

We drank several shots in succession. The old man soon became drunk, and the more drunk he became, the purer and more cultured his speech became. Crossing his legs and looking first at Sasha and then at me, he said quickly and very clearly, lowering his voice:

"None of us knows what is hidden in the other's heart. For example, the frank conversation you and I are having is nothing but an insane, suicidal divestment of our clothes. But if you take off your clothes in the street in the literal sense of the words, you'll be taken to the local precinct, fined, publically censured, and that's all! But candor and the taking off of one's spiritual clothes is impermissible! Who knows, some of my words or one of my ideas may sting you in your most sacred, most tender spot and burrow in so deeply that the poisonous splinter can only be pulled out at the expense of my life! So you will be longing to kill me and to save yourself! Who and what can prevent you or any other person, for that matter? Which of us knows how much hostility is felt by another toward us? And what causes it? An ill-chosen word, the way you eat, the shape of your nose. By the way," he turned to me, "are you Jewish?"

"No," I replied, feeling my nose. "Why, do I look it?"

"Yes, a bit. Now, those Jews are a wise people. They live in fear. And not in fear of God, but fear of man. They regard everyone as a potential enemy. And rightly so. What can be more terrible than man? A wild animal kills in order to satisfy his hunger. It doesn't give a damn for ambition, for the lust for power, or for seeking a career. It isn't given to envy! But take us: can we know who is thirsting for our blood, or whom we have offended without knowing it? Offended by our very existence? We know nothing. . . ."

"Wild animals fight to the death over the female," said Sasha.

Gennadi Vasilevich frowned:

"That's a different matter. That's the instinct of procreation. Wild animals have wisdom and simplicity; they do not fall in love. But take man . . . man has only to fall in love and he's ready to commit any base act, any crime. It wasn't for nothing that the Romans used to say *femina mors anime* —woman is death to the soul. But I'm not talking about that. I ask you, Sasha, and you, Anatole, are you certain that there are not people among your acquaintances and friends who might kill you? As for me, I'll say that I don't intend to! But death . . . You are young and haven't thought about it, but I'm an old man. I lie here at night on this divan—look at it, it has a wooden back—twisting from side to side, knocking the wood with my elbow and thinking 'That's how it'll be in the coffin—wood on both sides, wood on top, wood . . .' "

He drew a breath; his head was shaking very slightly.

"Nothing can be foreseen. Nothing helps, neither caution, nor solitude—nothing! And yet they waste their time arguing, reasoning, fussing about . . ."

"Who's they?" I asked.

"Those . . . ignorant fools," answered the old man in a tired voice.

He got up, staggering, and pulled back the gray curtain revealing bookshelves along the entire wall. Gaudy writers bound in brightly colored calico burst into the room like the Tartar horde, tearing the semblance of security and the deceptive tranquility of middle-class comfort to shreds. With the horde came the squeaking, cumbersome carts of philosophical systems, the curved mirrorlike sabers of self-analysis, the blunt battering rams of universal pessimism, the stallions of civilization with the yellow froth of misanthropy on their bared teeth, trampling to bits, to a pulp, into a pancake, the gray-bearded evangelists who hold their commandments up to an apathetic heaven as they decompose into atomic dust. . . .

"People are ready to drown each other in a spoonful of water," sighed Chuprov, pouring out the remains of the vodka.

. . . Chuprov and I walked along the empty streets. At the crossroads stood solitary policemen on duty. The neon signs of grocery stores shone bright, and our heels tapped sharply and sonorously along the sidewalk, but even that sound, which I normally like so much, didn't please me. Public Murder Day was exactly a week away.

6

Revolt—you wouldn't dare:
Run away—you couldn't if you tried,
And it's all the same thing, anyway;
What would be the soldier's lot—inglorious death
Or undying glory . . .
                                    —George Bolotin, "The Halt"

I stopped going to work. I called up the editorial office and said I was sick. I lay on the bed, or wandered about the room and spent hours drawing faces on the wrapping paper in which some sausage had been delivered.

The only person who came to see me during all this time was Volodya Margulis; he kept asking me an idiotic question, as soon as he arrived: "But, do they expect to gain from this Decree?" "They" was the government. I kept silent while Volodya, who was glad that I had no personal opinion, began explaining to me that the whole weird business was not only inevitable but lay at the very basis of socialist teachings.

"Why?" I asked.

"Well, of course it does. It's all quite correct: they have to legalize murder and make it a commonplace occurrence, so that's why they're not explaining anything. Before, they used to explain things and spread propaganda."

"You're talking nonsense! When was that?"

"During the Revolution."

"You're wrong there. The Revolution was neither made that way nor for that purpose."

"What about 1937? It was the same thing. Complete freedom of extermination. Only at that time there were trimmings to go with it, while this time there's nothing. Kill and that's all! And anyway, at that time there was a complete apparatus with tremendous personnel at the service of the murderers. Now you do it yourself. Self-service."

"Oh, dry up, Volodya! Your anti-Soviet monologues have stopped being funny."

"What's wrong; are you taking the side of the Soviet regime? Do you think that you ought to stand up for it?"

"For a real Soviet regime, of course I ought to."

"You mean one without communists? Like in Sholokhov's *And Quiet flows the Don?*"

"Go to hell!"

"That's a very convincing answer!" said Volodya sarcastically. "And you . . ."

"That's enough," I said.

We lapsed into silence, and he went off in a huff.

I lay down on the bed again and began thinking. The reason the Decree had been announced just didn't concern me. There was no point in looking for scientific justification and jabbering about the Revolution. I don't like doing that. My father was a commissar in the Civil War and I think he knew what he was fighting for. I don't remember him very well— he was taken away in 1936, one of the first, but after my mother's death I found his letters. I read them and I don't think that people of my generation have any right to talk loosely of those times. We can and must each decide for himself. That's all that is left for us, all that we are in a position to do, but it's quite enough. Too much, in fact.

Arbatov, the old poet from Danilov Boulevard, had irritated me. I not only didn't want to, but couldn't kill anyone! But others might want to and might be able to. And their victim might be me, Anatole Kartsev! Just as on the day of my last meeting with Zoya, I again thought about my enemies. That one couldn't. That one might want to, but would be afraid. That one might try with a stone or a brick from around the corner. Who else, who else was there? No, that one wasn't an enemy of mine. Not an enemy? How did I know? Perhaps he was! And anyway, why should my enemies be the only ones who might kill me? Any passer-by, any drunk or crazy fool might shoot me in the face just to see me thrash my legs about in agony. Spilling my life onto the sidewalk. My nose getting sharper, cheeks hollowing, and jaw dropping. My eyes coming through the hole in my skull, my arms, my words, my silence, my sea, my sand, my women, my clumsy poetry . . .

Damn it! To hell with it! I can't let them kill me. I must go on living. I will hide, barricade myself in; I'll spend the day at home. I don't want to die. I don't want to! Never speak evil of the living.

Stop! I must get a grip on myself. I must calm down. I'll buy some food the night before and won't go out at all on Sunday. I'll lie on my bed and read Anatole France. I like Anatole France very much. *Penguin Island, Revolt of the Angels.* There's also "Anatole France in a Dressing Gown." Whenever I spent the night with Zoya, she used to make me put on Paul's dressing gown and was terribly amused. At that time I didn't know why it pleased her so much, but I do now. She was imagining that she had become a widow and married me. I wonder how she intended to kill Paul? She was going to stay home on Sunday. The neighbors would also be there. Of course, people might break into the apartment. The front door would have to be secured. I would steal a crowbar from a building site nearby and bar the door. Hit them on the head with the crowbar. If they broke in, I would hit them with the crowbar like dogs. I was recently at a dog show. I very much liked the Borzois with their long narrow heads like dueling pistols. Would I be able to fight a duel? Pushkin's bullet hit one of D'Anthès' buttons. If I go out on Sunday, I'll have to put a cigarette case in the inside pocket of my jacket on the left where the heart is. *On the Left Where the Heart Is* is a novel by Leongrad Frank, a very boring one. But Bruno Frank is quite different; he wrote a book about Cervantes. And what would Don Quixote have done on August 10th? He would have ridden to Moscow on his Rosinante and interceded for everyone. On his own personal Rosinante. An eccentric with a copper bowl on his head, he would have ridden across Red Square, ready to break his lance in the name of the Beautiful Lady, in the name of Russia. On the Moscow streets of 1960 the poor knight would have sought his friend and fellow thinker—the Ukrainian boy who had once sung of Granada. But the marks of the lances are now covered over with cobblestones, and the holes made in the ground by the staffs of regimental banners are filled with asphalt. He would not find anyone, this visionary from La Mancha, no one! That much I know for certain. Who are the people who would follow Don Quixote? Margulis? Igor? No, no; if they fight at all, it's only for themselves. Each fights for himself, each decides for himself. Wait a moment, who was it said recently: "We must each decide for himself!" Yes, it was me who said it; why have I taken it on myself to judge others? Are they better than I? Am I better than they?

I jumped up from the bed and looked with disgust at the pillow still indented from my head. Was it me who had been lying there? Was it me who had wanted to stock up with grub and bar the door? Was it me shaking like jelly in fear of my precious skin? Was it me who nearly dirtied his pants with fright? So what good am *I*, me with my splendid passion for unmasking and despising others, with my stinking detachment? Pontius Pilate, betraying his own soul every day—what good am *I*?

Yes, everyone answers for himself. But for himself, and not for the person other people want to make you. I answer for myself, and not for a potential self-seeker, police spy, chauvinist, or coward. I cannot let them kill me and thereby save their own lives.

Wait, though: what shall I do? I'll go out into the street tomorrow and shout: "Citizens, don't kill each other! Love your neighbor!" and what will that bring? Whom will I help? Whom will I save? I don't know, I don't know at all. . . . I may perhaps save myself, if it's not too late.

7

Stay here! Where are you going?
In senseless gloom, in blind fury—
Aren't the angels skimming over the heads
Of the howling crowd;
Haven't thousands of reptiles crept from the bogs,
Having forgotten the power of terrestial laws;
They hiss with huge gaping mouths,
And mothers have miscarriages.
Stay here! Life itself has summoned you
By the heralds of those who are herded here, on earth.
Drink it in, take your fill of inspiration
From the meaninglessness of the Day of Judgment!
                    —George Bolotov, "To You, Poets!"

On August 10 I got up at eight o'clock. I shaved, had breakfast, and read a little. No matter what I started doing, I kept thinking that I ought to go out of the house because of the loudspeakers blaring stirring marches outside, and the cats sauntering in zigzags across the roadway, delighted by the sudden dearth of people, and also the fact that my neighbors didn't go to the kitchen or the toilet, but did everything in their own rooms.

At about eleven o'clock I got dressed, put the cigarette case in my inside pocket as I had planned, and went out onto the landing.

I walked down the stairs slowly and noiselessly, so that when I bumped into my neighbor from the third floor on a landing, it was a surprise for both of us. She gave a scream; her net shopping bag full of bottles flew aside and hit against the banister. There was a sound of breaking glass and yogurt poured out onto the landing through the mesh of the bag. The woman slipped in a thick pool of yogurt and sat down heavily on the stairs with a gasp. I ran to help her. Then she let out a second scream and closing her eyes, feebly began pushing me away with trembling hands.

"Tolya, Tolya," she burbled. "I used to hold you . . . in my arms . . . when you were small . . . Your mother . . . Tolya! . . ."

"Anna Filippovna, what's the matter? There's broken glass here, you'll cut yourself!"

She opened her eyes, and slowly raised her leaden face toward me.

"Tolya," she said, "I . . . I . . . thought . . . I bought the yogurt for my granddaughter . . . Oh, Tolya!"

And she burst into tears. Her heavy, swollen sixty-year-old body shook. I helped her up and picked up the bag.

"Zina is sick and Boris is away on a business trip, that's why I went to get the yogurt. . . ."

Zina, her daughter, who had been in the same class at school as me, came running down from the third floor in an unfastened dressing gown.

"Mamma! What's the matter? What have they done?"

"Nothing, Zina, nothing. I fell down. . . ."

"But I told you . . ." began Zina.

"Zina, take your mother home and I'll go for the yogurt."

I took the long, yogurt-soaked loaves of bread out of the bag and gave them to Zina.

"Tolya, what about the money?"

When I had cleaned up the yogurt and gone into the street again, it was even hotter, as steamy as before a storm, and I carried my jacket on my arm, forgetting about the protective cigarette case. I felt very upset; I kept seeing the cadaverous face of the woman from the third floor and hearing her incoherent and desperate babbling: "Tolya, Tolya . . ."

I went along Nikitsky Boulevard. It was the same as ever —cheerful, neat, and tidy, and covered with the tiny shadows of leaves, like a dappled horse. Except that today there were no children. Teen-age boys, in shirts with rolled-up sleeves, lounged on benches, spitting over their shoulders onto the grass, and an elderly man was going down the path through the middle, arrogantly sticking out his chin and leading an enormous unmuzzled dog on a leash.

When I reached Arbat Square, I saw people running. They were hurrying somewhere behind the old subway station, but I couldn't see exactly where; the movie theater was in the way. I ran across the street and pushed through the crowd.

On the ground a man lay with his head to the wall. He was in the same position as the corpse depicted in Sasha Chuprov's poster: he was lying slumped to the side, with one leg bent at the knee and his arms spread out. A red stain had spread over his shirt, a white one, from Vietnam; I have one too—my sister bought it for me in the spring. He was absolutely motionless and the sun was reflected in the narrow toes of his fashionable shoes. Somehow I didn't realize at first that the man was dead, but when I did, a chill ran down my spine. But it wasn't the murder, or death, which shocked me, but this almost mystic realization of Chuprov's wild vision. Why was he lying in exactly the same position? His head was almost resting against the frame of an ad which showed a dashing black-and-white dancer announcing a ten-day exhibition of Ossetian art and literature. Next to it hung a tattered Polytechnic Museum notice: "G. S. Gornfeld, Economist, will give a lecture on 'Planning and Organization of Labor in Industry . . .' The rest was torn off.

The onlookers were quietly exchanging comments:

"He's only a kid."

"Perhaps he's still alive?"

"Of course not! He's dead. I held a mirror to his mouth, this one from my bag."

"But who did it?"

"The woman selling flowers says that a tall, tanned fellow came up to him and shot him. He called to him, and when the boy turned around, he shot him."

"Who turned around?"

"Heavens, the dead boy, of course."

"And would you believe it, not a militiaman in sight!"

"They're always around when they're not needed."

"Wait a minute, mister, what has the militia got to do with it?"

"What do you mean? A man has been killed!"

"So what?"

"God, you young fool! A man has been killed, I tell you!"

"Go easy, mister. Who you kidding? Don't you read the papers? Today it's allowed!"

"Don't raise your voice, young man, in the presence of the dead. Newspapers are newspapers, but there's such a thing as conscience."

"You're holding the wrong end of the stick, mister. Do you think that conscience and a government decree are two different things? If I were you, I'd stop that kind of talk!"

"You'd better get out of here, young man, before I bash your head in."

"He's really got some fight in him, that old man!"

"We ought to chase the flies off the body, it looks bad."

"All this means, folks, is that a hoodlum can go and do someone in like this and nothing will happen to him!"

"You should read the papers, lady. They say: 'Free extermination.' Don't worry. They'll kill the ones that deserve it, and that's all."

"And who deserves it?"

"They know over there who deserves it. They don't issue decrees for nothing."

"His clothes may be stolen. His shoes . . ."

"Looting is forbidden. This is a government matter."

I pushed my way out of the crowd and went away.

I don't remember now where I wandered, how many streets and squares I walked through, or how I reached the Red Square.

I went right up to the Lenin-Stalin Mausoleum.

The bulging, rectangular, boxlike square was filled right up to the roofs and domes with the dense and palpable veneration of many centuries. The bare concrete rows of parallel grandstands, the three-tiered cubes of the tomb, the right angles of the low parapet, the wall with its unsophisticated double-toothed battlements—this whole pattern which was familiar to me and loved by me from childhood, from the cradle, immutable and uncompromising, like a drawing in a geometrical theorem, suddenly impinged upon my mind, heart, and soul. We are given: an idea; we are asked to prove: the implementation. And the geometricians, hardened by their zeal, keep drawing and drawing, resting the paper on the backs of people bowed before them, keep on drawing and do not notice, or do not want to notice, that the paper is torn, that the pencil is broken, that it has turned into a scourge that makes furrows in the skin and the flesh! Stop! We cannot go on, we cannot pay this price! They are people, after all. He did not want it—he who was the first to lie behind these marble walls! . . .

Someone pushed me over. I fell, and before I could get up again a man had thrown himself on top of me. He gripped me by the throat, but I jerked back my head and freed my neck. We rolled about, hitting our heads against the cobblestones, clinging to each other and vainly trying to get a hold on the slippery, recently washed stone with our feet. I glimpsed the blue sky, the vivid colors of St. Basil's Cathedral, the red marble of the tomb, and two motionless statues with rifles, guarding the corpses. We rolled over to the feet of the sentries, where I was finally able to push him away by thrusting my knee in his stomach. He let go and I jumped up, stumbled, and stepped on a sentry's foot. My adversary also jumped up and I punched him in the jaw, once and then once more. He fell down again, crawled a little, tried to get up, but his arms were too weak and he sat sprawled against the Mausoleum. Spitting blood, he rasped:

"Go on, then, kill me!"

I picked up my jacket lying on the parapet and said, breathing hard:

"You son of a bitch . . ."

He replied: "It was for the Motherland . . ."

I glanced around at the sentries. They were standing just as motionless as three minutes before, except that one of

them, squinting downward, was staring at the dusty mark
left by my heel on his polished boot. . . .

I went home.

8

The Lord offended a shell:
He took a prickly grain of sand
and hurled it
Into its defenseless mouth.

And if Something comes into your house,
Where is the refuge from evil?
And a pearl grew there
Like a white globule, like a
transparent grain.
                    —Richard O'Hara, "The Lagoon"

I celebrated the anniversary of the October Revolution in
the same company. After long discussion it was decided to
get together at Zoya and Paul's place; they had a separate
two-room apartment, a tape recorder with recordings of Vertinsky and Leshchenko,[11] and lots of spare plates—in other
words, the women decided it would be best to go there.

When I was told the party was going to be held at their
place, I decided I wouldn't go, but then . . . then I thought:
"Why the hell shouldn't I, after all? They are my friends, the
food there is good, and as to what I know about Zoya . . .
we can pretend that I don't know anything."

I wasn't quite certain if Zoya cared whether or not I went,
so I told Lilya that I still didn't know if I was going out at all
that day, that I wasn't in a very good mood and that Zoya
should call me the night before—by then, I would know for

---

[11] *Emigré* Russian singers. Vertinsky voluntarily returned to the Soviet
Union after World War II. Leshchenko was evidently deported from
Bucharest to the Soviet Union in about 1948; his fate is unknown. Foreign
recordings of Leshchenko, smuggled in by returning Red Army soldiers,
circulated widely in the postwar years.

certain. In my own mind I had decided what I would say and do during the conversation.

And Zoya telephoned me.

She greeted me as though nothing had happened, asked about my health, and whether I planned to come. She talked to me and I answered her and heard her breathe into the mouthpiece of the telephone. She said:

"Please come, Tolya. I very much want you to. I'll expect you. If you don't come, you'll spoil my holiday."

I said into the phone:

"If I come, Zoya, I won't come alone."

"Who will you be with?"

"You don't know her," I said.

Zoya paused for a fraction of a second and then said:

"Well, of course, come with anyone you want, you know we'll all be glad to meet your friends."

And we hung up.

"You don't know her," I said. That was the honest truth: I didn't know myself whom I was thinking of.

In my mind I went through all the women I knew, the unmarried ones, naturally. There were quite a few of them, but the trouble was that they might interpret the invitation in quite the wrong way; and I didn't have the slightest desire to get involved in any new affairs. Perhaps I ought to go alone? Then I suddenly felt childishly spiteful and decided that at all costs I must prove to Zoya that I didn't give a damn about her. I decided to call Svetlana. She worked as an artist in our publishing house. She was twenty-three, very pretty, obviously interested in me, and unassuming enough not to get any wild ideas. She was very pleased when I invited her, but then became coy, and said she would feel awkward as she didn't know anyone and she "just wasn't sure . . ."

"Nonsense, Svetlana," I said. "They're all very nice people, as long as you're not worried by their getting tight and singing rude songs, and perhaps using swear words. . . . Any-

way, I'll wait for you tomorrow at nine-thirty at the corner
of Stoleshinkov Street, where the bookshop is."

When we arrived they had all been at the table for some
time. The bottles were a third empty, the men had taken
off their coats, and someone was already dying to sing. But
the festive atmosphere had not yet been spoiled. Cigarette
butts were not yet sticking up from the plates and people
were still drinking out of their own wineglasses.

When we walked in they all began to chatter loudly and
happily, and looked hard at Svetlana.

"This is Svetlana," I said. "I hope you'll be good friends."

"Svetlana, dear, come over here," crooned Lilya. "These
men have got completely out of hand; they eat and drink and
pay no attention to us. But we can't do without them, can
we?"

"You can't do without us!" Paul roared with laughter.
"We . . ."

"Svetlana, here's your glass," Igor poured her some dry
wine. "Maybe you'd like some brandy? I won't dare offer
you vodka."

"No. No thank you, really not," said Svetlana with a rather
forced smile.

"Tolya, where have you been; why haven't you been to
see us? Misha keeps asking 'Where's Uncle Tolya? When is
he coming to see us?' " Emma, Volodya's wife, rested her
bosom on the table and rounded her mouth and eyes, imitating her son. As always, she was dressed loudly and without
taste.

"You all right?" Zoya handed me a glass of vodka.

"All right," I answered.

"Good health! Good health, you late-comers!" Paul leaned
across the table to clink glasses with me. "I was afraid that
you wouldn't come. Zoya and I . . ."

"Paulie, you're spilling your drink."

"Sorry, my dear . . . Zoya and I . . ."

"Paul, pass the salad, please."

"Zoya and I . . . Why don't you let me finish what I'm saying?"

"I just wanted to ask you to pour me some wine too."

The noise was increasing. There was now no longer any general conversation. Igor was flirting with Svetlana for all he was worth; Lilya, jumping up from her chair, now had her arm around a tall young man whom everybody called "Yura the geologist"; Volodya was already reading out some verse by a fashionable young poet, bad verse with sloppy rhymes like dangling shoelaces. He was being baited by a sharp-nosed girl, who called out that the poet was a hack and that his poetry was worthless.

"A hack, maybe, but what about his civic courage?" shouted Volodya. "Worthless, maybe, but *Komsomol Pravda* attacks him!" [12]

Everyone was having fun. Paul started to set up the tape recorder. Emma was eating her salad. Yura the geologist was saying: "We're so unused to mayonnaise." I drank down three glasses and for some reason got mad.

"Listen, friends," I said, shouting above the din of the party, "You know how I love you all dearly!"

"Tolya!"

"Tol-ya!"

"It's terribly stupid of us to get together so seldom," I continued. "When was the last time we met?"

"The last time?"

"Yes, indeed, when was it?"

"I know!" shouted Lilya. "The last time we met was at our *dacha!* When they announced Public Murder Day!"

Everyone suddenly quietened. Even the tape recorder, which had just begun playing, stopped with a squeak. Emma alone continued speaking, by sheer force of inertia:

"And they've organized hot lunches in our school . . ."

---

[12] The implication being that he must be good if he is denounced in the press.

But glancing around at the silent faces, she too fell silent. The pause went on and on, and became embarrassing.

"Yes, indeed," said Igor, "so much time has passed since then, so many events. August tenth . . ."

"Zoya and I," shouted Paul, "Zoya and I had a quiet day. . . . We watched television and had the tape recorder. . . . The next day at work they asked me . . ."

They all suddenly came to life:

"And I told him: 'You'll be the first person I'll club to death! You son of a . . .' and I told him what I thought of him . . . ."

"In Odessa some crooks got hold of the Chief of Police. He was in uniform of course. So you know what they did? They made him put on some old rags and then let him go. Do you see, they let him go! Then they ran after him and finished him off! They were tried later on."

"Well? Well?"

"They were convicted of robbery!"

"Listen, listen to what happened in the writers' colony at Peredelkino! Kochetov[13] hired himself a bodyguard of thugs from outside Moscow. He gave them food and drink, of course. And some other writers also hired people—you know why? To get rid of Kochetov!"

"Well, and what happened?"

"What happened! There was a fight, that's what happened! The thugs fought each other!"

"Listen, does anybody know how many victims there were?"

"Not many in the Russian Republic: seven or eight hundred, maybe a thousand. A man in the Central Statistical Bureau told me."

"So few? That can't be right!"

"It is right, it is right. They broadcast the same figures. The foreign radio, of course."

"What a slaughter there was! The Georgians went for the

---

13 See p. xxxii of the Introduction.

Armenians, the Armenians went for the Azerbaijanians . . ."

"The Armenians went for the Azerbaijanians?"

"Yes, in the High Karabakh. That's an Armenian region."

"And what about in Central Asia? I bet there was quite a lot of fighting there."

"No, there was no fighting among themselves there. They killed all the Russians . . ."

"Have you read the letter from the Central Committee?"

"Yes!"

"No, we haven't! Tell us about it."

"First, the Ukraine. There the Decree was taken as a directive. And what a mess they made of it! Teams of young communist activists were given blacklists; well, the word got around right away about the lists. You couldn't keep a thing like that secret. And so special teams had nothing to do; all those on the list decamped. So the whole thing was a fiasco. Not only that, but the Central Committee has tossed out fourteen regional-committee and two area-committee secretaries for cheapening a great political idea and overdoing things!"

"Really?"

"It's absolutely true. But in the Baltic states no one was killed."

"What, no one killed?"

"No, no one."

"But that's a provocation!"

"It certainly is! They ignored the Decree, and that's that. The Central Committee letter mentions the inadequacy of political-educational work in the Baltic states. They've also fired someone there."

". . . running along the street, shouting and firing! Bursts of machine-gun fire at the windows! Where did he get the machine gun from? He teaches at the Aviation Institute . . ."

"We locked the door, lowered the blinds, and played chess . . ."

"I said to him: 'Don't dare, think of the children!' But he

said 'I'm going outside!' He was grinding his teeth. Misha was crying . . . I only just managed to talk him out of it . . ."

"There's an article in *Izvestia* by what's her name, Elena Kononenko. On the educational importance of the Day for young people. She somehow tied it up with the polytechnization and the virgin lands . . ."

"You should have seen the cartoon in *Crocodile!* The guy is lying down . . ."

"The only thing Zoya and I regret is that we didn't have any friends around . . . things would have been a bit more cheerful. . . ."

It's over, it's over, it's over! These unspoken words burst through the anecdotes, through the nervous laughter, through the digs at the government. It was the first time since Public Murder Day that I had heard people talking about what had happened. Until that moment, whenever I had raised the subject, people had looked at me rather oddly and changed the conversation. Now and then I found myself thinking a weird thought: "Maybe I dreamed it all?" But now it's over! And now we're celebrating the Forty-third Anniversary of the Great October Socialist Revolution!

The four of us, Svetlana, Zoya, Volodya, and I, kept silent while the whirlwind of impressions, reports, rumors, and facts went around and around, hung in the air like a brightly colored rainbow, and splashed the beige wallpaper with foam:

"Everything was peaceful and quiet on our expedition. We couldn't do anything—there was dense forest all around us. If it's him today, then it's your turn tomorrow . . ."

"Our neighbor committed suicide at dawn. . . . He was a quiet old man, a waiter in the 'Prague' Restaurant . . ."

"I couldn't sleep the whole night, I kept thinking I heard someone scraping . . ."

I recalled that on the night of August 10th I had gone out and seen two sanitation trucks moving along the Sadovaya Road; they covered a broad front, and spurting out jets of

water, kept washing and washing the roadway and side-
walks. . . .

Catching Svetlana's eye, I silently motioned toward the
door. She went out, and a moment later I followed. It was
cozy and quiet in the kitchen.

"Well, Svetlana, do you like it?"

"I don't understand, Tolya. At first they were all really
very nice, but then when they began talking about that . . .
Why are they so pleased about it?"

"They're pleased that they're still alive, Svetlana."

"But they all hid! They've been . . ." Svetlana broke off,
looking for the right word. "It was terror!"

"Terror?" I took hold of her by the shoulders. "Svetlana,
do you realize . . . ?"

No, she didn't. She didn't know that this one word of hers
had answered the question which millions of bewildered
people had been asking themselves and each other. She
didn't know, this girl, that she was now the match for our
great men of state—those watchful guardians of the peoples—that she was now quite up to the standard of the papers
wisely rustling in their darkened private offices, the discreet
and respectful words murmured by their advisers—the whole
thing which is solemnly called Power with a capital P. She
thought she had spoken this word to me alone, but she had
inadvertently thrown it in the faces of huge government
buildings, confronting the miles of black-and-white news-
print which crisscross the country every day. She had chal-
lenged unanimous opinions of general meetings, and all the
diabolic clatter of tanks which carry the gaping muzzles of
guns to ceremonial parades.

I kissed her and said:

"That's enough of that, Svetlana. I want to kiss you, I've
been wanting to for a long time. Haven't you noticed? . . ."

. . . And so, having seen Svetlana home, I return to my
room. I go along familiar streets, along lanes which I could
walk through blindfold. Luxurious lampshades like crino-
lines show pink through tulle curtains. Young lovers linger

in doorways and cannot bring themselves to part. The stone statue of Timiryazev[14] is thoughtful, as thoughtful as the finger placed against his forehead. A radio is blaring somewhere; there is a squeal of brakes from a car somewhere; groups of happy people returning home from parties, like me, are making a lot of noise. Somewhere in their rooms, on their own particular floors, people sit muttering swear-words, poems, and declarations of love.

This is Moscow speaking. I go along the street, along the quiet, cozy boulevard, feeling my notebook in my pocket and thinking about what I have written. I think that what I have written could have been written by any other man of my generation or of my destiny, who loves this damned, this beautiful country just as much as I do. I have judged it and its people; I have judged myself both more severely and less severely than I should have done. But who will reproach me for that?

I go along and say to myself: "This is your world, your life, and you are a cell, a particle of it. You should not allow yourself to be intimidated. You should answer for yourself, and you thereby answer for others." And the endless streets and squares, embankments and trees, and the dreamy steamships of houses, sailing as a gigantic convoy into obscurity, answer me with a low hum of unconscious assent and surprised approval.

This is Moscow speaking.

---

[14] A Russian botanist (1843-1920), much honored in the Soviet Union.

REFERENCES TO ORIGINAL RUSSIAN SOURCES

Boris Pasternak, "Bezlyubye," *Volya Truda,* Nos. 60 and 62, November 26 and 28, 1918.

Evgeni Zamyatin, "Revolyutsya, literatura i entropia," *Litsa,* Izd. imeni Chekhova, New York, 1955.

Victor Shklovsky, "Literatura i kinematograf," I. Ladyzhnikov, Berlin, 1923.

Sergei Esenin, "Rus Sovyietskaya," *Sergei Esenin, Sochineniya,* Volume 2, Moscow, 1956.

Konstantin Paustovsky, from *Vremya bolshikh ozhidanii,* Sovyetsky Pisatel, Moscow, 1960.

Isaac Babel, "Doroga," *30 dnei,* No. 3, March 1832.

Alexander Grin, "Sozdanie Aspera," *Ogon i voda, rasskazy,* Federatsia, Moscow, 1930.

Boris Pasternak, "M.Ts.," *Stikhotvoreniya v odnom tome,* Izd. Pisatelei v Leningrade, 1933.

Boris Pilnyak, "Krasnoye derevo," *Opalnye Povesti,* ed. Vera Alexandrova, Izd. imeni Chekhova, New York, 1955.

Mikhail Zoshchenko, "Pered voskhodom solntsa," *Oktyabr,* 8 and 9, Moscow, 1943.

Vladimir Polyakov, "Pozharnik Prokhorchuk" (rasskaz v rasskaze), *Smeyatsya pravo ne greshno,* Izd. Isskustvo, Moscow, 1953.

Lev Kassil, from "Dorogie moi malchiki," *Izbrannye Povesti,* Sovyetsky Pisatel, Moscow, 1948.

Julia Neiman, "1941," *Literaturnaya Moskva,* Volume 2, Moscow, 1956.

Nikolai Chukovsky, "Brodyaga," *Literaturnaya Moskva,* Volume 2, Moscow, 1956.

Ivan Kharabarov, "Nekhozhenoi tropoi," *Kazakhstanskaya Pravda,* August 2, 1959.

Yuri Kazakov, "Otshchepenets," *Oktyabr,* July 1959.

Vladimir Tendryakov, "Troika, semyorka, tuz," *Novy Mir,* No. 3, 1960.

Ilya Ehrenburg, "Lyudi, gody i zhizn," *Novy Mir,* No. 1, January, 1961.

Evgeni Evtushenko, "Babi Yar," *Literaturnaya Gazeta,* September
    19, 1961.
Nikolai Arzak, "Govorit Moskva," unpublished in Russian. Copyright
    Kultura, Institut Littéraire Maisons-Laffitte, Seine-et-Oise, France.